S0-CAT-981

A volume of a series in religion, edited by
LUTHER A. WEIGLE, DEAN EMERITUS OF
THE YALE UNIVERSITY DIVINITY SCHOOL, *and*
CLARENCE P. SHEDD, STEPHEN MERRELL
CLEMENT PROFESSOR OF CHRISTIAN METHODS,
YALE UNIVERSITY DIVINITY SCHOOL

CHRIST
IN THE GOSPELS

An Introduction to His Life and Its Meaning

By

HENRY M. BATTENHOUSE

PROFESSOR OF ENGLISH LITERATURE
CHAIRMAN OF THE DIVISION OF LANGUAGE
AND LITERATURE, ALBION COLLEGE

THE RONALD PRESS COMPANY · NEW YORK

Copyright, 1952, by

THE RONALD PRESS COMPANY

———

All Rights Reserved

The text of this publication or any part
thereof may not be reproduced in any
manner whatsoever without permission in
writing from the publisher.

Library of Congress Catalog Card Number: 52–6181

PRINTED IN THE UNITED STATES OF AMERICA

32.9
332k

LIFE Pacific College
Alumni Library
1100 West Covina Blvd.
San Dimas, CA 91773

L.I.F.E. College Library
1100 Glendale Blvd.
Los Angeles, Calif. 90026

Dedicated to the memory of
Frederick W. Schneider, John L. Nuelsen, Milton S. Terry,
Doremus E. Hayes, and Frederick C. Eiselen,
beloved teachers who instilled a deep reverence for the
Word of God in those whom they instructed therein.

022297

PREFACE

The study of the four Gospels and of the life of Jesus Christ with which they deal may be variously attempted. If the reader is in search of a story, he will find that of Christ especially beautiful. If he chooses to make the Gospels the basis of his daily worship, he will find in them God's plenty. If his approach is that of a historian, he will have much opportunity for analysis and hypothesis. Or, finally, if he reads as a theologian, he will be appreciatively exploring what Saint Paul calls the "breadth, and length, and depth, and height" of the world as revealed in the love of God.

The aim of this volume is to unite, in as introductory and simple a manner as possible, these four types of study. We shall try to give a rightful place to the Gospel story and its devotional use, emphasizing at the same time the history and meaning of the narrative. For to Christians of any age, the Gospel is more than a charming story or an ethical philosophy. It is divine history and revelation; and we shall be concerned to discover how this judgment of the facts is substantiated in the records of the four Evangelists.

The book is primarily designed to be used in the college classroom. It is hoped that it may also be found useful to teachers of Bible classes and to others in search of a wider understanding of the basis of our Christian faith. The topics listed for discussion at the close of the text are intended to serve as a guide to further investigation by assembled groups or individual students.

Acknowledgment is made to Floyd V. Filson who, in the interest of a good cause, read the manuscript and gave the author his valued comments; to Carl O. Schniewind who kindly offered his services as Curator of Drawings and Prints of the Art Institute of Chicago in the preparation of the illustrations;

to Vernon Bobbitt for his assistance in making the photographs of the engravings and woodcuts available; and to the publishers from whose works the author of this volume has been privileged to quote excerpts of prose and poetry.

HENRY M. BATTENHOUSE

Albion, Michigan
January, 1952

CONTENTS

PART I

God in Human History

PART II

The Gospel Record

PART III

The Earthly Life of Christ

CONTENTS

x   CONTENTS

ILLUSTRATIONS

MAPS

PART I

GOD IN HUMAN HISTORY

Chapter 1

HISTORY AS DIVINE DRAMA

I

NATURE AND DESIGN

We live our temporal lives in a world of nature. In it there are physical laws. The star and the atom, alike, obey them. There is organic life, following biological stages through birth, growth, degeneration, and death. The plant or animal cell, in its diagram on the chart, appears to be a world in itself, at once a record and a symbol of life's complete cycle. In it, growth struggles against decay, life contends with death, its apparent decisive victor. And man, measuring out his life by that pattern, might well agree with the seventeenth-century poet[1] who held that

> That age is best which is the first,
> When youth and blood are warmer;
> But being spent, the worse and worst
> Times still succeed the former.

There is also a social order in which human beings participate. On the lower level this order is instinctive, as in the societies of ants and bees; on the higher level it is intellectual and purposive, as in the founding of families and the planning of institutions and states. In society, as in the cell, this order involves the struggle for survival: a tension is set up between the forces that build and those that destroy. Only, whereas in nature whatever is hereditarily strong survives and is considered good, in human society there is the obvious conflict with evil which is often demonstrably mighty for no natural reason but that men have willed it so.

[1] Robert Herrick.

3

This tension between good and evil is an observable fact in individual and social experience. We note how it involves men and nations, the innocent with the guilty; and we can see, on closer study, how upon it, and upon the intelligence which in the conflict is added to the will, human society depends for the building of moral character. The pattern of selective values woven within this area of tension constitutes what we may call our culture. Out of it, in the course of the years that pass into generations, we form our concepts of truth, beauty, and goodness; and these together make up the world of civilized life in which we live—the world of science, literature, and art, of social custom and decorum as represented in good books, music, houses of good architecture, and in valiant behavior and gentle manners.

But this world, so offered to us in nature and constructed by man, is of and by itself incomplete. We see it everywhere limited by the facts of relevancy and contingency: everything in it depends upon something else; and the whole scheme or structure of civilization, and of life itself, seems always to be hanging unbalanced in mid-air, or resembling an intricate machine set for perpetual motion but from which the secret of the power to impel it to movement is withheld. The world, our common sense tells us, is not self-moved. Its motion, as the poet Dante's higher theological knowledge perceived it, is "by the *Love* impell'd that moves the sun in heaven and all the stars."

But more especially, in our search for the ultimate meaning of life, we are compelled to go to history. Here more closely, at our own door on the road through the centuries, we confront our task and ask for the vision to accomplish it. Secular history, like all else in the order of nature, is characterized by the facts of incompletion and tension. It is the long record of the conflict between man's flesh and his spirit, of his desire to pit his soul's strength against the world, of his endless war with time that presents itself in "withered stumps" of his wasted years, or echoes its hollow "Hurry up please its time" in the malignant air.[2]

Viewed as a mere continuation of events, history is meaning-

[2] See T. S. Eliot, "The Waste Land," Part II, "A Game of Chess," *Collected Poems* (New York: Harcourt Brace & Co., Inc., 1936), p. 73.

less. It reads like an attempted story without order, without justified action or plot. Only when viewed as drama does it present something of which the reasoning faculty can take hold. Only in the ensuing scenes and acts does the argument unfold; and then usually only in flashes of sudden insight, in the clash of conflicting ideas, as in the crisis or climax of some great play. It is as if the shining truth hidden away in the events were a sword, useless in its sheath until drawn for battle by the Red Cross Knight in some dividing and sacred enterprise.

Even our ordinary lives, in their daily round of duty, take on character and achieve significance when measured out in episodes of a larger design. So discerned, the little acts we do daily have a meaning to us, are given a setting of peculiar worth, and carry with them a kind of fatefulness seen only in the larger retrospect out of which all history is written. Anticipation and retrospect, we note on close observance, furnish the materials of our daily history. "It can happen at any time," we say. Events accumulate. Time ripens, as the grain for the harvest. Then, as the parable in the Gospels tells us, comes the day of ingathering, of reaping what we have sown. By this pattern civilizations rise and fall. That is the panoramic picture of history; and its end, or the moment when its meaning is made known, is its day of judgment.

II

PROVIDENCE AND WORLD EVENTS

World history, accordingly, may be looked at in two ways. Viewed as an aspect of physical nature, and in a secular sense, it seems to be altogether man's achievement, his search for the happy or contented life and its exploitable values; and this search is begun and continued within a pattern of an endlessly recurring cycle of events. According to this view, as there has been no beginning of happenings, so there can be no end. Nothing is either old or new except for its transitory moment within the revolving cycle. Birth and death are endlessly repeated phenomena; good and evil appear as alternating currents issuing from time's dynamo. So, too, hope and despair alternate in a

perpetual round. The *end,* if anything whatever by this conception of history, is not the goal or destination but the exhaustion
of all things. It is simply and finally the cessation of life.

But the facts of history point to another view which has
man's highest reason to commend it—a reason based on the fact
of divine revelation. It is, in fact, the only view that makes
human history possible by lifting man's life above the enveloping
cycle of trivial things suggesting a caged squirrel, or a piece of
driftwood floating toward the vortex of an engulfing whirlpool,
and gives to it the positive and horizontal direction of a traveler
taking a journey. It is the view that history is the story of
God's work in the world, for man, in and through man, and
together with man, in human events. According to this view,
God is Himself not confined to these events, or indeed wholly
represented in them, but transcendently operative in them: in
institutions and nations, in the natural aspirations of peoples
and in their failures; and His divine will is not merely influenc-
ing, but fully and finally determining all earthly destinies toward
a purposeful and peaceful end.

So considered, history is the record of a divine providence,
not only—as we read in *Hamlet*—in the fall of a sparrow, but
in the rise and fall of nations. It is this religious conception of
life and of the world to which, for example, Arnold Toynbee
gives expression in his statement that what is apparent is that
civilizations rise and fall, while that for which they exist, namely
their religious faith, tends to endure. In reviewing the entire
record, we may now go one step further to say that the light of
truth toward which men have been led has been for all time
fully revealed in the history of Jesus Christ. The divine drama
of history is the drama of human redemption. Its theme is the
restoration and perfection of that divine "image" which is "the
capacity to know and to love God," [3] but which has been distorted and corrupted by the "fall of man" or the fact of sin.

It was in such a setting that the prophets of the Old Testament looked on history. In this pattern of human events, seen
against a background of a divine world order, they saw a great
and wondrous purpose at work. God was making history, not

[3] Saint Augustine, *Confessions.*

simply by being Himself present in it as the great First Cause, the symbol of a natural or cosmic law, but rather by using history as the special and chosen instrument of His willed plan to save mankind from the power and consequences of evil, and so to effect the redemption of the world. These men of great insight, the prophets, regarded history as the vast area of tension between the natural course of events and the divine purpose to be wrought through them. History was viewed by them in simple grandeur as the fruitful field of God's activity and special revelation. Here was God's tillage, the land into which the plow could be put, the seed sown in grace, and the harvest gathered in judgment. By this view the history of the Hebrew people was one of many seasons full of such sowing and reaping. It was the proving ground in which, age after age, Israel was to be winnowed as wheat for that day of rich planting represented in the New Testament as the coming of the Kingdom of God, the era of plenteous grace and of final judgment inaugurated by the advent of Messiah in the person of Jesus Christ.

Everywhere on the pages of the Old Testament we see the scene re-enacted in pictures of challenge and response. Abraham leaves the fertile soil of Chaldea for rugged Canaan, seeking "a city whose builder and maker is God." Jacob wrestles with the angel, imploring to be blest. Israel wanders in the desert between memories of Egypt's fleshpots and visions of God's presence in the pillars of cloud and fire. Elijah, on Mount Carmel, calls his people to an eventful decision between letting the God of their fathers make history through them and degenerating to the gross nature worship of the cult of Baal. Similarly, Isaiah calls upon the king of Judah to trust God for the safety of Jerusalem; Amos declares that the merchants of Israel must reckon with divine justice in measuring out the grain in the market place; Jeremiah challenges Jerusalem to believe in its divine destiny at the moment when the city is besieged and falls. Ezekiel is confronted with a vision in which he sees the ruined state of Israel come to life again in the picture of the resurrection of an army in a valley of dry bones.

It is obvious that in such a chronicle there is more than the mere listing of transpiring events. The truth borne in upon

us is that in Holy Scripture we have the record of divine history taking place within human history. The men who committed this history to writing themselves sensed that what was happening was of momentous importance to the world. Indeed, it seemed as though a miracle transpired before their eyes. They were aware that this history was in fact God's work, and that it was often at variance with the wills of men who saw but dimly, if at all, the divine handwriting in the events happening before them. But the prophetic writers were divinely inspired men; and it is recalled that, on one occasion, one of them, seeing with a clear prescience what was to happen, heard the stern voice of God saying: "I will work a work this day in Israel that will set this people's teeth on edge."

Clearly, it was not by gradual evolution from barbarity to mildness that the Kingdom of God was to come. Instead, its advent was to be by the Word of God to be heard in the world through the voice of a trumpet announcing the resurrection of the spiritually dead, and a call to arms against the hosts of evil. The Kingdom of God might at first, it was true, come without observation; but once having arrived, it was to force men to decision in a great roll call and battle of dividing. Consequently, throughout prophetic history, there is this noticeable conflict of wills, this onrush of opposing purposes by means of which divine history seeks to break into human history, reversing nature's order that ends in decay and death, making sin bitter and justice sweet, and turning despair into hope and death into triumphant life.

It is a radical transvaluation of life's values that we see taking place before our eyes as we turn the pages of the Bible. It is as though the recorded events of history, together with the involved circumstances of nature itself, were presented to us in a gradually unfolding and overwhelming picture of the meaning of life; and that we were having these events presented to us, not now through their external circumstances, but *from within* —as though we were to go into a spacious, but as yet darkened, historical gallery of art and were to see the lights turned on, one by one, above the great paintings on the walls.

This prophetic way of looking at life from within calls for

the use of symbolism. It calls for the poet's method of allegory in the treatment of his chosen theme. We see this method forcefully applied, for example, in the prophet Isaiah's parable of the vineyard in Isaiah 5. In the parable, Israel is regarded as Jehovah's vineyard, planted and tilled by God Himself; but, after much tillage, being found bearing only wild grapes, it is, paradoxically, laid waste by its Owner and allowed to yield briers and thorns, with the express command to the clouds that they "rain no rain upon it."

The parable's interpretation, held intact by the symbolism, that God's plan which never fails has thus far failed, prepares the way for a new conception of history. It demonstrates man's failure to make a new world by his own ingenuity and might. It is his failure to make of society a fruitful vineyard by his natural tendency to grow wild grapes. The redemption of man, within this setting, is God's task. Naturally, it involves man's activity, his cooperation with the divine plan; but the "kingdom, the power, and the glory" belong to God.

It is this plan of world redemption that makes the Bible a book of divine revelation, giving it, beyond its antiquarian interest and acknowledged literary worth, the title of Holy Scripture. For it is Holy Scripture to us by reason of the fact that in it God speaks His word and His will for all mankind: first, in anticipation, through Israel's history; and finally, in fulfilment, through the Messianic mission of Jesus Christ. Through this close tie that binds together the Old and New Testaments, the Gospels, too, become divine history; and especially so, since, as Saint John's Gospel tells us, the very Word of God became flesh in His Son whom as Christians we call Christ our Lord. This evident orderly plan of the Bible, which is of one piece and throughout centered in the theme of man's redemption, presents us with a structural pattern for our special study of the Gospels and their Christian message.

Chapter 2

THE GOSPEL AS HISTORY

I

THE CHRONICLE OF REDEMPTION

Christianity is not a mythical religion. Its gospel record is not a story invented to meet a merely rational need. Its source is the truth reaching us from beyond history; the occurrences which issue from it lie within history's range. The gospel is a divine event of which the church is the outward historic sign. The Christian community on earth, called into being by the gospel, had a beginning and, in the consummation of things, will have a victorious end. Being involved in world history, it shares the temporal vicissitudes of the human race, reflects world currents of influence, has its periods of rise and decline. Its place in the world may therefore be pointed out, carefully studied, and appraised.

But the Christian faith is not simply to be explained as the product of an evolution in time. It has its own history, fitly called *Heilsgeschichte,* the history of God's special and purposeful action for man's salvation. It is characterized by epochs and crises, prophecy and fulfilment, times of grace and of judgment; and the philosophy, or meaning, of that history is offered to the world in the facts of the incarnation and resurrection of Christ, his ascension and acknowledged lordship, and, since then, in the prolonged historic dispensation of the Holy Spirit. These events, presented to the reader in theological terms, have the same textbook value as have the very useful terms that are applied, for instance, to the study of geology and anthropology. And the truths they encompass are to the Christian vastly more than something antiquarian, something about which it is curiously interesting to have a cultural knowledge. They offer, in

fact, the most acceptable framework for man's understanding of his divine origin and destiny, and have the immediate effect of determining his attitude toward life in this world.

Moreover, by these facts of divine history, and the theological truths they hold, world history is itself made and changed. After making due allowance for the stress on a divine providence which natural religion offers, it is granted that a new force has been released in the world through the Christian faith, a new law of life and an effectual source of power, that, as a matter of record for all to read, has "lifted empires off their hinges and turned the stream of history into new channels." [1]

Prophets and poets alike have pictured the divine mystery of the Incarnation associated with the historic fact of the birth of Christ. By this event was begun that dispensation of divine grace foreseen by the ancient prophet Isaiah, and reviewed in its fulfilment by the poet John Milton in the hymn from his "On the Morning of Christ's Nativity," in which he said:

> The Babe lies yet in smiling infancy
>   That on the bitter Cross
>   Must redeem our loss,
>   ...for from this happy day
>   The Old Dragon under ground
>   In straiter limits bound,
> Not half so far casts his usurpëd sway,
>   And, wroth to see His kingdom fail,
>   Swinges the scaly horror of his folded tail.

As the Incarnation was more than the natural event of Jesus' birth, so the Crucifixion was more than the incident of his cruel death. It is the Cross, and not the martyrdom of Jesus, on which the Christian church has built its faith. Many heroes, we say, have died for their religious convictions. But Christ died for our sins. The heroism of martyrs is world history; the gospel of the Cross is *Heilsgeschichte*. It belongs to the special history of the divine plan of man's salvation. There is no other way in which the Gospels can be understood. To look on the life,

---

[1] C. E. Jefferson, *Things Fundamental* (New York: The Macmillan Co., 1923), p. 173.

the death, and the teaching of Jesus as offering us a great example is indeed helpful. We are enjoined by Saint Paul to "remember the Lord Jesus who said that it is better to give than to receive." And we know, too, that the challenge to take up the Cross, to follow in his steps, and to drink of his cup of suffering is a realistic even if humanly impossible undertaking. But this commandment presupposes an understanding of what the Cross means, as it is interpreted to us by the Gospels themselves within the setting of the life of the early Christian community.

Whatever moral strength we may get from reading the New Testament as inspiring literature, we must remember that its story—by which we here mean its report of historical events plus their meaning to the first Christians who were witnesses to them—is a theological one. It signifies that God was acting in the life of Christ, wondrously and according to His divine plan, yet always so as to reveal to us both the divinity and the humanity of our Lord. Thus, for example, the Evangelists tell us, after Saint Peter, the leader of the Twelve, that Christ "bore our sins in his own body on the tree." The clear intent of the witnessing record is to portray the Messianic person and mission of Jesus. The stress in it is everywhere on the fulfilment of a long-nurtured prophetic hope. The demonstrated certainty of this realized hope startles us. Everything, these witnesses declare, is authenticated history. The events are recorded and their meaning is made clear. The story's end is implicit in the beginning. The God of Moses and the prophets has spoken; and the life of Christ is the answer.

Or, on taking a nearer look at the Gospel record, we see Jesus presented to us in it, by varying stages, as the Davidic Messiah-King, the Suffering Servant of Jehovah, the Son of man, and the Son of God. Equally impressive, besides, is the fact that, whatever his role, Jesus' divine sovereignty is matched by an equally divine humility. The humanity of Jesus is not denied; instead it is everywhere affirmed. But—and this is a point of importance—the familiar pastoral portrait of the humble and rustic Jesus so long and generally regarded among us as the ideal example of humanitarian virtue is not to be found in the New Testament. The Jesus we see as we read through gospel

history, and remember unforgettably, is the one Saint Paul saw and of whom he wrote in what may be called the "little Gospel":

> Let this mind be in you, which was also in Christ Jesus: Who, being in the form of God, thought it not robbery to be equal with God: but made himself of no reputation, and took upon him the form of a servant, and was made in the likeness of men: and being found in fashion as a man, he humbled himself, and became obedient unto death, even the death of the cross. Wherefore God also hath highly exalted him, and given him a name which is above every name: that at the name of Jesus every knee should bow, of things in heaven, and things in earth, and things under the earth: and that every tongue should confess that Jesus Christ is Lord, to the glory of God the Father.[2]

From this affirmation of faith it is clear that the earthly life of Christ was much more than a commendable example in gracious and unselfish living. His humiliation is described as a kingly abdication, and is followed by his heavenly exaltation. The Cross, whereon "he must redeem our loss," is the gateway to the resurrection, the ascension, and the lordship of Christ in the world. And the good life enjoined on us as Christians is to be lived within the framework of this exalting fact.

The fires of modern revolutionary thought, we are aware, have attempted to destroy this ancient structure of God's and man's building. But its historic framework stands; and theology, rightly understood, is simply the recognition and tracing of its architectural design. It is this Christological view that lies behind the composition of the Gospels and gives to them the character of Holy Scripture. It was as the record, or witness, of divine revelation, and not as imaginative literature, that the New Testament first came to be written; and it is as such that it continues today to command our worshipful attention.

II

THE CONSUMMATION OF HISTORY

But the gospel, as divine history, is not only Christological. It is also eschatological: that is, its history has an end, an ulti-

[2] Philippians 2:5-11.

mate outcome, a final goal. This means, in the language of the Bible, that God's plan which had its beginning in Genesis is completed in Revelation. This divine plan involves the temporal order which is itself God's creation. Time, together with mankind living within its vast span, is to be redeemed, to be restored to the newness of its first creation, as of the morning of which we read in the opening chapter in Genesis:

> And God said,
> Let there be light: and there was light.
> And God saw the light, that it was good:...
> And God called the light Day.

To us, accordingly, who live within time's span, this redemptive purpose, conceived as divine history, has its beginning and its end in the eternal mind of God. The final goal of the Christian faith, the end toward which it is directed, is beyond history. We cannot, of course, conceive what lies so far beyond our reach. That outcome rests with God, of Whose nature we have the revealed and spoken word of Jesus Christ. Meanwhile, from where we now are, we look out upon a world of conflict between the powers of good and evil. As Christians, though involved in this conflict, we are not crushed by it. Rather, we see it as a part of the victorious enterprise of the Kingdom of God which, though now an accomplished fact since Christ is come, is yet awaiting its consummation in the fulness of time when not only men and nations but the whole of creation shall come under its compelling reign.

Until that time comes, as Christ himself said, the Kingdom of God "suffereth violence," calling us to action in its enterprise of war against evil. In this holy warfare there can be no discharge until evil is overcome and, in the words of the Book of Revelation, Satan is bound and cast into the fiery lake. Such a picture of world conflict, we are assured, is not to be regarded as incompatible with our Christian concept of peace. It carries with it the immediate peace that Christ has promised us in the midst of the conflict—the peace that is not of "this world."

Such is the world view the Gospels present to us. It is not an easy road to disarmament that we see as we read the four

Courtesy of The Art Institute of Chicago.

1. The Annunciation. Martin Schongauer.

Courtesy of The Art Institute of Chicago.

2. THE NATIVITY. Martin Schongauer.

Gospels through in their entirety. And this impression is further intensified as we follow the story of the Book of the Acts, the letters of Saint Paul, the record of martyrs and heroes in the Epistle to the Hebrews, and come at last to the climax of the battle of Armageddon in the Book of Revelation. The strong apocalyptic note, the note of extreme crisis, runs through the entire New Testament. Nor is it absent in the Gospel of John whose exalted doctrine of divine love is strangely interrupted by hostile controversy. We note, again and again, that the Gospel's very pronouncement of God's love stirs up the enemy's hate : there seems, indeed, to be a divine strategy in this controversy by which the evil enemy, symbolized in "the Jews," is baited and led on to self-destruction. And nowhere, until he writes his prison letters, does Saint Paul take off his Christian soldier's armor to say : "I have fought a good fight; I have finished my course."

But it is in the Synoptic Gospels of Matthew, Mark, and Luke, whose narrative is our primary source of early Christian tradition, that this note of crisis reaches its highest pitch. In them the parables and discourses of Jesus alternate between grace and judgment in accelerating tempo until, at the close of his public ministry, we hear the echo of the words that still ring through the ages : "Woe unto you, Pharisees ! Woe unto you, Capernaum and Jerusalem !" When, finally, in the "Little Apocalypse" in Mark 13, supplemented by Matthew 24-25, we read of the "abomination of desolation" spoken of by the prophet Daniel, we have a surprising sense of the great tribulation of the world in which the story of the gospel is involved, and forces on us its parallel picture of the suffering and chaos that have overtaken our twentieth century.

But if the scene of these chapters in Matthew and Mark is one of impending violence, and if the voice is one of warning, the message is one of hope. The Good News of the Gospel is never stilled; its light is not extinguished. From having been a lighted candle on a candlestick, it is now a sudden world-wide illumination; the Kingdom of God which came on the scene of the world almost without observation has suddenly appeared as a bolt of lightning that "cometh out of the east, and shineth even

unto the west," bringing with it the revelation of the Son of man. This is the outlook that the apocalyptic view of the Gospels gives us of the world of "man's disorder and God's design."

But it is not, we must note, the whole picture. By the side of it, on the pages of the New Testament, we see two others. The one presents to the world the cosmic figure of the Eternal Christ, the Son of God, with whom man may enter into immediate and mystical communion and of whom, in the Fourth Gospel, we read: "I am the light of the world: he that followeth me shall not walk in darkness, but shall have the light of life." [3] The other presents us with the earthly life of Jesus of Nazareth who taught in the synagogues and by the seaside, walked through the fields and talked of God's care for the birds and flowers, sat among the children in the market place and ate at the tables of the socially outcast; and who, while the multitudes touched him and "there went virtue out of him," said "Blessed be ye poor; for yours is the Kingdom of God."

To reconcile these divergent views of Christ's person and mission was not the ancient Evangelists' task. They stood so near to the events that the truth they saw in them was clear and majestic before their eyes. Time, circumstance, and social setting contributed to individualize their viewpoints. But whatever change the situation and the years brought with them, their conception of the gospel of Christ was not distorted nor dimmed. We who look at the Gospels from this distance have a natural desire to harmonize and reconcile them. Our perspective offers us a challenge to take the various passages in them apart and place them together again to make a complete pattern. But we shall, at last, have to content ourselves with the narratives as they are. Their interconnection presents us with both a literary problem and a theological task. The Gospels, we must remember, were not written to make literary history but to record a divine historical event; and, while called upon to analyze them, we shall probably come nearer to their final synthesis and meaning by following the path taken by the reasoning insight of Saint Paul who saw in the mystery of the Gospel the reconciliation not only of divergent views but of all things.

[3] John 8:12.

Two rivers that in the lowlands run far apart, taking into them the soil and following the course determined by the surrounding terrain, may at their source be fed by the same alpine spring. Yet we know that even their glacial fountain does not account for them. The sun, the winds, and the clouds generate them; and behind the process of their generation is the designed order of the universe. By our study of nature we trace this process; but the reason for the creation of such a cosmic order is, at last, incomprehensible to us. We say it pleased God to make and have it so; and by saying this we do not demonstrate the fact of creation but our faith in the divine Creator.

It is exactly so with the history of the Gospels. As we look at them we see in the stream of the narratives the evidence of surrounding ideas. Thoughts from Judaism and Hellenism, for example, intermingle with the current of the story as it passes through the life of the early Christian community. To detect them is easier than to extract them; and the greater wisdom is in recognizing that, no matter what additional ideas the narratives may carry with them, they are not for that reason less genuine in their essential content. The river's life is in the water that flows from its original spring.

Chapter 3

THE EARTHLY LIFE OF CHRIST

I

THE GOSPEL OF THE KINGDOM

Not all the history of Christ is of this earth. If it were, we should have a biography of Jesus but no gospel of salvation. The apostles and evangelists are in agreement in considering the facts of the Incarnation and the Resurrection as integral parts of the story they have to tell. The fact that Christ was born to bring us redemption, and raised from the dead for our eternal hope, is the New Testament's central theme. The record summarily affirms that the earthly life of Christ is, above all, the revelation of this fact through the process of human history; and the public ministry of Jesus, viewed in its widest aspect, is a sign from heaven attesting to the mighty, gracious, and redeeming work of God.

That such was the belief and verdict of the early church is proved by the notable emphasis given to the events of Jesus' divine birth, his death, and his resurrection, in the telling of the gospel story that was later to be written down by the four Evangelists. This emphasis is pointed out to us, for example, in the Apostles' Creed; and it survives, to this day, in the Christian calendar in the seasons of Christmas, Good Friday, and Easter. No biography of Jesus—except one with a hidden fourth dimension, so to speak—can explain the magnitude of these events in the tradition of the church. They belong, by their very truth, to a history written with Unseen Hands, in words of indelible meaning, of which sentences like these are the typical prefatory signs:

And the angel said . . . behold, I bring you good tidings of great joy: . . . for unto you is born this day in the city of David a

Saviour.... Jesus, knowing that all things were now accomplished,
...said: It is finished.... And the angel answered and said...He
is not here: for he is risen, as he said.[1]

Nevertheless the earthly life of Christ is an essential part of
the Gospel narrative. It has its origin in a child born in Bethlehem, nurtured in Nazareth, and growing to manhood in Galilee.
Luke the Evangelist mentions the boyhood of Jesus, saying that
he "increased in wisdom and stature, and in favor with God
and man." The years of his growing manhood are passed over
in silence by the record, indicating that neither his education
nor his secular vocation were of any special interest to those
who told the story. It was not a life story, in the usual sense,
that they were writing, nor a character study of a famous personality. Rather, it was the history of a momentous *event* associated with Jesus' birth, his earthly life, the words he spoke, the
mighty works he wrought, and the manner in which, to the
surprise of all except the understanding and wondering few, he
took upon himself the office of the long-awaited Messiah,
thereby giving to his death the signal meaning summed up in
the New Testament account as the "Gospel of Jesus Christ."
Therefore in reading the story of Jesus' earthly life, we are
not to look for any carefully outlined order or succession of
events but rather for their *meaning* as it is interpreted to us in
the reported words and acts of Christ. And it will be our
particular aim to see the summarized meaning of these forego-
ing events set forth in the one great and united Act of Christ's
death and resurrection, by which he called into being the Christian church, together with its continued "acts," in the redemptive history of the world. Guided by this approach to the
gospel literature, we shall not lose sight of its purposeful theological content. It will no longer sound to us simply like a
romantic story about Jesus. It will become to us the greater
history of the action of God in and through the life of Christ.
The earthly scene will not be less familiar. The man Jesus will
not be withdrawn from us into a mere symbol of divine truth;
but, in and through the record, we shall see the evidence of

[1] Luke 2:9-11; John 19:28, 30; Matthew 28:5, 6.

Christ's humanity, and of how in him our true humanity—as by the first creation it was intended to be—is fully restored to us. And so looking at the Cross, we shall be challenged to say with the centurion: "Truly this man was the Son of God." [2]

We are accustomed to speaking of Jesus' ministry in its threefold activity: as that of preaching, healing, and teaching. It began with the announcement that the Kingdom of God had come. A new age had begun in fulfilment of prophecy. It was the Messianic age, signalized by the special outpouring of God's spirit in heavenly grace. It was the time of sowing for the harvest yet to come, of building the new house of Israel upon a permanent rock, and of lighting a candle in that house that should never be put out. We shall see in the following chapters how this task was accomplished.

Jesus probably began his preaching in Capernaum and Nazareth. We read that while the people heard him gladly, some seeds fell on hard ground; that from the very beginning, the winds of opposition were gathering to beat upon the house to extinguish the burning light. But "God was with him," the Gospel narrator tells us, and a fire of evangelism was started in Palestine that was not to be put out. The storm of opposition quickly fanned the gracious hearth fire into a spreading flame of judgment and, in its enmity to Jesus' preaching, the old Israel with its historic institutions was all but swept away and burned to the ground. At last, in the darkness and earthquake of the Crucifixion, the veil within the temple was torn away, laying bare before the world the mystery and historic purpose of God's kingdom.

The four Evangelists stress the fact that Jesus' preaching was everywhere accompanied by miraculous healing. The people were even more astonished at his deeds than at his words. His miracles, say the records, were manifestations of God's power and of Jesus' authoritative word that the Kingdom had come; they were also the signs of its greater and future coming, when mankind was to be healed of its sin and the eyes of men were to be opened to the full meaning and ultimate goal of human history.

[2] Mark 15:39.

It is not difficult to see this dual significance of the miracles as we read the account of them. Jesus' compassionate healing of one blind man's sight was clearly the sign of God's compassion and power to heal this world of its blindness; the healing of the demoniac was typical of what was again and again to happen in Christian history when, by the power of the Gospel, the souls of men were to be loosed from the demonic grip of evil. The multitudes, then present, sensed that fact and rejoiced in it; the more intimate disciples were held in awe by what they surmised but could not explain; and we who live today, after the centuries, cannot withhold our witness to the Gospel's great ministry of healing.

But overshadowing all else, as a mighty work of God's doing, was Jesus' resurrection. It too, was typical of what faith in Christ thereafter was to do; for everywhere, as the Gospel was preached, the blind were to see, the lame to walk, and the dead to rise at the word of him who was "the resurrection and the life."

II

THE TRAINING OF THE TWELVE

To his ministry of preaching and healing, Jesus added that of teaching. The Kingdom of God was to be established with power. But this event was not to take place arbitrarily or without men's help. It was to be a communal, not a private enterprise; and participation in it presupposed a fundamental knowledge of its great design. Assuming the role of Master, Jesus undertook to instruct his disciples in the new law or way of life involved in the great hope of the Messianic kingdom. They were to be the remnant of the people Israel from which, as from a bolt of cloth woven at the loom, the new Israel of God was to be reconstructed, after the pattern of the divine *Ecclesia,* later to become the historic Christian church. More simply, the disciples were to be the first Christians. For a time, indeed, it looked as though they might also be the last Christians to live on earth. For so great was the urgency of Jesus' preaching, so immediate the popular response and so intense the opposition to it, that many who heard him, including

the disciples of John the Baptist, were persuaded that the end of the age was near. The record suggests that Jesus at first may himself have shared the expectant hope that the Son of man would soon appear to bring the Heavenly Kingdom to a glorious and final consummation.

In the midst of this early crisis, Jesus gathered his close followers around him and taught them. The content of his teaching was evangelistic. The mood of joyous but solemn anticipation in which the disciples went forth as missionaries to the people of Galilee illustrates the urgency of the prophetic and practical task before them. They were commanded to go without delay, without staff or purse or bread, expecting to be welcomed, yet prepared to be rejected, to preach repentance and to heal the sick; and such was the prompt urgency of their mission that they were bidden to shake off the dust under their feet as a sign of judgment against the cities that refused to receive them. In this mood, apocalyptic almost from the start, Mark's Gospel tells us, Jesus began his ministry.

As we follow the synoptic story into its next stage, we see the tension temporarily released. The scene changes. It is as if, in traveling with the narrative, one came from a steep hill country to a broad fertile plain. "And he spake many things unto them in parables," says Matthew. Parable follows parable in a wondrous exposition of the Kingdom of Heaven. The Kingdom is like the little mustard seed, the baker's leaven, a treasure hidden in a field, a pearl of great price. Holding apprehension in abeyance, these stories breathe divine good will like a gentle south wind in a sheltered valley. The setting, temporarily, is within, not beyond, history. It is in the area of what has been called "realized eschatology," the area of gospel ethics in which the kingdom of God is proclaimed as having come. The refrain of this aspect of Jesus' teaching is heard in the words: "Blessed are the meek, for they shall inherit the earth"; "Lay up for yourselves treasures in heaven"; "When ye pray, say, 'Our Father which art in heaven'"; "He that heareth these sayings of mine and doeth them I will liken him unto a wise man, which built his house upon a rock." [3] With

3 Matthew 5:5, 6:20; 7:24.

such teachings, and others, he astonishes his hearers who marvel at his word of authority.

But the tension is not long released. When hostility to Jesus springs back to enclose him as in a barbed fence, his instruction becomes more private. Its general theme is the doctrine of cross-bearing. The Kingdom of God has begun to suffer violence; its adherents are being sifted as wheat after harvest; and the Twelve who follow Jesus closely are frankly puzzled at what they see and hear. The early note of urgency changes to one of foreboding. The Master's words are more impassioned; the parables are more incisive. Many withdraw from following him. "Will ye also go away?" they hear him say to them. When Peter answers for them: "To whom shall we go; thou hast the words of Eternal life," their commitment to him is sealed. The lessons in cross-bearing follow; and the disciples are told that they too must drink the cup of suffering with him.

Viewed summarily, it is clear that the teaching of Jesus is here, as at the beginning, enveloped in the apostolic preaching of the gospel of Christ the Messiah. The instruction is implied in the proclamation of the Good News. Through Jesus' ministry of teaching, the living plant of the gospel is brought into the laboratory for the examining test. Within, at the center, is the nucleus of the divine incarnate Word; around this nucleus lies the connective tissue of Jesus' ethical teaching. The *Kerigma* and the *Didache,* together, form the Gospel's organic cell.[4]

Finally, on the night before his trial and crucifixion, Jesus unveils the truth before them. His death is to be more than a martyrdom; it is to have the world-wide meaning of the Second Isaiah's picture of God's Suffering Servant who is to give his life as a ransom for the sin of the world. And the disciples, thereafter, are not to be left comfortless; for the Holy Spirit is to be with them to the end of time. Then, when God's will on earth is accomplished, they are to join him at the Messianic feast of the consummated heavenly kingdom. The bride, which is the church spotless and beautiful, will be beside the Bridegroom who is Christ, and joy will reign unending.

[4] See C. H. Dodd, *History and the Gospel* (New York: Charles Scribner's Sons: 1938).

Chapter 4

THE HISTORIC CHRISTIAN CHURCH

The Faith Takes Form

Memorable days followed, for the disciples, between the earthly life of Christ and the birth of the Christian church. They were meditating on his command, "Go preach . . . and teach," and were waiting between the Ascension and Pentecost for the promised Holy Spirit. So commissioned and expectant, they were being prepared to be the first Christian evangelists and apostles.

Chronologically, one period in history had ended and another had begun. But there was no gap or any cleavage between what had already happened and what was yet to take place. For an unbreakable bond had already been formed in the disciples' minds between (1) the Jesus of Nazareth whom they had followed and (2) the Christ of their newborn faith. Peter's confession, "Thou art the Christ, the Son of the Living God," had forged the chain that was to bind them together. And the gospel story, soon to be given to the world, was the record of this consolidating fact. Here, in Peter's words, was the story's vital core of truth:

> Jesus of Nazareth, a man approved of God among you by miracles and wonders and signs, . . . delivered by the determinate counsel and foreknowledge of God, . . . crucified and slain; whom God hath raised up; . . . being by the right hand of God exalted, and having received of the Father the promise of the Holy Ghost; . . . whereof we all are witnesses.[1]

The gospel was now a transpiring event in history. But the story that the apostles were to tell required of them both insight

[1] Acts 2:22-33.

and retrospect. It could not be told until the events had become history. And as we have heretofore said, there could be no history to relate until the events had taken form—the form which, in the words of Aristotle, the soul gives to the body—and so had come to have a meaning. All this, of course, could not happen in an instant. Time and perspective were needed, and above all, the gracious activity of the Holy Spirit in the church, to crystallize the events and to give them the pattern of the Gospel message. As by comparison in some newly opened area of land first villages appear, then from them larger towns grow, which in time become great cities, so by the preaching and teaching of the Word the four Gospels and the Christian communities that nurtured them came into being.

These several communities at first were small. Then presently in Jerusalem, in Antioch, in Caesarea, and after that in Ephesus and Rome, the churches grew and became large and strong. Preaching places multiplied; catechumens, or converts, were instructed; and, in the course of time, the words and acts of Jesus, often retold and so remembered, were given their appropriate setting in the existing narrative of his earthly life and were safeguarded against willful alteration by a deep reverence for the original gospel account of eyewitnesses and apostles.

Thus the wondrous story grew and assumed the form of an oral tradition. Christ was preached and men believed. The gospel had free course. It was the life of those who were called Christians, a Life beyond life; and through it God was again making history that was mightily to affect the secular history of the world.

Logically, therefore, and chronologically, before the gospel became recorded history, it was a declaration of Christian faith. The focal center for both was the passion story. It was the death of Christ, and his resurrection, that wrought in the disciples the great change and made apostles of them. They now understood what Jesus had meant when he had so recently said that the Son of man must suffer death and rise again. On Easter morning, John reminiscently records, they ran to the tomb, their anticipative hearts running before them; they saw

and they believed. Almost at once the truth of Holy Scripture was unfolded before them. Jesus was indeed Messiah: the crucified Suffering Servant of Jehovah had risen as the glorious Son of man; he was, of a truth, the world Savior, the Son of God. Sustained by this revelation that had not come to them by "flesh and blood," their faith leapt within them. They began to preach Christ, as the Gospels later recorded, first in Jerusalem, then in Samaria, and after that in "the uttermost parts of the world."

Looking at the entire historic scene, it is not difficult to see how the picture of this mighty work of God, this divine drama of human redemption, exhibited itself to the minds of the apostles. It was the Cross that stood at the center of the scene. There, in the darkest hour of their hope when their eyes were blinded, God had revealed Himself, had spoken to the world His Word of life. The passion story was therefore the pivot of their gospel message. Around it all else that they preached revolved; and from it, as on rays of light from a hilltop, the gospel they proclaimed traveled backward into prophetic history and forward into the ages yet to come. Looking on Jesus' birth, they saw in it the incarnation of the Son of God. And reviewing, from this lighted hilltop of the Cross, his earthly life, his ministry of preaching, of teaching, and of healing, they beheld in it the fulfilment of God's covenant with mankind in signs of His enduring mercy, His just judgment, and His purposeful plan of world redemption.

How this gospel history assumed its present literary form we shall see in a later chapter. It is enough to indicate here that the four Gospels, in the making, passed through two major periods or stages. The first represented the oral tradition; the second, the narrative's literary composition. The stress, in the beginning, was on the living Word. Just as, by comparison, the Word became flesh, so the living gospel took literary form. The narrative, as we know it, is the embodiment of the divine gospel which was before the four Gospels. Yet the coming of Christ is the primary historic fact: for, obviously, the preaching of the gospel did not bring Christ into the world; rather Christ came into the world that we might have a gospel to preach.

Therefore, in outlining our task, the historic order we are to keep in mind is this: first, the event through which God Himself entered history by giving Christ to the world; second, the gospel of world redemption preached by the newly established church; third, the gathering together of the body of gospel tradition based on the preaching and teaching of the Word and given its setting in the principal events in the life of Christ; fourth, the final composition of the four Gospels out of the material so collected and edited.

Finally, the proportioned length and accent of the total Gospel narrative indicate clearly how central and exalted the Cross of Christ was to the faith of the early Christian community. From it, as though it were a hardy and already mighty tree, the Christian movement grew, gradually spreading its branches over Palestine and letting its seeds be carried by apostolic preaching to the far corners of the Mediterranean world. The church, so taking root, was of God's own planting. It drew its first nourishment from the soil of Judaism where the Law, the prophets, and the Sacred Writings of Israel were its fertilizing environment. There, in a favorable and providential setting, as the parable of the mustard seed tells us, the Kingdom of God flourished, attracting the attention of men until their thoughts lodged in it like birds nesting in a tree.

II

TRADITION AND EVANGELISM

Before the century ended, therefore, the gospel message had been transplanted throughout Palestine, Syria, Asia Minor, and to important parts of Europe. Through the spread of Hellenism into these regions the people living there, and even those in Palestine, were acquainted with Greek ideas. The influences of Alexandrian philosophy and of the appealing Mystery Religions of the East must have made themselves felt in many of the communities to which the first missionaries carried the Christian message.

But the faith of these early Christians was not a mere catchall movement of sundry philosophies or simply an out-

spread net in the stream of floating ideas. It was, indeed, as men of the world then thought, a narrow way, cutting through the life of the time by a "strait gate," and entrance into it, as Christ himself had said, was through a "needle's eye." This very singleness of purpose was its safeguard against strong inroads of ideas. Wherever such ideas from Hellenism, for example, were welcomed, it was to help interpret Christian truth and not to add something alien to its content. Similarly, the influence of Judaism did not determine what Christianity was to be. For, according to the records, it was the Christian faith's initial and increasing separateness from Judaism that made it the movement it became. Neither hereditary Jewish influence nor Hellenistic environment could account for the Gospel or explain it. It was, as the apostolic age interpreted it, a new creation.

The first Christian community, the writer of the Book of the Acts tells us, kept close to the teaching of the apostles. It avoided pagan contact, stressed its communal life, recognizing the eucharistic nature of that life in the daily breaking of the bread; and the members of the community, we know, lived in a state of expectancy of Christ's earthly return—an expectancy that nurtured the deeply implanted gospel truths from which the evangelistic preaching of that and the ensuing generation directly stemmed. A striking example of this earliest gospel, in its condensed and living form, is to be found in I Corinthians 15, where Saint Paul writes:

> ... brethren, I declare unto you the gospel
> Which I preached unto you,
> Which also ye have received,
> And wherein ye stand;
> By which also ye are saved, ...
> How that Christ died for our sins, according
>   to the scriptures;
> And that he was buried, and that he rose again the
>   third day; ...
> And that he was seen of Cephas,
> Then of the twelve: ...
> Then of all the apostles.

Tested in the crucible of the Roman Empire, the gospel tradition, at first oral, was gradually committed to writing. It is clear that much besides this central core of Christian teaching remained to be included in order to make the gospel story complete. The earthly ministry of Jesus was not ignored; it was presupposed as a necessary part of this story of salvation. Without it we should have the climax of the divine drama without its preceding "mighty acts" of God. The "situation in life" would be lacking, as also would the background of Old Testament history which sets the stage for what, in the language of dramatic criticism, is called the argument, of which the divine and especially suitable prologue is presented to us in the opening chapter of the Book of Isaiah, in these words:

> Come now,
> Let us reason together,
> Saith the Lord:
> Though your sins be as scarlet,
> They shall be as white as snow;
> Though they be red like crimson,
> They shall be as wool.

In the course of the first century, or by about A.D. 50, the oral gospel tradition had become firmly established. Besides the passion story, the parables of Jesus, his great sayings, and more particularly the "pronouncement stories" that had become the texts of inspired apostolic preaching were being widely circulated among the early Christians whose chain of growing churches extended northward from Jerusalem to Antioch and westward to Rome. In every community, as Christians met, the story was told, accompanied by the celebration of the Eucharist commemorating Jesus' passion and signifying continually that the risen Christ was making himself known to them "in the breaking of the bread." So the new faith was deeply implanted; and so it grew and spread.

Soon, as Luke the Evangelist tells us, these apostolic communities began to be known as churches, and the beginning of the expansion of Christianity into a worldwide religion was under way. It was in these churches, principally at Jerusalem and Caesarea, at Antioch, Ephesus, and Rome, that the collec-

tions of stories were made which, during the years between
A.D. 50 and 100, became the literature of our present Gospels of
Matthew, Mark, Luke, and John. The four Gospels, accord-
ingly, differ in certain details from one another; yet, underlying
them, we find the original tradition of the apostolic faith in
Christ as the Messiah and the Savior of the world.

Thus, in review, we see the life and gospel of Christ unfolding before us in three definite aspects. There is, first, the living
fact, having a divine source: the fact of God's revelation of
Himself in the person of Christ as the eternal Word becomes
flesh in the earthly life of Jesus of Nazareth; and for the understanding and exposition of which we must go to Christian
theology. In the second place, we may approach the gospel as
world history: as having its origin and moving in its expansion
amid the circumstances of time and place, limited to the sphere
of human activity in which, by the eternal will of God, the plan
of redeeming mankind was made operative and given a setting
in life, and in which also the story of the gospel could be enacted,
treasured, and reported. Finally, we may view the gospel as
literature, complete in its range of outlook, its expression of the
faith of the early church, yet not of the primitive church only
but of a great world movement, rich, expansive, and many-sided
—a literature replete with poetry, the poetry of the gospel whose
theme and glory is the song of man's salvation.

It is with this threefold approach that we shall now enter
upon our more detailed study. And we may consider our aim
well achieved if, at the end, we shall have attained something
of the serenity and assurance of John the Evangelist whom
Robert Browning pictures in the poem "A Death in the Desert";
where, surrounded by his disciples, the apostle thinks of the time
yet to come when men will ask,

> Was John at all, and did he say he saw?
> Assure us, ere we ask what he might see!

And, looking out into the future, as if at our own century, he
answers their questionings with this testimony for all the world
to read:

> ...it was so; so I heard and saw,
> ...I saw, I heard, I knew.

PART II

THE GOSPEL RECORD

Chapter 5

THE ROMAN WORLD

I

The Land of Palestine

For us Palestine is a land of pleasant pictures and sacred memories. Its very place names have rich associations for us. Bethlehem, for example, is synonymous with Christmas; Jerusalem, with royalty and tragedy; Gethsemane, with Jesus' agonizing prayer. The Lake of Galilee, the Jordan River, and the Dead Sea are to us almost a story of our lives, the allegory of the history of nations and civilizations.

To the first Christians Palestine was not simply their ancestral home; it was the land also of their religious faith. The blood and dust of their fathers were in its soil; the God of their fathers was the country's very soul. They could look back on a thousand years of national history. Geographically, Palestine was on the border of three continents. It was itself Asia's frontier facing the Mediterranean Sea, the gateway to the Western world. Toward the south and west lay Egypt, ancient and fertile and civilized, but pagan. In ancient historic times it had been Israel's friend, its enemy, its conqueror, its ally, and its rich granary. Beyond Egypt stretched the vast land mass of Africa, half desert, half jungle, and savage. Situated on this threshold of civilizations, Palestine was coveted territory. Nineveh on the Tigris, and Babylon on the Euphrates, wanted it as an outlet to the sea; the centuries of Pharaohs claimed it as their rightful possession; Rome, at last, included it in its ironbound domain, ruled it with legal justice, tolerated its social and religious tradition, kept a watchful eye on its uprisings, and sought, as much as possible, to integrate it into the great empire.

The topography of the land is an interesting natural phenom-

enon. In the distant north, Mount Hermon rises nine thousand feet above sea level. From this snow-covered peak the clear waters rush precipitately to the Lake of Galilee, from which the Jordan River cuts a deep gorge through the region of the Decapolis, past Samaria and upper Judea, where it empties into the Dead Sea, 1293 feet below the ocean's level. This geological rift provides Jericho, for example, with a tropical climate which is in marked contrast to that of Jerusalem situated in the exhilarating hill country not far away. But the road up the mountains is steep; and one can see why the historic capitol, built on the high plateau of a great rock, was commonly kept safe against marauding caravans. Beyond the Judean hills lay Philistia, the land of ancient Israel's old enemy. Ashdod, Ashkelon, and Gaza, its principal cities, still stood in New Testament times, and the road through them led conveniently down to Egypt. Northward, on the coastal plain, was Joppa; below it and inland, the town of Lydda; and farther to the north, the seaport city of Caesarea—all three of them as intimately associated with the early missionary activity of Peter as Gaza and Azotus were with the evangelism of Philip.

Almost in the center of Palestine, yet strangely isolated from the Jewish community by a racial and historical tragedy, was the region of Samaria. Naturally rich and beautiful, it had in ancient days been famous for its vineyards, pastures, and fields of grain. When Israel was still a primitive people and the land was known as Canaan, the sacred shrines of Schechem and Shiloh had been established there. Bethel had been the place of Jacob's angelic dream and of Amos' fiery prophecy; Dothan and Sychar were remembered from patriarchal times. But Samaria had fallen at the assault of Assyria; its fertile valleys and grazing land had been repopulated by people of mongrel blood; and the spirit of the Samaritans had suffered a long and a pitiful humiliation. Yet Samaria was an integral part of Palestine. It was on the road from Judea to Galilee; and we read, in John's Gospel, that Jesus "must needs go through Samaria," where he visited Jacob's well—and where, according to the wider teaching of the Gospel record, by his offer of himself as the dispenser of

Living Water, he annexed forever all the Samaritans of this world to the Kingdom of God.

One of the most interesting areas of Palestine is the great Plain of Esdraelon. Its natural fertility and its place in Hebrew history are alike extraordinary. The map shows it as opening from the west, above Mount Carmel, letting in the influence of the sea, its warm enchanting air, its commerce, its culture; and it stretches like a vast luxurious corridor across lower Galilee to the Jordan. Coursing through the plain is the valley of Jezreel, famous in history for its association with the treachery of Jezebel and the furious chariot ride of Jehu. And there, like a giant overlooking the domain, stands Mount Gilboa where Gideon fought the Midianites and King Saul died in defeat fighting the Philistines. There, too, by the river Kishon that runs to the sea, is the battle ground of Megiddo where Deborah, long ago, had called the settling tribes of Israel to battle for the holding of the land, and where, as we read in her song commemorating the victory:

> The kings came and fought, . . .
> They fought from heaven;
> The stars in their courses
> Fought against Sisera.
> The river of Kishon swept them away,
> That ancient river, the river Kishon.[1]

But it is in Galilee, among its hills and by its lake, that gospel history has some of its most distinctive setting. There, in a region native to the first disciples, are the villages rich in their association with the life of Christ. The towns of Capernaum, Bethsaida, Cana, Nain, and Nazareth, all near or within easy reach of the lake, are hallowed by the words of Scripture that cluster around them like ivy around an old historic chapel. As one reads these Galilean sections of the Gospels, the very hillsides are green again with grass, the fields ripen to the harvest, the birds nest in the hedgerows near where the farmer plows or the shepherd herds the sheep; one sees again the houses that seem asleep in the village of Capernaum nestled by the lake;

[1] Judges 5:20-21.

and the fishermen's boats with their white sails are anchored in one's memory forever as one sees Peter sorting the fishes or drying his nets.

The region north of Galilee is mountainous, and far up from the seaports of Tyre and Sidon are the forests of Lebanon whose cedars once adorned the Temple at Jerusalem. In the Anti-Lebanon range, to the east, stands Mount Hermon at an altitude of nine thousand feet; and on its southern slopes was the city of Caesarea Philippi, built by Philip the tetrarch of Trachonitis, the just and friendly ruler into whose territory Christ and his disciples withdrew to escape the treachery of Herod Antipas, the "fox." There, in the vicinity and seclusion of the hills surrounding Mount Hermon, tradition most favorably places the story of the Transfiguration.

In the upper territory east of the Jordan was Gadara, one of the confederation of ten cities known collectively as the Decapolis. The region between the rivers Yarmuk and Jabbok is infrequently mentioned in New Testament history. But ancient Gilead, then called Perea, and spoken of in the Gospels as "beyond Jordan," was well-known territory. The land of Moab, below Gilead, was famous as the sepulcher of Moses and later as the home of Ruth. The Jordan Valley, below the Jabbok, became the dramatic scene of the preaching of John the Baptist; and toward the south, in the tropical area where the river Arnon flows into the Dead Sea, stood the fortress of Machaerus in which John was imprisoned, and where, on the instigation of Herodias, he was cruelly put to death. It was through Perea also that, according to Saint Luke, Jesus journeyed on his way to Jerusalem to give himself up in his great sacrifice on the cross.

II

THE EMPIRE AND ITS CULTURE

The early Christian community was never allowed to forget that it was a part of the larger Roman Empire. The Roman domain, in the first Christian century, was vast, orderly, and just. It extended as far eastward as the Euphrates and westward to the Atlantic; and from the Rhine and the Danube in

the north to the African desert. Altogether, it comprised a fairly rectangular area of 3,000 by 2,000 miles. Its system of government was provincial. The administration of the colonies was simple, tolerant, efficient. Such comparatively quiet areas, for example, as Africa and the islands of the Mediterranean were governed by proconsuls who were responsible to the senate; others, more subject to disturbance, were ruled by either propraetors or procurators who were directly responsible to the emperor. These imperial deputies were usually of equestrian rank. The propraetors, particularly, were prepared for the exercise of discipline, having with them five imposing lictors, or attendants, carrying the fasces composed of bundles of rods encasing axes with projecting blades, the symbols of Rome's authority. The province of Syria, of which Palestine was a part, was subject to this imperial legate's rule.

But the exercise of this rule was limited by the fact that Palestine was a semi-independent state. In New Testament times, generally, it was composed of three little kingdoms: the Trachonitis, Galilee, and Judea. These kingdoms had once been the dominion of Herod the Great. At his death, in 4 B.C., this dominion was divided among his three sons, the Trachonitis going to Philip until his death in A.D. 34, after which it went to Agrippa I, until A.D. 44, and then, after an interval, to Agrippa II. Galilee, together with Perea across the Jordan, passed into the hands of Antipas who was deposed in A.D. 39; and Judea, together with Samaria, was inherited by Archelaus, who also was deposed in A.D. 6, after which the state was alternately ruled by appointed procurators and the two Agrippas.

Domestic disturbance and arrogant despotism accounted for much of this change in rulership. It kept the land and the people in that state of continued unrest which was to give an historic setting to—though it could not of itself explain—the note of crisis in the gospel story. By this situation, as we shall see, the stage was set for the events that were to make gospel history.

To bind together all the provinces and to make them accessible to Rome, the empire built its famous roads. Durably constructed of cement and stone, marked with milestones and furnished with military guards, these highways offered rapid

transit to troops, encouraged commerce, provided the Romans
with the necessities of a civilized life, and opened the empire
to the interchange of ideas and the influence of a widening
cosmopolitan culture. In Palestine one such road led from
Jerusalem to Antioch and through the Syrian Gates to Tarsus
and Galatia; another followed the coast from Caesarea to Sidon
into upper Syria, and from there westward to Miletus or to
Ephesus. By means of these open throughfares, and of the
supporting ships on the Mediterranean as the season of safe
navigation permitted, persons who were strange to one another
continually met, races intermingled, the Jews were dispersed
throughout the empire, the Greek language became known in
Asia and Africa and Europe, and the pagan peoples of the empire began to feel the unrest of a moral and religious awakening.

If the Romans furnished the institutions for promoting the
civilized life of the first Christian century, the Greeks infused
into them their vigorous and cultivated spirit. The Greek
genius was volatile and intellectual. It entered and filled the
body of this Roman giant with its own soul. In the Greek
colonies their native literature, art, and philosophy were allowed
to flourish: Ephesus had its temple of Diana; Corinth was famous for its culture and humane studies; Athens gloried in its
freedom of thought, its men of wisdom, and its poets; Tarsus,
in Asia Minor, had its own university; Alexandria, in Egypt,
was a renowned center of learning in which, as early as 250 B.C.,
the Old Testament was begun to be translated in a Greek version
called the Septuagint.

To promote the dissemination of this lively culture, Greek
slaves, like the famous Epictetus, were brought to Rome, allowed
to become freed men, and invited to instruct the patrician families in the teachings of Plato, Aristotle, and the Stoics. Jews in
the empire, even in Syria, became Hellenists, adopting the Greek
language, its ideas, and its customs. This Hellenization of the
entire Mediterranean world accounted for the fact that the New
Testament itself was written in Greek. Saint Paul used the
language with masterly skill. Saint Peter, at one time but a
Galilean fisherman, learned to speak it and to write in it; and it

is altogether probable that Jesus understood it and knew how to use it.

But while the educated persons throughout the empire could console themselves with such philosophies as Stoicism and Epicureanism, the masses of humanity were left without hope except as they found it in the Eastern faiths known to us as the Mystery Religions. Four of them, especially, deserve to be mentioned: (1) the worship of Cybele, the earth-goddess; (2) the cult of Isis and Osiris, Egyptian in its origin, stressing the preparation for the life after death; (3) the Eleusinian Mysteries, centering in the ceremonial act of eating the ground meal dedicated to Demeter, the Grain Mother and goddess of the harvest; (4) Mithraism, of Persian origin, which represented to the Eastern mind the struggle of the soul with evil as symbolized in the conflict between darkness and light.

These mysteries, at first, were purely naturalistic. But, with the progress of civilization, they came to assume a definite moral and spiritual significance, emphasizing men's need of a cleansing from sin and a hunger for communion with God. They witnessed to the fact that a world wandering in darkness was seeking the light, and that enlightened men were not content with bare physical existence. Saint Paul, surrounded by these influences in the middle of the first century, sensed this deep and pitiable need, and summed it up in its fulness as he stood on Mars Hill, in Athens, and said:

> Ye men of Athens, I perceive that in all things ye are too superstitious. For as I passed by, and beheld your devotions, I found an altar with this inscription, To THE UNKNOWN GOD. Whom therefore ye ignorantly worship, him declare I unto you.[2]

The empire attempted to fill this great void in the hearts of men by the introduction of the cult of emperor worship. But no state religion could meet the needs of a people in whom, through progressive culture, the faculty of reason had become discriminative and the conscience alive and sensitive. Fortunately, the wisest of emperors, like Augustus, Tiberius, Claudius, and Vespasian, did not press the cult's observance. When

2 Acts 17:22-23.

Caligula, in A.D. 40, and particularly Domitian, in A.D. 90, determined on being tendered the homage of the deity of the state, it was the Christians who demurred and suffered.   We can well understand why the title *dominus et deus,* applied to Domitian, was abhorrent to them, and why the writer of the Book of Revelation felt compelled to associate this ruler with Nero, disguised as "the beast"; though Nero, aptly described as the "incarnation of the persecuting spirit of the empire," for reasons perhaps obvious enough, did not demand to be regarded as a god. Actually an idiot, he preferred rather to be called an actor and an artist.

Chapter 6

THE PRIMITIVE CHRISTIAN COMMUNITY

I

ISRAEL'S RELIGIOUS HERITAGE

The early Christians were aware of their rich racial and religious heritage. The Hebrew scriptures lay open before them. There, on its sacred pages, were the stories of Israel's patriarchs, heroes, and prophets, men of great courage and faith in God. First among them all was Abraham, who

> As God's first adventurer stood forth
> One star-wrought night, on a familiar hill,
> And saw the Chaldean dawn, remote and chill,
> Etching old Ur along the lonely north,
> And bowed himself to his loved earth, and rent
> His garments, crying he could not go ... and went.[1]

Others followed, men of valiance and vision: Joseph who, returning good for evil, provided food for his father and brothers; Moses, who beheld the glory of God in the burning bush and led the children of Israel from Egypt to the land of Canaan; Joshua, at whose trumpet call Jericho fell; Samuel, who heard the voice of God at the dawn of Israel's national history; David, who set up the kingdom and sang of the wondrous goodness of the Lord, his God. After him came the kings and prophets: kings good and bad; and prophets like Isaiah, Jeremiah, Ezekiel, Daniel, Amos, and Hosea. From them every Jewish youth—and all the first Christians were Jews—learned that the Lord Jehovah was with His chosen people, guiding its destiny, teaching it to walk in His ways, and preparing it to be a light to the Gentiles and a blessing to mankind.

[1] Nancy Byrd Turner, "When Abraham Went Out of Ur," from *Star in a Well* (New York: Dodd, Mead & Co., Inc., 1935).

41

Then, as now, no one could listen to the reading of a great chapter of Hebrew history and not be deeply moved. The realization of the justice and mercy of God was as comforting to them as a rock or a cloud to dwellers in a burning desert. God would not forsake His people. He could not forget Israel: His disciplining hand was upon it; His love and pity were those of a Creator toward His human creature. Such divine solicitude, instilled by the teaching of the prophets, could not go unheeded. It awakened in the Jewish people a deep consciousness of responsibility, particularly because of the humiliation that the nation had suffered when Jerusalem had fallen and Israel had been taken into exile.

The experience of exile had been a shocking one. Devout men were asking: Why had God permitted the nation He loved to suffer this humiliation? The answer, the later prophets had the faith to declare, was in God's own plan for Israel's greater future. By its very suffering Israel was to heal the broken heart of mankind. It was to be, said the Unknown Prophet of the Exile, Jehovah's Suffering Servant, chosen of God to endure, in silence, all the world's sorrow, its sin, even the accusation of being "stricken and smitten of God." Yet the prophet, in his prescience of things to come, could hail this divine servant as blessed, saying,

> When thou shalt make his soul an offering for sin,
> He shall prolong his days; ...
> The pleasure of the Lord shall prosper in his hand.
> He shall see the travail of his soul,
> And shall be satisfied.[2]

When the remnant of the nation returned from Exile to re-establish the Jerusalem Community, it remembered these words and took heart from the hope they inspired. The result was a deepening of inward piety within the community, a strict re-emphasis on the keeping of the Ezra-Mosaic law, and an intense nurture of the Messianic hope that filled the true Israelite's mind with expectancy as he repeated Isaiah's words:

[2] Isaiah 53:10-11.

> The people that walked in darkness
> Have seen a great light:
> They that dwell in the land of the shadow of death,
> Upon them hath the light shined. . . .
> For unto us a child is born,
> Unto us a son is given:
> And the government shall be upon his shoulder:
> And his name shall be called
> Wonderful, Counsellor, The mighty God,
> The everlasting Father,
> The Prince of Peace.[3]

It was on this foundation that the religious faith of Judaism was built. The priestly observance of the temple worship tended further to deepen the consciousness of sin and the desire to seek deliverance from it. Besides this, the nobler aspect of Phariseeism, reflected in its pure monotheism and the moral fervor it engendered, was a challenge to the entire Roman world in which, through the "Dispersion," the Jews were either forced or invited to settle.

The temple and the synagogue were Judaism's chief institutions. There was but one temple, and it was in Jerusalem. It was the symbol of the people's racial and spiritual unity and of its allegiance to God. There, in the daily morning sacrifice, and in the mystery of the Holy of Holies, every devoted son of Israel, however far away in one of the Roman colonies, felt himself to be represented in the presence of Jehovah. Wherever he might be, engaged in secular pursuits in Rome, or Corinth, or Ephesus, or Alexandria, he remembered the historic days on which the feasts and fasts were held: the Passover, the Feast of Unleavened Bread, the Feast of Tabernacles, and particularly the Day of Atonement; and on those days he looked with longing toward the sacred city, brooded solemnly on his people's past, and renewed his fervent faith in the coming of Messiah.

By contrast, yet intimately bound to this temple worship, there was a synagogue in almost every Jewish community. It was, first of all, simply a place of assembly. Its atmosphere was free and democratic. It was conveniently built, often close by

[3] Isaiah 9 :2-6.

a lake or stream; and there was in it no ban on conversation which, in an Oriental setting, might easily be lively, colorful, and assertive. Its supervision was in the care of a body of elders who, in the more tranquil areas of the empire, were given a considerable amount of authority in civil matters.

But the primary use of the synagogue was religious and educational. In it the Scriptures were read and prayers were said, and a scribe or rabbi might address the people on some aspect of the canonical law. Thus the history of Israel became a topic of familiar knowledge; and the story of Moses and the prophets, and large portions of such later sacred writings as the books of Psalms, Proverbs, and Job, were so well learned and taken to heart that, in villages like Capernaum and Nazareth, as well as in Jerusalem, men, women, and children, meeting together in the synagogues on the Sabbath day, could repeat with one accord:

> O how I love thy law!
> It is my meditation all the day....
> How sweet are thy words unto my taste!
> Yea, sweeter than honey to my mouth!...
> Thy word is a lamp unto my feet,
> And a light unto my path.[4]

It was in this setting that the primitive Christian community began its historic existence. But an event had occurred that had made a great difference. Christ the Messiah had come, fulfilling the expectation of Israel, satisfying the world's longing for deliverance from sin, and establishing a new law and way of life. And the wondrous thing had happened in Palestine, before men's very eyes: the blind had received their sight; the lame had walked again; the evil spirit had been driven out of helpless, wretched souls; and the gospel of salvation had been proclaimed to the world.

The people had received the Messiah gladly. But the rigidly legalized minds of the leaders of a now long-established Judaism had turned against him. When the conflict had reached its crisis, they had allowed the Messiah to be crucified. But he had

[4] Psalm 119:97, 103, 105.

risen from the dead and had been accepted as the Lord of life by those who had believed in him. At first the disciples had lived in fear of persecution. But their faith had sustained them. They had banded themselves together into a little company of faithful followers, rehearsing among themselves the events of Christ's life and death and resurrection, and living daily in joyous expectation of his earthly return to establish his kingdom. We read in the Book of the Acts that the number of converts increased rapidly and that the Christian community, so established, "continued steadfastly in the apostles' doctrine and fellowship, and in the breaking of bread, and in prayers."

II

THE APOSTOLIC FAITH AND MESSAGE

It soon became evident that there was both a similarity and a difference between the early Christian community and the adherents to classic Judaism. The first Christians had no desire to separate themselves from their Jewish kinsmen. They were themselves Jews. The history of Israel was very real to them, especially its providential and prophetic message; and they found on the pages of Holy Scripture, as they read them, a glowing confirmation of their faith in Jesus as Messiah. The simple wonder of his birth, the gracious words that fell from his lips, his miracles, the judgment he pronounced on this sinful world, his assumption of the role of the predicted Suffering Servant of Jehovah, his death and resurrection—all these events, as they rehearsed them, took on the significant meaning of divine history.

What had happened, and many of them had witnessed, was indeed God's doing. Through signs and wonders associated with the life and person of Jesus, God had wrought a mighty work in the world, even as Israel's great prophets had predicted. The consummating event that Judaism had so ardently awaited had come to pass. Yet the leaders of Judaism had rejected Jesus as the Christ, and were now opposing the faith of those who believed in him. Such opposition could have but one cause: their eyes were not yet opened that they might behold him. But

those among the Jews who beheld and believed were baptized and accepted to membership in the newly established church.

Thus, beginning with the twelve disciples—after the place made vacant by Judas' betrayal and tragic death had been filled —the Christian community took root and grew. Devoted to the common cause, they kept together, shared each other's possessions, distributed of their income to the poor, followed the instruction of the original disciples who were now called apostles, assisted one another in the faith and fellowship of the risen Lord, and so lived in peace, gladness, and simplicity of heart that they were looked on in favor by all the people.

We note with interest that Peter, who, with James and John, was closest to Jesus during his earthly ministry, distinguished himself as the first leader of the early church. There was a good reason to expect such leadership of him. For, as the Gospels inform us, it was he who, in the time of crisis in Galilee, had addressed the Master with the revealing words: "Thou art the Christ, the Son of the living God." And it was this confession that now made of Peter the rocklike character that early Christian tradition declared him to be. Therefore, when the time came for the church to proclaim itself openly and to make a public confession of its faith, this sturdy apostle stood up to speak.

The story of his first sermon is preserved for us by Saint Luke in the Book of the Acts. Its historic setting was the season of the Harvest Feast, or Pentecost, fifty days after the Resurrection. The disciples were assembled for the hour of worship when, suddenly, the Holy Spirit descended upon them. In the midst of the gracious visitation that befell them, the call came to Peter to preach to the people of Jerusalem. What he said was important both for its content and its evangelistic appeal. Here, for the first time, men heard the gospel of Christ as it was to be preached during apostolic times and later throughout the centuries of Christian history; and it was from this preaching of the living Word that, before the first century ended, the New Testament, including the four Gospels, was to take its final literary form.

What this original gospel contained, and how it was pre-

sented, is therefore of special concern to us. The following outline may be accepted as a general summary of the text as we find it recorded in the second chapter of the Acts, in its twofold setting of the prophetic Book of Joel and the historic scene of Pentecost:

1. Jesus was truly the Messiah sent of God to establish His kingdom.

2. Jesus' death was not simply a tragic event of history. It was God's plan for the redemption of mankind.

3. Jesus' resurrection was by the power of God. It is the proof of his Messiahship.

4. Christ the Messiah is now become the Lord of life. He is given a place on his throne by the right hand of God; and he will, in due time, come again in glory to consummate the reign of his kingdom.

5. Of these facts the disciples, now become the leaders of the new Christian movement, are the true witnesses.

6. The new dispensation of the Holy Spirit is now at hand. God is prepared to do a mighty work in the world through the outpouring of His spirit.

7. Signs and wonders, both of grace and judgment, are yet to be witnessed before this mighty work is fully accomplished.

8. This time, yet to come, will be one of great dividing and decision; and, during it, "whosoever shall call on the name of the Lord shall be saved."

9. This, therefore, is the Day of Grace in which men are called to repentance, to baptism for the remission of sins, and to the promised possession of the gift of the Holy Spirit.

10. This time of grace is signalized by the apostolic word of warning: Save yourselves from this corrupted generation of the children of the world.

Peter's eventful sermon was to bear rich fruit. Before long the Christian community in Jerusalem was enlarged by the conversion of a number of Hellenists, or Greek-speaking Jews of the Dispersion, who had once lived in the outlying areas of the

empire and were now returned to their native land. One of them was Stephen, the first Christian martyr. His awakened mind and devout spirit had found in the gospel of Christ the Messiah the exact fulfilment of the hope of the world. Having now been appointed to an office in the church by the laying on of the apostles' hands, he was filled with the Holy Spirit and began to preach. The great freedom with which he recited the history of Israel, stressing the persecution of the prophets, and reaching a climax with the story of the death of Christ, aroused the opposition of the conservative leaders of the Jews. Stephen was stoned, calling on Christ to forgive his enemies. In the persecution that followed, most of the newly converted Hellenists left Jerusalem, returned to their former homes in the areas of the Dispersion, and carried the "Good News" of the gospel of Christ with them into the empire. Thus the blood of this first martyr became the seed of the church.

As the result of this brief but intense period of persecution, new Christian communities now sprang up almost everywhere. Philip the evangelist went to Samaria, was gladly received, and, as Luke's history records, preached "the things concerning the kingdom of God, and the name of Jesus Christ," and "baptized both men and women." After that he went southward on the road toward Gaza, met the Ethiopian treasurer, interpreted the death of Christ to him in the words of Holy Scripture, baptized him into the faith and fellowship of the new church, and sent the gospel on its way with him into Egypt.

It is pertinent to our study to note that the passage of the Book of Isaiah used as Philip's text was that which centered in the Suffering Servant of God, and read:

> He is brought as a lamb to the slaughter;
> And as a sheep before her shearers is dumb,
> So he openeth not his mouth.[5]

This text, and the fifty-third chapter of Isaiah in which it was found, began very early to be the basis of apostolic preaching and to prepare the way for the special emphasis which the four Gospels were to place on the passion story; and there is an

[5] Isaiah 53:7.

added significance in the fact that, even before the Gospels were composed, Saint Paul made that great chapter the foundation of his doctrine of the Cross.

Meanwhile, acting in behalf of the Jerusalem community, Peter extended his apostolic mission to Joppa by the sea, and northward to the Roman port of Caesarea. He did so, Luke tells us, impelled by a vision. Besides, it is said that, while in Joppa, he lodged in the house of "Simon a tanner." Among the Jews tanning was an "unclean" occupation; but Peter, no doubt remembering how his Master ate with publicans and sinners, resolved to follow where the Holy Spirit led him. When, after that, Cornelius, a Roman centurion, sent for him, he went up to Caesarea, driven as by a voice whose echo the Mediterranean, as he journeyed up the shore, gave back to him: "What God hath cleansed, that call thou not unclean." When Peter rose to speak in Cornelius' house, he said: "Of a truth I perceive that God is no respecter of persons; but in every nation he that feareth him, and worketh righteousness, is accepted with him." [6]

Peter's sermon, here as before, centered in these fundamental facts: Jesus was sent of God; he went about doing good and healing the oppressed; he was nailed to the Cross, but God raised him from the dead; he has revealed himself to his disciples who are his chosen witnesses; his apostles are now commanded to preach Christ as "ordained of God to be the judge of the quick and the dead"; and all who believe in him are to be saved from their sins.

But the apostolic community was still awaiting the arrival of its greatest leader. He appeared in the person of Saul of Tarsus, later called Paul. With him the name "Christian," first applied to the disciples in Antioch, under the ministry of Barnabas, became known throughout the Roman empire. His conversion released the faith of the followers of Christ from the restricting nurture and tradition of Judaism and made of it a world religion. Without the apostleship of Paul, as we may judge the facts, the followers of Jesus would have remained but a sect within Judaism, or the adherents of a cult in the eyes of the Romans who observed it. But such a statement, we should

[6] Acts 10:34, 35.

add, begs history's question: for it is the assumption of prophetic history that God willed it so; and it was on this assumption that Paul knew himself to be called to preach Christ, not to the Jews only, nor to the Greeks alone, but to all men.

Beginning in Antioch, Paul's evangelistic ministry took him first into Asia Minor, then to Greece, and finally to Rome. Everywhere, as a result of his preaching, churches were established. These churches, like the apostle himself, were "new Creations"; they owed their new existence to God's saving power to redeem men from bondage to sin and to make them free. It was this note in Paul's message that made so great an appeal to people everywhere in the empire: men hungered for deliverance, not merely from the yoke of Rome but from the chains of sin. To them the gospel Paul preached was a new "righteousness"—a door miraculously opened to a new and wonderful way of life. The key to this door, he told his hearers, was love. "God loved us while we were yet sinners," he declared with impassioned reasoning to Jews, Greeks, and Romans as he journeyed through Galatia to Macedonia and Corinth. He delighted in founding new Christian communities, in seeing them grow. He worked with consuming zeal, in generous recognition of the work of others, giving God the glory; and he has left us his own commentary on what happened, in these words: "I have planted; Apollo has watered; but God giveth the increase." When his missionary activity ended, Christianity was on its way toward becoming the world's great historic religion.

Chapter 7

THE EARLIEST GOSPEL

I

THE STORY AND ITS SETTING

It has already been suggested that the Christian gospel and the church came into existence together. Both had their origin in the ordered history of revelation. As the church was the new Israel, so the gospel was the law of the new historic dispensation. All that had occurred, within Bible times, was now understood by the first Christian disciples as one continuous Action of God in the world. The "once unspoken, but now spoken, Word of God," in the fulfilment of time, had "become flesh." More directly stated, this self-revealing Act of God was represented in the life of Christ. It was from the life he lived as the God-man, and from his enacted deeds, that the church came into being and that the history of the gospel was begun. And it was to commemorate this life and these enacted deeds that the gospel tradition was later put into writing by the four Evangelists. The Gospels, accordingly, are the record of the divine history begun with the story of Abraham, continued with the acts of Moses and the prophets, and consummated in the life of Jesus Christ.

But before this spoken Word, so offered to the world and accepted, could be committed to writing, it was to be tested in the crucible of experience. There, as the purified and authorized gospel of the church, it gradually crystallized into the basic narrative of New Testament history. So two decades passed, between A.D. 30 and 50, during which, by the preaching of the apostles, the gospel was transmitted from community to community throughout Palestine and to the farther colonies of the Roman world. This crystallization of the oral gospel into a

body of tradition was not accidental. It grew out of a desire to safeguard and present the exact truth about Christ: first, his eschatological message of the Kingdom; second, the treasured account of his earthly life; third, the divine purpose of his death and resurrection; finally, his acknowledged spiritual lordship of mankind. Those who themselves remembered the words of Jesus, and those also who, a few years later, heard the testimony of eyewitnesses, were alike eager to preserve these precious sayings in a form as exact as possible. This reverence for the gospel story, together with the disciples' consciousness of being guided by the Holy Spirit—the spirit of truth-telling as well as truth-revealing—tended to keep the oral tradition intact until the time came for its incorporation into the permanent narrative of the four Gospels.

These four Gospels, we may gratefully say, are now ours. Their narratives lie open before us, letting us look at their major similarities and minor differences. We are aware, as we read them through, that each Evangelist expresses, besides the events he records, his own viewpoint. Yet we note how strikingly alike they are when they stress the same incidents and sayings. Within this area of similarly stressed events we know we can look for the body of oral tradition that was so carefully guarded against being altered or modified by the free exercise of the tendency toward individual interpretation. That this tendency existed, then as now, may be assumed; and the minor divergencies among the Gospels support this assumption. But the major differences among them, especially those between the Synoptic Gospels of Matthew, Mark, and Luke and the Gospel of John, point to another fact, namely, that each of the four Gospel writers had access to some source or sources, oral or already written, with which the others among them were not acquainted.

All this makes it clear that while the gospel story was freely circulated among all the Christian communities, not all of them had access to the same body of oral tradition. It is therefore necessary to look carefully at the entire gospel record in order to find in it the earliest, or primitive, gospel message which was first preached and taught by the apostles, treasured by them, and so kept intact until the time came for it to be incorporated

into the complete narrative as it now exists. The task of finding this original gospel imbedded in the oral tradition has lately attracted the attention of New Testament scholars whose findings have become known to us under the name of *form criticism*.

The method of approach of the form critic is analytical. His viewpoint is prevailing theological. He sets out to find in the existing narrative those passages which indicate why and how the gospel was first proclaimed to the world. He asks: What was the essential message of the writers of the New Testament? The answer, indicated or implied on almost every page of its sacred text, is this: it was the message that Jesus was the Christ, the expected Messiah, the Savior of the world. This great truth was openly preached, first to the Jewish communities in Palestine, then to Jews and Gentiles alike in the colonies of the Roman empire. It was taught to the new converts who needed to be instructed in the doctrine and the fellowship of the Christian faith. It helped the community of Christians to bear their earthly trials, and to nurture in them a comforting eternal hope. This gospel, so preached and taught, was to them the core of the meaning of Christ's coming into the world. That meaning, simply expressed, was religious; and the interpretation given to it, in the very beginning, was a theological one.

A closer examination of the content of this earliest gospel shows it to have been, generally, of a fourfold nature. There was, first of all, the compelling message of the Kingdom of God. Christ had come to announce that the Kingdom was at hand. God was prepared to do mighty things in the world. In an era of divine grace He was to pour out His heavenly spirit on mankind: the blind were to see, the lame to walk; the evil demon was to be driven out of suffering humanity, and peace and good will were to be offered to the longing hearts of men everywhere. Thereafter would come a time of judgment. If men repented, they were to be saved; but evildoers were to be cast forth from God's presence; they were to be as the bad fishes sorted from the fisherman's net, as chaff burned in the fire, as the unready guest excluded from the wedding feast at the time when Christ the Bridegroom was to sit down with his bride, the church, in the everlasting banquet of the consummated heav-

enly kingdom. This feast of grace was prepared for all who wished to come. Christ, through his birth, his death, and his resurrection, had put everything in readiness for them. He had established his church on earth, and already here and there in Palestine, and presently in the empire, people were gathering to form Christian communities. It was God's will that the gospel should be preached everywhere and that the church should be built in every land as a witness of God's plan to redeem the world.

Next to the proclamation of the Good News of the Kingdom was the teaching of its divine law. The Kingdom was not only an event in history; it was also a way of life. Christians were to be guided by it in their daily living, in their relation to one another, to the world, and to the business to be transacted in it, and in their general labor and waiting for the great day of the fulfilment of their Lord's promised return.

Until that day came, Christians must needs live in the world; but they were not to be of the world. Their lives were to be like lighted candles in a dark room. They were to live humbly as behooved the followers of Christ: to be merciful, just, pure in heart; to expect and even to rejoice in persecution, not fearing death; to keep the commandments, but to exceed them by avoiding retaliation; to go the second mile; to love even their enemies. They were to refrain from judging others, to trust God's mercy for themselves, to be wary of evildoers—wolves in sheep's clothing. They were to discipline themselves to enter into the Kingdom by the strait gate and the narrow way, and to lead lives of true piety, giving to the poor, avoiding a show of being religious. And they were to remember their communal need of each other and of God's daily grace, as this need was summed up in the prayer their Lord himself had taught them in the words:

> When ye pray, say:
> Our Father which art in heaven,
> Hallowed be Thy name,
> Thy Kingdom come,
> Thy will be done
> In earth, as it is in heaven.

Give us this day our daily bread.
And forgive us our debts,
As we forgive our debtors.
And lead us not into temptation,
But deliver us from evil.[1]

In addition to the proclamation of the Kingdom, and the teaching of its law, there was a third element in the content of this earliest gospel. It comprised the events of the earthly life of Christ.[2] In their history, his birth, death, and resurrection were the focal points; for in them the early church found gathered together both the prophecy and the fulfilment of the doctrine of the Kingdom of God. Christ was to be born as the Davidic Messiah, carry the world's sin with him to the Cross as the Suffering Servant of God, rise triumphant from the grave as the Son of man, and be enthroned in heaven as the Son of God at the right hand of the Father.

Yet in focusing attention on the Incarnation, the Crucifixion, and the Resurrection, the human life of Jesus of Nazareth was not allowed to fade from the picture. To remember Jesus as he lived on earth, taking upon himself our complete humanity, sharing our infirmities, our laughter, and our tears, was not something incidental to the faith of the early Christians. For some of them had themselves been with him, heard the words he had himself spoken, and seen with their own eyes the mighty deeds God had wrought through them. The memory of these words and deeds was treasured up by the apostles, together with the special event of Christ's passion and death; and these together, from the beginning, were joined into the integrated body of the gospel tradition. Peter's preaching, and Paul's after him, stressed both the humanity of Jesus and the divine history of his life as indispensable to the historical setting of God's plan and drama of our redemption. Without this especial stress the human relationship involved in the divine purpose

[1] Matthew 6:9-13.
[2] In a larger sense, the life of Christ comprises the entire gospel. The gospel is the gospel of the life of Christ. The events here referred to are to be understood as composing the gospel's divine history. Similarly, the law of the Kingdom is not to be interpreted legalistically but as the life of Christ operative in the community of believers.

of Christ's coming would have been obscured and gradually lost. Christ had lived on earth and among men; and the glory of the Lord had been revealed that "all flesh might see it together." This solid fact was also a part of the Christian gospel.

Finally, the Christian community had a faith with a forward look into the great and awaiting future. To its devout adherents Christ was now the ruler of mankind, and to them the time was not far off when he would come again to claim his own for himself in the Father's kingdom. In the words of the ancient parable, the vineyard of God was now being tilled and kept by his chosen husbandmen who were intent on having a rich harvest ready for their Lord on his return. To this trust every leader in the Christian community must and would be faithful. To have faith and to be faithful was the twofold command entrusted to them.

But the time would come, soon or late, and the end of the age would be at hand. It would be a time of sifting, of the burning of the chaff, of an ingathering of the harvest of the redeemed. Then, with the consummation of all things, the vineyard of God's kingdom was to yield the wine of an immortal life, when the Master, now the Bridegroom, would sit beside his bride, the church, at the banqueting table in God's heavenly kingdom and joy would reign eternally. In anticipation of this fulfilment, the disciples needed the continuous outpouring of heavenly grace in the person of the Holy Spirit. And the comfort they could give one another as they looked into the future was that contained in what Saint Luke later so carefully recorded in his Gospel, and in the Acts,

> Of all that Jesus began both to do and teach, until the day in which he was taken up; after that he through the Holy Ghost had given commandments unto the apostles whom he had chosen; to whom also he shewed himself after his passion, by many infallible proofs; being seen of them forty days, and speaking of the things pertaining to the kingdom of God.[3]

[3] Acts 1:2, 3.

II
THE ORAL TRADITION

In this fourfold material comprising the gospel story there lie imbedded certain units or sections, called *pericopae,* preserved for us in their original setting in the present literary narrative of the Evangelists. These units, kept intact and safe from change by their use as oft-repeated texts for evangelistic preaching, and as topics for the instruction of converts in the Christian community, are of special interest to us today as we try to answer the question of how the gospel began to assume the form which in a short time crystallized into the oral tradition.

In these units, discoverable in their present context by their literary style and their historical-social setting, some scholars who follow the method of form criticism have sought to find a record of the very words (*ipsissima verba*) of Christ as they were spoken by him in the hillside towns of Galilee or in the region of Judea. It has, indeed, been shown that certain passages which in our Gospels have a markedly poetical structure may readily be translated from the Greek into the Aramaic language in which Jesus spoke to the people of his time. When such a translation is made, it can be seen that the poetry of these passages, having the rhythm and repetitive quality of an utterance of Old Testament prophecy, would tend not only to make them easily communicable but to protect them against any change as they passed into the hands of the later Gospel writers.[4] Here—to choose but one type of passage or literary unit—is an example of the traceable and essential gospel, the living word of Christ the Word of Life, directly communicated to us from the sacred text:

> O Jerusalem, Jerusalem,
> That killest the prophets,
> And stonest them which are sent unto thee!
> How often would I have gathered thy children together,
> Even as a hen gathereth her chickens under her wings,

[4] See C. F. Burnev. *The Poetry of Our Lord* (New York: Oxford Book Co., 1925).

And ye would not!
Behold, your house is left unto you desolate.
For I say unto you,
Ye shall not see me henceforth, till ye shall say:
Blessed is he that cometh in the name of the Lord.[5]

Here also, very significantly, we have evidence of the intrinsic Christological character of the earliest gospel tradition. Passages like the one just quoted prove that we do not have simply the record of the conversation and the practical admonition of a very humanitarian and pious Jesus but of the historically manifested word of God. The truth impresses itself on us that Christ was not simply an extraordinary personality whose virtues we are to emulate, but that he was the Son of God from whom we are to receive the eternal and living Word—even the Word that strikes through us, riving our sinful hearts, placing our lives under its judgment, and replenishing them with its efficient grace.

These units, or pericopae, as the form critic calls them, are given a general classification for us under the terms of parables, poetical sayings, controversial dialogues, and pronouncement stories. Beyond them, looming before us in its great portent, is the story of Christ's passion, no longer an aggregation of units but a solidified narrative. The list of these units, as we should expect, is large. Actually, it is not limited to the four Gospels but includes sections of the letters of Paul, the epistles of Peter, the Epistle to the Hebrews, and the Book of the Acts. The following is a typical and illustrated record of them:

1. *The Passion Story*
   The core or nucleus of the gospel tradition.
   Now one consolidated and complete unit.
2. *Pronouncement Stories*
   Examples
   The Feast with Publicans and Sinners. Mark 2:15-17
   Jesus' Blessing on the Children. Mark 10:13 ff.

[5] Matthew 23:37-39.

3. *Parables*

    Examples

        The Lost Sheep. Luke 15:4-7

        The Pharisee and the Publican. Luke 18:10-14

4. *Poetical Sayings*

    Examples

        The Children in the Market Place. Matthew 11:16-19

        Jesus' Lamentation over Jerusalem. Matthew 23:37-39

5. *Controversial Dialogues*

    Examples

        The Charge of Sorcery. Mark 3:23-26

        The Question of Divorce. Mark 10:1-10

6. *Miracle Stories*

    Examples

        The Healing of the Withered Hand. Mark 3:1-5

        The Demoniac in the Synagogue. Mark 1:23-27

7. *Aphorisms*

    Examples

        The Law and the Prophets. Matthew 11:13-15

        The Blessedness of the Disciples. Matthew 13:16-17

8. *Eschatological Discourses*

    Examples

        Parable of the Unfaithful Vineyard Keeper. Mark 12:1-9

        Parable of the Ten Virgins. Matthew 25:1-13

        Parable of the Messianic Feast. Matthew 22:1-14

A detailed example of how these gospel units may be tested for their authenticity is offered in the two simple parables of the Hidden Treasure and the Costly Pearl. Their setting in the context of Matthew 13 is that of a collection of parables defining the kingdom of God. Here, presented in clear relief, is the gospel's central truth, radiant like a diamond in a cluster of pearls. The parable itself is a typical form of illustrative story found nowhere in the New Testament but in the Synoptic Gospels—a fact that is itself sufficient proof of Jesus' use of it. Besides, the literary *form* of the parable is itself inseparable

from its inner *content* and so tends to preserve the actual words
which keep the thought intact.

It follows, therefore, that the apostles, in using the parables,
whether in preaching, in teaching, or in open controversy with
the Jews and Gentiles, would usually quote rather than para-
phrase them among the people. Moreover, the general tone of
the parables was at variance with popular sentiment: it made
investment in the kingdom of God seem a rash and foolish
thing. A man finds a treasure hidden in a field and he hastily
buys the field to own the treasure. Or a man discovers a pearl
and parts with all his property to own it. Is the kingdom of
God made up of such rash and foolish men—of speculators who
will not play safe? Yet it is precisely this risk that Jesus com-
mends and himself assumes. Such words give no evidence of
an easy adjustment to a later situation within the expanding
church. They are hard and firm words; they present the Christian community with a testing alternative, an "either/or"; they
stand in their own right in the setting of Christ's earthly life
and are clearly authentic.

We are not to think of these pericopae as at first wholly
disconnected preaching or teaching units. Rather, there was
from the beginning a sustaining root from which they grew, as
clusters on a vine, whether as groups of sayings, or parables,
or stories of miracles, as in Mark 2, Matthew 13, and Luke 15;
and the passion story well illustrates the tendency toward an
integrated narrative in which the words and acts of Christ are
fully assimilated by the intent and design of the divine drama.
In the story of Christ's passion, the fusion of the elements is
complete. To return to our illustration: it is as if the vine's
cluster of grapes had been pressed together into an outpouring
stream to give us the gospel's full story and to symbolize its
deep meaning.

The obvious tendency, in the formation of the gospel tradition, was twofold: (1) to collect and arrange the sayings of
Jesus by topics, and (2) to give to the collection the authentic
setting of Christ's earthly life. For it was clearly not enough
to have these great imperishable truths to preach; they needed
to be associated in some historic order and trustworthy manner

with the life of him from whom they derived their meaning. This need was, first of all, applicable to the passion story in which it was necessary to explain why and how Christ, whom the early Christians acknowledged as Lord and adored, was by the Jews and Romans put to death as a malefactor. A carefully kept record of the events in the life of Christ was therefore not incidental to the telling of the gospel story. It was not something of which the apostles, under whose guidance the oral tradition took shape, were ignorant, or to which they gave the afterthought of their own invention.

The earthly life of Christ and his living gospel were from the beginning an integrated story consisting of reportable units of the mighty words and deeds of him who was born of the Virgin Mary and baptized of John, who gathered his disciples about him, preached and taught the advent of the Kingdom, incurred the enmity of the Jewish leaders, and, after that—in the language of the Apostles' Creed which was later to preserve, for all time, the essence of the passion story—

> Suffered under Pontius Pilate,
> Was crucified, dead, and buried; . . .
> The third day he rose again from the dead:
> He ascended into heaven,
> And sitteth at the right hand of God the Father Almighty;
> From thence he shall come to judge the quick and the dead.

In a word, the oral tradition was, from the first, both Christological and historical. Story and doctrine were united in its initial crystallization. We are, therefore, not to think of the earthly history of Jesus as a later addition to the gospel of Christ, or that, contrariwise, the simple story of Jesus of Nazareth was gradually and radically changed by an addition of the theological ideas of the Gospel writers and the teachings of Saint Paul. It is enough for our present study to say that, while the life of the early Christian community was reflected in the gospel tradition, it was not the creation of that community. Historically speaking, the gospel coexisted with the church; and the apostolic age prized its tradition too highly to distort it.

It is important to remember that Saint Paul also was of that age. He shared the gospel tradition. He did not create it. When, in the year A.D. 48 or 49, he began his eventful ministry in the Roman colonies outside of Palestine, the church in Antioch had been firmly established. Barnabas, his colleague on his first missionary journey, had been careful to instruct him in the new faith; and, as we may infer from Luke's account in Acts 12, he had heard the story of Jesus' earthly life from Peter himself, from whom Mark had also first learned it. That Paul's preaching generally resembled Peter's is clearly noticeable: both apostles began with an account of Old Testament history; and both reached the climax of their discourses with the story of the Crucifixion and Resurrection. If Paul made use of concepts current among the adherents of the Asiatic Mystery Religions, it was to make plain the greater mystery of the gospel of the Cross and not to translate that gospel from its setting in prophetic history into speculative ideas associated with certain pagan cults. How greatly, besides Jesus' earthly history, the Apostle respected also the authority of our Lord's social teaching may be seen, for example, in his reference, in I Corinthians 7, to the institution of marriage.

But what finally impresses us is the fact that, among all the apostles, it was Paul who saw most clearly the world-wide implications of the historic event of Christ's coming. The majesty of Paul's conception of Christ and of his prophetic-redemptive office, as symbolized and re-enacted in the Holy Eucharist, is nowhere in the New Testament given a more natural historical setting in the life of Jesus than in these now-treasured words:

> For I have received of the Lord that which also I delivered
> unto you, that the Lord Jesus, in the same night in which he
> was betrayed, took bread; and, when he had given thanks,
> he brake it, and said:
> > Take, eat: this is my body, which is broken for you;
> > This do in remembrance of me.
> After the same manner also he took the cup,
> when he had supped saying:
> > This cup is the new testament in my blood;

This do ye, as oft as ye drink it, in remembrance of me.
For as often as ye eat this bread, and drink this cup,
Ye do shew the Lord's death,
Till he come.[6]

We may say, therefore, that by the year A.D. 45 the oral tradition was in the complete form in which it was ready to be committed to writing. The four strands of the narrative had during the fifteen preceding years been closely bound together to represent what has been called the *Kerigma,* the *Didache,* the *Gnosis,* and the *Eschaton* of the gospel.[7] Briefly interpreted, the essence of the Kerigma was that the Kingdom of Heaven was at hand. The Didache had to do with the manner in which those who awaited the Kingdom's coming were to conduct their lives in an earthly society. The Gnosis represented a deeper inquiry into the life of Christ as the revelation of God. And by the Eschaton was meant the divine plan of the goal of history and the end of all things.

In summary we may say that the vital cord of this tradition had been the preaching of the gospel of the Kingdom. Next to it, and intertwined with it, had been the teaching of the Kingdom's law and rule of life. Surrounding these two strands, bound up with them and not merely their covering fabric, had been the doctrinal history of the earthly life of Christ. And, finally, giving to gospel history the goal of a divine plan, there had been discovered in—not added to—this entire tradition the eschatological order, or doctrine, of the final consummation of all things. So entrusted to the future, the tradition awaited its permanent incorporation into written history.

[6] I Corinthians 11:23-26.
[7] See C. H. Dodd, *History and the Gospel* (New York: Charles Scribner's Sons, 1938), chap. ii, pp. 41-77.

Chapter 8

FROM TRADITION TO LITERATURE

I

The Gospels' Literary Structure

Reading through the Gospels, eagerly, and in the light of their revealed truth, is a deeply moving experience. Here is a story four times told, interspersed with sayings whose very familiarity has the sound of footsteps at the door—variously expected, insistent, disturbing, and consoling. The convincing reason is that in every turn of the narrative the reader has been waylaid and confronted by the Word of God. There has been no way of ignoring or escaping the fact, as Francis Thompson has expressed it, that "Fear wist not to evade as Love wist to pursue." For such reading, after the first few pages, has not been a mere examining of the records to see if by some chance any evidence of first-century history has been left unverified in ferreting out the gospel facts. Instead, it has been a lesson in listening, and a discipline of the soul, to follow the story's continuing tension and release, suggesting these words of the poet's familiar refrain:

> Still with unhurrying chase,
> And unperturbèd pace,
> Deliberate speed, majestic instancy,
> Came on the following Feet,
> And a Voice above their beat—
> "Naught shelters thee, who wilt not shelter Me." [1]

Such an absorbing reading of the Gospels leaves other valuable and guiding aftereffects. One of them, and the first in

---

[1] Francis Thompson, "The Hound of Heaven," from *Poems*, 1893. Used by permission of Dodd, Mead & Co., New York, publishers.

importance, is the vivid impression one gets of two diverse facts. The first is the Gospels' striking differences; the second is their remarkable agreement. A common lofty theme unites them while, at the same time, they show an independence that points equally to an originality of composition and to the use of a variety of sources. The likeness is most marked among the Gospels of Matthew, Mark, and Luke; the divergence is most vivid and wide in a comparison of those Gospels with the Gospel of John. This divergence is noticeable from the start, and continues throughout the narratives, until we reach the passion story, when all the Gospels come together, like four streams to form a deep river running to the sea, indicating, as we have already said, the purpose of the combined tradition to find its fulfilment in the world-wide church.

One notices at once, and particularly, the wide use of the parable in the first three Gospels, and its conspicuous absence in the Gospel of John where the argument, or dialogue, takes its place as a vehicle for the teaching of the doctrine of the person of Christ. John's substitute for the parable is the allegory. Events in the life of Christ become signs of what he himself is to the world: the encounter with the woman at Jacob's well becomes an invitation to drink of the water of life; the feeding of the five thousand offers the occasion to announce himself as the bread of life; through the healing of the blind man he becomes the light of the world; by the raising of Lazarus he declares himself to be the resurrection and the life.

The stories John chooses, accordingly, are types symbolizing great truths. Time, place, and circumstance in them have an ideal setting. The truths themselves are timeless; they are set over against the world represented in the Jews; and, by this means, a tension is set up between the Word and the world, a challenge demanding a response. The silence of the world is its denial of the Word, and thereby the world is judged. The earthly history of Christ is not denied. Christ's coming is the world's judgment. But to those who respond to the challenge the response means life eternal, here and now, a gift of God's grace, a revelation of divine truth.

This symbolical use of Jesus' earthly history is not absent

in the other three Gospels. In them, too, the mighty works of God are signs that His kingdom is come among men. But the whole record is given a more strictly historical setting. The kingdom of God is regarded as history. The events are set together in a careful order of sequence, especially in the Gospel of Luke in which an attempt is made to write a complete biography of Jesus. The miracles, parables, pronouncement stories, and discourses, of which we have previously spoken, are so arranged as to lead up very naturally to the passion narrative as the climactic event of the gospel story. The order of events, though not more intentionally chronological than that of John, is better suited to a continuous story having an auspicious beginning in Judea, a period of expansion followed by a crisis in Galilee, and a climax in Jerusalem; and the schematic or topical arrangement of the material in the first three Gospels is seen to have been formally subjected to this unifying purpose and dramatic design. The total effect upon the reader of the narrative of these three Gospels, accordingly, is one of pleasing harmony. The three Evangelists, in the main, see eye to eye in their accounts of the words, deeds, and sufferings of Christ; and it is for this reason that New Testament scholars habitually speak of them as the Synoptic Gospels.

But while this narrative-topical agreement among the Synoptic Gospels is general and genuine, it is not the whole story. To assure ourselves of this fact we need only turn again to their opening chapters and to observe what we find there. We note, first, that Matthew and Luke begin their narratives with birth stories which resemble one another closely without being identical. We observe, too, that both Matthew and Luke present us with similar though not identical genealogies, and that they give them different places in the narrative.

At the beginning of Luke's Gospel we read of the birth of John the Baptist, but note with some surprise that Matthew does not record it. Nor does Mark who does not record any infant stories of Jesus at all but begins his Gospel with the prophetic message of John. To complete the comparison, Matthew alone tells the stories of the visit of the Magi and the flight to Egypt; while Luke, its seems, not wishing to be out-

done in originality and in his adoration of Christ, includes the stories of the infant's presentation in the temple and of the child Jesus among the doctors. After that, as if having found a story of great dramatic significance, Matthew, Luke, and Mark join in recording the preaching of John in the wilderness of Judea; and to add to our interest, after these divergences, they use, for whole sentences together, the very same phrases in relating John's message culminating in the words: "I baptize you with water . . . He shall baptize you with the Holy Ghost." But though whole phrases of the three narratives are literally alike, there are characteristic differences even in this climactic statement of John's sermon; for Matthew alone writes: "I baptize you with water *unto repentence";* and Matthew and Luke, together, go beyond Mark to record: "He shall baptize you with the Holy Ghost *and with fire."*

From this initial comparison of the first three Gospels, there issue several clear facts. There is in them, first of all, an unmistakable tendency toward harmony and an equally undeniable evidence of independence. Next, it is observable that when the Evangelists agree they often do so literally, using identical phrases and following the same sequence of thought within a given episode. Here, we must conclude, is proof of the use of some documentary source; for it is not likely that all three Gospels could record so literally certain material that was still only available in the form of an oral tradition. This source, it must be inferred, either was a now lost document used by all three of the synoptic evangelists, or it was itself, in whole or in part, one of our existing Gospels used freely, yet independently, by the other two. That the Gospel of Mark served as a primary source to the writers of both Matthew and Luke is now an established opinion of synoptic scholarship.

The evidence for this opinion has a twofold ground. The one may be called historical; the other, literary. Mark's Gospel is fundamentally simpler than the other two narratives. There is an abrupt brevity in the sequences of its various episodes that suggests a closeness to the events it records. It is not the brevity of condensation but of the bare thought. The record

has the character of immediate action rather than of prolonged contemplation. The typical Markan story begins with a
"straightway" of some deed or act of Jesus, and ends with a
terse reference to the astonished crowds standing by and listening to his words of authority. The first chapter of the Gospel
illustrates this instancy of time and closeness to the scene, as,
for example, in verses eighteen and thirty-three: "And straightway they [the first disciples] forsook their nets, and followed
him"; "And all the city was gathered together at the door." In
a word, the language and the episodes alike indicate that the
tension set up between the announcement of the kingdom of
God and the open response to it is greater, and that therefore
the issues are more closely drawn toward the impending crisis in
Mark's narrative than in those of Matthew and Luke. It is,
on this ground, more reasonable to assume that Matthew and
Luke drew upon Mark as they desired, according to their several
aims, than to hold that Mark is but a lesser transcript of one
or both of the longer narratives of Matthew and Luke.

But it is in the order of events of the combined narrative
that the dependence of Matthew and Luke on Mark is most
clearly established. Though Matthew and Luke write more
elaborately than Mark, they do not do so without a definite plan
and a good reason. Each of the two Evangelists sets out with
his own aim and in the end accomplishes it.

Matthew, for example, will go along with Luke for some
distance in his account, item after item, using many of the
same phrases, stressing the same noteworthy facts. Then,
quite unexpectedly, after this almost identical order of sequence,
he will interrupt his narrative long enough to include a chapter
on the teaching of Jesus; after which, from all appearances,
having considered himself long separated from his companion,
he rejoins Luke at the exact place where, a little while ago, he
had abruptly left him. Throughout his Gospel we see Matthew
doing this same thing five times, each time to introduce a body
of Jesus' teaching or public discourse, and so furnishing us
with a clear view of the pattern of his narrative. Luke, similarly, in a place where it suits his purpose, interrupts the parallel

record for the space of nine chapters [2] in order to introduce a group of parables and incidents. He then returns to pick up the thread of the narrative at the exact point where it was broken off. This intermittent joining of the two accounts may seem strange to us until we look at Mark's Gospel and find that, when Matthew and Luke thus keep together, their combined story is exactly parallel to that of Mark. It is very evident that Mark is here their main source. The priority of this Gospel is thereby established.

But what shall we say of the interpolated discourses and parables which so evidently caused Matthew and Luke to break away from Mark, their primary source, in order to provide a place for this additional material in the synoptic record? Clearly, such parables and discourses were available to Matthew and Luke. And that they were no longer in the form of an oral tradition, but existed in writing, is implied by the literal care with which, for example, the collections of the sayings of Jesus are used by the two Evangelists. Matthew, as we have said, breaks them up into five groups; Luke, on the other hand, distributes them to various parts of his narrative. But their identity as a documentary source is readily discovered, even though it must perhaps be assumed that Matthew and Luke had before them different versions of it. Among scholars of the Synoptic Gospels this source has become familiarly known as Q. It antedates the Gospel of Mark. The Evangelist Mark seems himself to have incorporated sayings of Jesus from it into his own Gospel. Its early origin as a written source was the natural outcome of the need of the early Christian church for such a collection of Jesus' teachings to be used among its converts.

Containing, besides the discourses best preserved for us in Matthew's Gospel, also certain incidents of the life of Christ, the source called Q may be said to have been the first written Gospel. We can readily picture the impression it made on those who heard it read in the early Christian communities established in Caesarea, in Antioch, and elsewhere in the empire, and

[2] Chapters 9:51-18:14.

appreciate the place of honor they gave to it by the side of the dramatic story of Christ's life and death and resurrection recorded in Mark's Gospel. And we are therefore able to understand the reason why Matthew and Luke felt themselves impelled to bring together both the mighty acts of Jesus and his great teachings into one complete narrative for the ages yet to come. In Matthew's hands the story retained its strong Markan stress on the self-sacrifice and Messiahship of Jesus; under Luke's guidance it expanded into a Gospel of world outlook, envisioning and glorying in the universal saviorhood of Christ. But both Matthew and Luke adhered loyally to the primitive tradition they found imbedded in their documentary sources. Both were careful authors and editors; and both, in their task, believed themselves to be overshadowed and guided by the Holy Spirit.

On looking further into Matthew and Luke, we discover that Mark and Q were not their only sources. For Matthew and Luke are seen to contain sections of material not to be found in Mark, and not attributable to any of the then current versions of Q. Many individual strands of the gospel tradition were in existence in Palestine and Syria between the years A.D. 70 and 85. Some of them had been put into writing; others survived in oral form. Two such strands, or fragments, supplied the infancy stories with which Matthew and Luke began their Gospels. Matthew, using one source, found in it the accounts of the visit of the Magi and the flight to Egypt; Luke, with access to the other, told of the birth of John, the temple presentation of the infant Jesus, and the boy Jesus sitting in the temple among the doctors. Another and more important body of tradition, perhaps circulated orally, was that of a special passion narrative which provided Luke with such stories as the trial before Herod, the penitent thief, and the appearance of the risen Christ to the disciples on the road to Emmaus.

But the most significant of these independent sources was that on which Luke drew for the writing of what is called the "Greater Interpolation," found in Chapters 9:51-18:14 of his Gospel. Here, for the space of nearly nine chapters, the

Third Evangelist gives us a collection of incidents and parables equalled nowhere else in the New Testament. The richness of this source can be measured by noting in it such parables as those of the Rich Fool, the Pharisee and the Publican, and the Prodigal Son.

Altogether, while Matthew's Gospel contains almost all of Mark, and only a rather small amount of the story not also to be found in Luke, there is in Luke, by comparison, much more material that can be called original. This originality is, besides all else, apparent in the arrangement of the topics as they pass under his reverent but scrutinizing observation. Everything indicates that Luke wrote with his sources before him, acknowledging his debt, as he himself said, to others who had worked with the existing tradition and the written documents to which he had access. That he weighed questions involving the priority of sources, giving precedence to certain accounts over others, omitting and selecting from what he had at hand, carefully weighing the evidence, and giving the entire narrative the historical order and literary structure he desired, is made sufficiently plain to us as we study the Synoptic Gospels analytically and with deserved care.

In summary, we note with satisfaction that the Evangelist himself lets us observe his entire plan of procedure when, with a sensitive recognition that he is recording the living word of God, he begins his Gospel by making these prefatory statements: (1) that others before him have undertaken to present an orderly account of the gospel story; (2) that his sources are the record and testimony of "eyewitnesses and ministers of the word"; (3) that he attempts his task only after much careful study leading to an "understanding of all things from the very first"; (4) that his object is to verify the historical nature of the Christian tradition and its underlying faith. How well he accomplished what he set out to do is amply demonstrated in the combined history of Luke-Acts.

II

THE DOCUMENTARY SOURCES

In order to get a clear insight into the synoptic problem, it will be helpful to place the incidents recorded in the three Gospels side by side in a manner that will indicate the reasons, *first,* for regarding Mark as the earliest of the first three Gospels, *second,* for assuming that, before Mark was written, there existed one or more versions of a documentary source now conveniently called Q, and, *third,* for holding the equally valid assumption that both Matthew and Luke—but Luke to a greater extent than Matthew—made use of still other written and oral sources of the gospel story current in and around Palestine at the time of the composition of these two Gospels.

Such a parallel arrangement will illuminate for us the entire picture of the gospel story. The table on pages 74-78, prepared by Wade, lists the items, or passages of the text, in three columns, placing those of Mark in the first column and numbering them in the order of their sequence in that Gospel.[3] The comparison is made illuminating and simple by taking note of these four guiding points:

1. The parallel passages found in *all three of the Gospels,* or in *both* Mark and Matthew, or in *both* Mark and Luke, have the same prefixed Arabic numeral.

2. The parallel passages found in *both* Matthew and Luke but *not* recorded in Mark—passages generally attributed to the source called Q—are marked by Roman numerals in parentheses.

3. Passages found in only one of the three Gospels are printed in italics.

4. The manner in which Matthew and Luke change the order of sequence of events, or passages, in Mark's narrative can readily be seen by noting the position of the Arabic numerals in the second and third columns.

[3] This table is found in G. W. Wade: *New Testament History,* 1922, Chap. vii, pp. 148 ff., and is used by permission of E. P. Dutton & Co. publishers, New York.

We can observe, with little difficulty, how this outline may be put to several important uses. First, a list can be made of the passages to be found in all three of the Gospels. These passages can then be compared for their likenesses and differences in thought and literary structure. Next, the passages in which Matthew or Luke, alone, follows Mark can be grouped together for special study. After that, a list of the passages found in both Matthew and Luke, but not recorded in Mark, can be made. This list may be regarded as a working copy of the lost document Q. Finally, the italicized passages and larger sections found in only one of the three Gospels can be noted and studied for clues to the extent and the character of the sources to which each of the three Evangelists alone had access.

This documentary study may be regarded as fundamental to a thorough literary knowledge of the New Testament. It prepares the way to a discovery of the oral tradition that lies behind the written narrative of the gospel, and helps us to find in this tradition the individual units, or pericopae, in which the evangelistic message of the early church is vitally and doctrinally preserved. Here, it has previously been noted, we find the essential gospel of Christ, the living Word, speaking directly to us and to the world—the word of grace for which the world is waiting, and of judgment which it does not wish to hear, but to which it must give heed, and by which it will at last be judged.

The study of the synoptic problem is not yet complete. It challenges us, in every age, with further questions. Among them, perhaps the most significant concerns the literary origin of the Gospel of Mark. Did not Mark, too, rely on several sources? If so, what were they? How much of the tradition of the Roman church is directly attributable to the words of Peter and to the teaching of Paul? Again, to what source did Luke go for the great parables found only in his Gospel? The existence of Q may, or perhaps must, be assumed; but how can its range and quantity be established in order to account for its precise use by the Evangelists, including its possible use also by Mark?

SYNOPTIC CHART

MARK	MATTHEW	LUKE
	(i) Genealogy of Jesus.	*Birth of John.*
	(ii) Birth of Jesus.	(ii) Birth of Jesus.
	Visit of the Magi.	*Circumcision and Presentation.*
	Flight into Egypt.	*Finding in the Temple.*
1. Preaching of John in the wilderness of Judaea.	1. Preaching of John in the wilderness of Judaea.	1. Preaching of John in the wilderness of Judaea.
	(iii) Substance of John's preaching.	(iii) Substance of John's preaching.
		26. John's imprisonment.
2. Baptism of Jesus in the Jordan.	2. Baptism of Jesus in the Jordan.	2. Baptism of Jesus in the Jordan.
		(i) Genealogy of Jesus.
3. Temptation of Jesus.	3. Temptation of Jesus.	3. Temptation of Jesus.
	(iv) Details of Temptation.	(iv) Details of Temptation.
4a. Departure to Galilee.	4a. Departure to Galilee.	4a. Departure to Galilee.
4b. Preaching there.		4b. Preaching there.
		Preaching at Nazareth.
		24. "Is not this Joseph's son?"
5. Call of Peter, Andrew, James, and John in Galilee.	5. Call of Peter, Andrew, James, and John in Galilee.	
6. Healing of possessed at Capernaum.	4b. Preaching in Galilee.	6. Healing of possessed at Capernaum.
	(v) Sermon on the Mount.	
	9. Healing of leper.	
	(vi) Healing of Centurion's servant.	
7. Healing of Peter's mother-in-law.	8. Healing of Peter's mother-in-law.	7. Healing of Peter's mother-in-law.
8. Healing of many sick.	8. Healing of many sick.	8. Healing of many sick.
	(vii) Offers of Discipleship.	5. Call of Peter, James, and John in Galilee.
		Miracle of the Fishes.
9. Healing of leper.	20. Stilling of the storm.	9. Healing of leper.
	21. Healing of *two* demoniacs.	
10. Healing of paralytic at Capernaum.	10. Healing of paralytic at Capernaum.	10. Healing of paralytic at Capernaum.
11. Call of Levi (Matthew).	11. Call of Matthew (Levi).	11. Call of Levi (Matthew).

12. Debate about fasting.	12. Debate about fasting.	12. Debate about fasting.
	22. Healing of Jairus' daughter.	
	23. Healing of woman with issue.	
	Healing of two blind men.	
	Healing of dumb man.	
13. Plucking ears of corn on Sabbath.		13. Plucking ears of corn on Sabbath.
14. Healing of withered hand.		14. Healing of withered hand.
15. Appointment of the Twelve.	15. Appointment of the Twelve.	15. Appointment of the Twelve.
	25. Directions to the Twelve.	(v) Sermon on the Mount (part).
	(viii) Message of John.	(vi) Healing of Centurion's servant.
	(ix) "Woe to the cities."	*Raising of widow's son.*
	(x) "None knoweth the Father save the Son."	(viii) Message of John.
		A sinful woman anoints Him.
	13. Plucking ears of corn on the Sabbath.	
	14. Healing of the withered hand.	
	(xi) Healing of blind and dumb man.	
His friends think Him mad.		
16. Controversy about Beelzebub.	16. "Beelzebub."	
17. His Mother and His Brethren.	17. His Mother and His Brethren.	18. Parable of the Sower.
18. Parable of the Sower.	18. Parable of the Sower.	17. His Mother and His Brethren.
Parable of the seed growing secretly.	*Parable of the Tares.*	
19. Parable of Mustard Seed.	19. Parable of the Mustard Seed.	
	(xii) Parable of the Leaven.	
20. Stilling of the Storm.		20. Stilling of the Storm.
21. Healing of demoniac.		21. Healing of demoniac.
22. Healing of Jairus' daughter.		22. Healing of Jairus' daughter.
23. Healing of woman with issue.		23. Healing of woman with issue.
24. "Is not this the carpenter?"		
25. Directions to the Twelve.		25. Directions to the Twelve.
	Parable of the Treasure.	
	Parable of the Pearl.	
	Parable of the Dragnet.	
	24. "Is not this the carpenter?"	
26. John's imprisonment and death.	26. John's imprisonment and death.	
27. Feeding of 5,000.	27. Feeding of 5,000.	27. Feeding of 5,000.

MARK	MATTHEW	LUKE
28. Jesus' walking on the sea.	28. Jesus' walking on the sea.	32. Peter's confession.
	Peter's walking on the sea.	33. The Transfiguration.
29. Dispute about eating with unwashen hands.	29. Dispute about eating with unwashen hands.	34. Healing of afflicted boy.
30. Healing of daughter of Syrophoenician woman.	30. Healing of daughter of Syrophoenician woman.	35. "Who shall be greatest?"
Healing of deaf-dumb man.		36. Forbidding one casting out devils.
31. Feeding of 4,000.	31. Feeding of 4,000.	*Rejection by Samaritans.*
Healing of blind man.		(vii) Offers of Discipleship.
32. Peter's confession.	32. Peter's confession.	*Mission of the Seventy.*
33. The Transfiguration.	33. The Transfiguration.	(ix) "Woe to the cities."
34. Healing of afflicted boy.	34. Healing of afflicted boy.	(x) "None knoweth the Father save the Son."
	Finding of stater in fish.	49. Question about the greatest commandment.
35. "Who shall be greatest?"	35. "Who shall be greatest?"	*Parable of Good Samaritan.*
36. Forbidding one casting out devils.		*Martha and Mary.*
37. Destruction of offending member.	37. Destruction of offending member.	(v) Sermon on the Mount (part).
	(xiii) Parable of Lost Sheep.	(xi) Healing of dumb man.
	(xiv) Forgiveness of offenders.	16. Controversy about Beelzebub.
		(xvii) Denunciation of Pharisees and Lawyers.
		Parable of Rich Fool.
		(v) Sermon on the Mount (part).
		Parable of the Fig Tree.
		Healing of an infirm woman.
		19. Parable of the Mustard Seed.
		(xii) Parable of the Leaven.

38a. Departure to Judaea.

38b. Question about divorce.
39. Blessing little children.
40. The great refusal.

41. Request of the sons of Zebedee.
42. Healing of blind Bartimaeus at Jericho.

43. Entry into Jerusalem.
44. Cursing of the Fig Tree.
45. Cleansing of the Temple.

46. Parable of the Vineyard.

47. Question about tribute.
48. Question about resurrection.
49. Question about the greatest commandment.
50. Question about David's son.

38a. Departure to Judaea.

38b. Question about divorce.
39. Blessing little children.
40. The great refusal.
    Parable of the Laborers.
41. Request of the sons of Zebedee.
42. Healing of *two* blind men at Jericho.

43. Entry into Jerusalem.

45. Cleansing of the Temple.
44. Cursing of the Fig Tree.
    Parable of the Two Sons.
46. Parable of the Vineyard.
    (xvi) Parable of the Marriage Feast.
47. Question about tribute.
48. Question about resurrection.
49. Question about the greatest commandment.
50. Question about David's son.
    (xvii) Denunciation of Pharisees and Lawyers.

38a. Departure towards Judaea.
    (v) Sermon on the Mount (part).
    (xv) Lament over Jerusalem.
    Healing of dropsical man.
    (xvi) Parable of the Great Supper.
    Counting the cost.
    (xiii) Parable of Lost Sheep.
    Parable of Lost Piece of Silver.
    Parable of the Prodigal Son.
    Parable of the Unjust Steward.
    Parable of the Rich Man and Lazarus.
    (xiv) Forgiveness of Offenders.
    Healing of Ten Lepers.
    Parable of Importunate Widow.
    Parable of the Pharisee and Publican.
39. Blessing little children.
40. The great refusal.

42. Healing of blind man at Jericho.

Zacchaeus.
Parable of the Pounds.
43. Entry into Jerusalem.

45. Cleansing of the Temple.

46. Parable of the Vineyard.

47. Question about tribute.
48. Question about resurrection.

50. Question about David's son.

MARK	MATTHEW	LUKE
51. The widow's mite.		51. The widow's mite.
52. Prediction of the end.	52. Prediction of end.	52. Prediction of the end.
	Parable of the Foolish Virgins.	
	Parable of the Talents.	
	The Sheep and the Goats.	
53. The Anointing at Bethany.	53. The Anointing at Bethany.	
54. Judas agrees to betray Him.	54. Judas agrees to betray Him.	54. Judas agrees to betray Him.
55. The Last Supper.	55. The Last Supper.	55. The Last Supper.
56. Prediction of Betrayal.	56. Prediction of Betrayal.	57. The Eucharist.
57. The Eucharist.	57. The Eucharist.	56. Prediction of Betrayal.
58. Prediction of Denial.	58. Prediction of Denial.	58. Prediction of Denial.
59. Gethsemane.	59. Gethsemane.	59. Gethsemane.
60. The Arrest.	60. The Arrest.	60. The Arrest.
61. *Young man with linen cloth.*		
62. Trial before the High Priest.	62. Trial before Caiaphas.	63. Denial by Peter.
63. Denial by Peter.	63. Denial by Peter.	62. Trial before the High Priest.
64. Trial before Pilate.	64. Trial before Pilate.	64. Trial before Pilate.
	Suicide of Judas.	*Trial before Herod.*
65. Simon of Cyrene.	65. Simon of Cyrene.	65. Simon of Cyrene.
		Address to the women.
66. The Crucifixion.	66. The Crucifixion.	66. The Crucifixion.
	Resurrection of Saints.	*The Penitent Thief.*
67. The Burial.	67. The Burial.	67. The Burial.
	Sealing of the Tomb.	
68. Appearance of an angel to the women.	68. Appearance of an angel to the women.	68. Appearance of *two* angels to the women.
	Appearance of Jesus to the women.	*Visit of Peter to the Tomb.*
	Assertion that the body was stolen.	*Appearance of Jesus on the way to Emmaus.*
	Appearance to the disciples in Galilee.	*Appearance of Jesus to the Apostles at Jerusalem.*
		The Ascension.

Notable progress has been made toward arriving at conclusions about the specific origin and content of these sources that lie behind the Synoptic Gospels, and toward finding a plan to designate their relationship to the narratives as they now exist. Among such formulated plans that of Canon Streeter [4] has found a very wide acceptance for its cogency and simplicity.

Assuming that Mark and Q were sources available to both Matthew and Luke, Streeter has established reasons for believ-

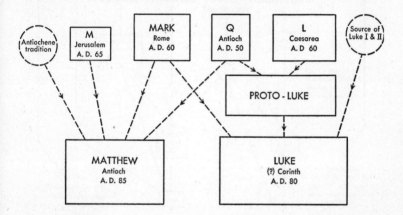

ing that Matthew had access also to a special document representing a collection of oral tradition current in the Jerusalem church. This document may conveniently be identified for us by the symbol M. In addition to the source M, the First Evangelist is believed to have made free use of information about the life of Christ conveyed to him in the form of an Antiochene tradition. Luke, similarly, is said to have used a written source which Streeter calls L, having behind it a tradition originating in or centering about the church in Caesarea. Streeter advances the interesting thesis that Luke, in or about the year A.D. 60, while at Caesarea and in close companionship with Saint Paul, prepared the document L out of the tradition current there in the Christian community; and that, a little later, he combined it with Q to create the document called Proto-Luke. This

[4] See B. H. Streeter: The Four Gospels (New York: The Macmillan Co., 1922).

amalgamated document is looked upon as having been, like Mark, a complete Gospel, and as comprising the main part of the present narrative of Luke. In the course of time a small body of carefully preserved and authenticated tradition, of Palestinian origin, and now to be found in Luke 1-2, was added to serve as a preface to the account of the Third Evangelist.

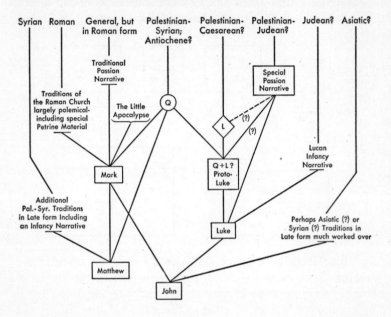

By this arrangement the combined traditions of Jerusalem, Caesarea, Antioch, and Rome are seen in one composite picture, as represented by Streeter in the chart on page 79.

Recently, scholars have attempted to look more intently into the background of Mark's Gospel.[5] The result has been the advancement of a "multiple-source" theory which, as Barnett says, stresses "the Palestinian and Syrian origin of the contents of the sources on which the authors of the canonical Gospels

[5] See B. H. Branscomb, *The Gospel of Mark* (New York: Harper & Bros., 1937), pp. 22-26; A. E. Barnett, *The New Testament: Its Making and Meaning* (New York: Abingdon-Cokesbury Press, 1946), pp. 113-17; and F. C. Grant, *The Growth of the Gospels* (New York: The Abingdon-Cokesbury Press, 1933), pp. 53-66.

relied." The aim of this theory is to put us into closer touch with the report of those who, in Luke's own words, were the original eye-witnesses of the events surrounding the divine history and person of Christ. The diagram [6] on page 80 is that of Grant's multiple-source theory of the origin of the Gospels. It includes the Gospel of John, whose special character and history will be the subject of our later study.

[6] Professor Grant writes on May 7, 1951: "I wonder if it [the diagram] doesn't need to be redrawn. The line from Q to Mark I think should be dotted. The last column (Asiatic?) ought to be headed Asiatic or Egyptian, with a question mark. And at the bottom of that column, it should read "Perhaps Asiatic, Egyptian, or Assyrian Traditions. . . ."

Chapter 9

THE GOSPEL OF MARK

THE AUTHOR AND HIS AIM

The Gospel of Mark is a compact and sturdy book. It suggests its own unmistakable Roman background and the reason why it was written. The circumstances of its origin are strikingly real. This fact is shown by the narrative's inner tension, by the author's feeling of suspension and release as he tells his story, and by the manner in which the entire history of Christ is given the active, episodic, and climactic character of a great drama. As one turns the pages of this Gospel and is impelled by the note of urgency in it, first, toward the intermediate climax of the Transfiguration, and then onward toward the major and final climax of the Resurrection, the question rises irresistibly: Out of what crisis was the Gospel born, and to what end did it come into being? The answer to these questions is found in Roman and Christian history. It lies in the fact that Mark's story was written in a context of tragedy and on an issue whose outcome was a transcendent victory for the cause of the Christian faith.

The Gospel has its general setting in the church at Rome. The situation points clearly to the persecution of the Christians during the closing years of the reign of Nero. The immediate motive for the writing of the Gospel was the shocking martyrdom of the apostles Peter and Paul. To get a picture of the evil character of Nero, and of his outrageous treatment of the Christians in the year A.D. 64, we need only to go to Tacitus, the Roman historian, who, without pity for those persecuted, wrote in the fifteenth book of his *Annals*:

Neither human help, nor imperial munificence, nor all the modes
of placating Heaven, could stifle the scandal or dispel the belief
that the fire [the burning of Rome] had taken place by [Nero's]
order. To stamp out the rumor, Nero substituted as culprits, and
punished with the utmost cruelty, a class of men, loathed for their
vices, whom the crowd styled Christians. Christus, the founder
of the name, had undergone the death penalty in the reign of
Tiberius, by sentence of the procurator Pontius Pilatus. . . .
First, then, the confessed members of the sect were arrested; next,
on their disclosures, vast numbers were convicted, not so much
on the count of arson as for hatred of the human race. And
derision accompanied their end: they were covered with wild
beasts' skins and torn to death by dogs; or they were fastened
on crosses, and, when daylight failed, were burned to serve as
lamps by night.

Such a situation clearly called for Christian heroism, and
Mark considered himself chosen to meet it with an account of
the cause for which men, in this crisis, willingly laid down their
lives. That cause was the resolute end toward which Christ
himself had offered his life on the Cross, not in martyrdom for
his convictions but in fulfilment of God's plan through his own
death to be the savior of mankind.

The story of Christ's life and death was of course familiar
to the Christians there. They had heard it frequently in the
preaching of both Peter and Paul. It had become the gospel
preached to them; the seal of its divine authority had been the
fact of Christ's resurrection; and the acknowledged lordship of
Christ was the bond holding them together in Christian fellowship and helping them to face this crucial ordeal. But Mark
now wished to give a complete and permanent expression to the
faith of these Christian martyrs by gathering together the
strands of tradition current in the Roman community and augmenting it by information that had come to him from Palestinian sources, including material from the source called Q.

That Mark was equipped to write the Gospel is fully verified
by the information the New Testament gives us of him.
Though his Roman name was Marcus, he was originally known
as John. His mother, whose name was Mary, was known to

have lived in Jerusalem at the time, or shortly after the time, of the Crucifixion. Her house was used as a place of worship, and Peter often lodged there. Barnabas, related to Mary, and Paul's early missionary companion, was Mark's own cousin; and Mark, in his youth, had himself accompanied Paul and Barnabas on the first missionary journey into Asia Minor. In Rome, years later, he had become Paul's close associate and, according to trustworthy tradition, the interpreter of the preaching of Peter. The inference is that Peter, a Galilean, preached to the Romans in his native Aramaic tongue, and that Mark translated the apostle's sermons into Greek and Latin. These assumed facts point directly to two conclusions: the first is that the Mark whom we thus know was the author of the Gospel; the second is that the Gospel contains much material traceable to the preaching, and perhaps also to the personal memoirs, of Peter.

These conclusions are corroborated by the ancient church fathers, notably by Papias, close to the year A.D. 130, and by Irenaeus who, writing in the year A.D. 177, said: "After the decease of Peter and Paul, Mark, the disciple and interpreter of Peter, himself also delivered to us in writing the substance of Peter's preaching." Modern scholarship interprets this statement as attesting to the trustworthiness of the oral tradition which was, in this manner, safeguarded by its close association with the great apostle who was an eyewitness to the events recorded by Mark under the title of "the mighty words and acts of God" spoken and wrought through the life and death and resurrection of Christ.

The Gospel of Mark is justly famous for its original and vigorous character. Once regarded as an abbreviated copy of Matthew and Luke, it is now known to be their source, and as having its roots directly and deeply implanted in the primitive Christian tradition. Its ancient symbol is the lion. The appellation is deserved; for Mark's is, in very truth, the Gospel of the "Strong Son of God." Though addressed to Gentile Christians, it retains the homely vigor of its writer's native surroundings and style. This is noticeable in his use of Aramaic words, which he first inserts and then explains, as, for example, when

he calls the disciples James and John "Boanerges," meaning the
sons of thunder, or lets us hear the agonizing cry of Jesus on
the Cross: "Eloi, Eloi, lama sabachthani?"—"My God, My
God, why hast thou forsaken me?" Without ornament, the
sentences are direct, the scenes vivid and often picturesque, the
action dramatic and intense. Episode follows episode in rapid
motion and descriptive detail. Place names are brought into
sharp relief within the story; things familiar are given a realistic
touch until they seem to come to life before the reader's eyes.

A few instances here will suffice to illustrate the tenseness of
this moving gospel drama in its natural Palestinian setting, in
which the Son of God himself is the divine hero and the transcendent theme is the world's redemption. John the Baptist appears, suddenly, clothed with camel's hair; his preaching is a
cry in the wilderness. Jesus' temptation is summed up in one
verse: he is in the desert with the wild beasts; but angels wait
on him. In Capernaum the whole city gathers at the door of
the house where he teaches and heals the sick. Later, a Syrophoenician woman comes to him in behalf of her demoniac
daughter. She will not take "No" for an answer; she will be
a "Gentile dog" if Christ will but say the healing word; and her
prayer is granted. Again in Bethany, before the day of Jesus'
passion, a woman enters the house, breaks an alabaster box, and
pours its precious ointment on his head; and Mark records
these words of Christ, boldly and truly:

> Verily I say unto you:
> Wheresoever this gospel shall be preached
> Throughout the whole world,
> This also that she hath done
> Shall be spoken of for a memorial of her.[1]

II

THE CONTENT AND ITS MESSAGE

Presupposing, according to Grant's chart presented in Chapter 8, that Mark had access to several sources in the writing of
his Gospel, we may now look a little more closely into the nature

[1] Mark 14:9.

of these particular sources. Behind them, as we have said, lay
the evangelic, or gospel, tradition. This tradition was at first
oral. It was kept alive and intact by the preaching of the Word
of God which had first been spoken through ancient prophecy,
then in and through the person and life of Christ, and finally
through divine revelation to the first apostles, as the gospel of
redemption for mankind.

Now an integral part of that consolidating tradition was the
added proof of what was even then taking place as the gospel
was being preached. A greater power had been released in the
world and its influence was being felt and outwardly demonstrated in every region of the empire to which the first missionaries had gone. And Rome, the very citadel of the empire, had
come to see its mighty influence, the effect of a power great
enough to challenge the opposition of Nero the "Antichrist."
All this demonstration, involving now also the death of the
Christian martyrs, was a witness to the lordship of Christ, to
the truth of what he had said and done on earth, to his resurrection, and to the establishment of his kingdom in the institution
of the church. It was nothing other than the life of Jesus as
the Son of God—the divine doctrine plus the earthly history—
that constituted the living body of the gospel tradition.

The strands of this tradition, as it came into the hands of
Mark, were mainly three. The one to attract our first attention
originated in Rome. It is regarded as having been strongly
polemical in character, as having its setting in the conflict between the Christian community and the empire, after the pattern of the Jewish opposition to Jesus, and heralding, for all
time to come, the historic conflict between the church and the
world. To this strand of controversial incidents and sayings
belong those associated, for example, with Jesus' healing, his
eating with sinners, his interpretation of the Jewish law, and the
demonstration of his authority and power by "signs and wonders." Woven into this main strand is the golden thread of the
preaching, or "memoirs," of Peter. To it the Gospel owes, particularly, its account of those dramatic incidents in which Peter
himself had a part. Among the most notable of them are these:
Peter's confession, "Thou art the Christ"; Jesus' rebuke to him,

"Get thee behind me, Satan"; the disciple's words on the Mount of Transfiguration, "Master, it is good for us to be here: and let us make three tabernacles, one for thee, and one for Moses, and one for Elias";[2] and his vehement denial of Jesus, when he said: "I know not this man."

Next in order, and the most important, is the body of tradition containing the passion narrative. It forms the climax of the story of Christ and gives evidence of a completely integrated account. Mark's use of it has all the traits of the vividness and realism for which his Gospel is famous. As we follow the accelerated and impassioned movement of the story, its heightened tempo, from the triumphant entry into Jerusalem to Gethsemane and Golgotha, and then to the resurrection morning, we are moved to say with the poet Richard Crashaw:

> Christ when He died
> Deceived the cross,
> And on death's side
> Threw all the loss.
>
> O strange and mysterious strife,
> Of open death and hidden life:
> When on the cross my King did bleed,
> Life seemed to die, Death died indeed.

Besides these sources accessible to Mark, there were two others of lesser quantity but distinct value. One of them was of Palestinian origin and was preserved in the form of a prophetic oracle after the pattern of the Book of Daniel. Its keynote is God's judgment upon "the abomination of desolation"—by which the Evangelist meant the execrable persecution of Nero and the wickedness of Rome. The oracle is called the Little Apocalypse, and is found in Mark 13. The other of the two secondary sources is Q. To what extent it was used by Mark, in one of its current versions, we do not definitely know. But of the "sayings of our Lord" preserved in it he had a sufficient knowledge to give them a secure place in his account. Perhaps the version of Q with which Mark was acquainted contained the

2 Mark 9:5.

so-called "Son of man" sayings of which this, recorded in Mark 8:38, is typical and particularly applicable to the writer's—and our own—time:

> Whosoever therefore
> Shall be ashamed of me and of my words
> In this adulterous and sinful generation;
> Of him also shall the Son of man be ashamed,
> When he cometh in the glory of his Father
> With the holy angels.

We recognize these sayings as strongly apocalyptic, having the style and tone of a chapter of Daniel's prophecy. Altogether, in Mark's Gospel, there are fourteen of them, and they reflect "a distinct theological point of view, a very primitive one, and pre-Markan." [3] What interests us especially is the manner in which the tension between the two conceptions of Christ as (1) the lowly Servant of God, and (2) the Heavenly Victor, is resolved by a doctrine of the Cross. It clearly resembles the central teaching of Paul and culminates in the climactic announcement of Jesus in Mark 10:45: "For even the Son of man came not to be ministered unto, but to minister, and to give his life a ransom for many."

The Gospel of Mark, as it now stands, falls into two major parts: (1) Chapters 1 to 9, and (2) Chapters 10 to 16:8. Each section ends with an exalting climax: the first, with the Transfiguration; the second, with the Resurrection. The central theme of both together is the Messiahship of Jesus, which is interpreted in terms of his acceptance of the way of the Cross as the will of God. Throughout the second section of the Gospel this way is also enjoined on all who would be his disciples. Messiahship and discipleship are the Gospel's two firmly implanted pillars. Between them the span of the story is by the road of greatness through suffering, of victory through humiliation, of eternal life through sacrifice unto death. It should be noted here that Chapter 16:9-20 is an appendix to the Gospel. To account for it, scholars today generally believe that it replaced the orig-

---

[3] See F. C. Grant, *The Earliest Gospel* (New York: Abingdon-Cokesbury Press, 1943), p. 63.

inal ending accidentally lost or worn away through constant use.
The contents of Mark are most conveniently outlined as follows:

1. Introduction: Jesus' Preparation for His
   Public Ministry   1:1-13
2. The Galilean Ministry of Jesus   1:14-9:50
3. The Journey from Galilee to Judea   10
4. Jesus' Ministry in Jerusalem   11-13
5. The Passion of Jesus   14-15
6. Conclusion: the Resurrection of Jesus   16:1-8
7. Appendix   16:9-20

For a brief summary of the Gospel we may turn to this writer's previously described account of the dramatic scene.[4]

The curtain rises. We look on Palestine: the Jordan River, the
hills of Nazareth, the shores of Galilee. We observe the moving
multitudes: first, seeking deliverance from human ills; then blessing the hand that gives them bread; thereafter, rising in protest
against him who is their best friend. In due time we reach Judea.
We witness there the rising tide of Pharisaic opposition; we hear
the fateful sentence of unjust condemnation; we suffer with our
hero the agony of Gethsemane and the cross. Then, as darkness
falls on Golgotha, the curtain lowers and the drama ends. Eagerly
we strain our eyes for one more look. In the center of the tragic
darkness a sudden light appears, dazzlingly bright, heavenly in its
splendor against the background of a dark but empty tomb. Enshrined in this circle of celestial light stands an illustrious and
kingly figure. It is the figure of the risen and living Christ. That
is Mark's picture. When the story has been told, the reader sees
"no man any more save Jesus only."

[4] See Henry M. Battenhouse, *New Testament History and Literature*
(New York: The Ronald Press Co., 1937), p. 85.

Chapter 10

THE GOSPEL OF MATTHEW

I

THE WRITER AND HIS READERS

The first page of Matthew's Gospel, in the Coverdale Bible of 1535, shows an engraving of the Evangelist writing his great book. The setting is Palestinian; the figure of the man is Jewish. He wears the turban, and his face has the rapt meditative intelligence of a rabbi. An angel speaks to him. It is the angel of the church, declaring to him in a mystery the fulfilment of prophecy and the giving of the new law. The illustration symbolizes the Gospel. It is in its very structure and essence an example of Holy Scripture. The law and the prophets live in it again; only now Moses is superseded by Jesus, and the old dispensation of the Jewish law gives way to the greater teaching of Christ. The new "remnant" of Israel is the church, and the widened hope of Messianism is the Christian evangelization of the world.

In looking into the literary history of Matthew's Gospel, one is first attracted to the high regard in which it was held by the ancient fathers of the church. It was known, among others, to Papias, Irenaeus, Ignatius, Justin, Origen, and Jerome. What they said of it is mainly recorded for us by Eusebius, the church historian. Eusebius himself said that Saint Matthew at first "preached to the Hebrews," and then "committed his Gospel to writing in his native tongue." He quotes Irenaeus as saying: "Matthew published his Gospel among the Hebrews in their own language." Origen is quoted, in these words, to substantiate this claim: "Among the four Gospels, ... I have learned by tradition that the first was written by Matthew, who was once a tax gatherer, but afterwards an Apostle of Jesus Christ, and

it was prepared for the converts from Judaism, and published in the Hebrew language." To this testimony Eusebius adds that of Papias, who writes: "So, then, Matthew wrote the oracles (Logia) in the Hebrew language and every one interpreted them as he was able." Two striking facts are brought out by these statements. The first is that the Gospel was widely known and revered; the second is that it was traditionally associated with Matthew the tax gatherer who became one of Jesus' twelve disciples.

Quite naturally, this testimony of tradition has invited men to a close study of the content of the Gospel in order to see how what is said of it can be verified. The result has been the opening up of the entire synoptic problem and the discovery of the source called Q, of which we have already spoken, and which is now believed to have owed its beginning to a "Collection of our Lord's Sayings in Aramaic made by Saint Matthew." A further examination shows that Saint Matthew the apostle did not write the Gospel as we now have it. The reasons are inherent in the nature and character of the Gospel. It was written in Greek; and its sources also, in so far as they were written and not oral tradition, were accessible to the author in Greek. The author himself was a Greek-speaking Jew. The atmosphere of the Gospel shows clearly that his thought had been nurtured on the history and teaching of the Old Testament. His mind, throughout the Gospel, dwells continually on Moses and the Prophets and on their New Testament counterpart of Christ and the Church.

Compared to Mark, whom he follows closely and whose interests are immediate and local, Matthew displays a world-wide outlook and looks into the future when the Gospel shall be preached to all the peoples and races of mankind. So wide, indeed, in his range of vision, so all-inclusive his grasp of history of divine revelation, that his account has been called "The Gospel." Beginning in its genealogy with Abraham, it spans the centuries to the birth of Christ, and from him, as the rock on which the church is built, it projects the vision of the reader into the ages yet to come, when

Many shall come
From the east and the west,
And shall sit down
With Abraham, and Isaac, and Jacob,
In the kingdom of heaven.[1]

This vast, anticipative, and at times intense outlook suggests a comparison with the writing of Saint Paul: first, in its ardent Jewishness; and second, in its broad and lofty universality. Here, in fact, we come to the crux of the Gospel itself and to the inherent paradox of the situation within which it came into existence. On the one hand, there was the Jewish community in which the Christian faith had taken root and from which it had taken much of its elementary nourishment. The Gospel of Christ, as it was at first preached, was both the fulfilment of Old Testament prophecy and the giving of the New Law. But, as time passed, there were also Gentile Christian communities in which the Ezra-Mosaic law was deemed to be of lesser importance by the side of the doctrines of the new birth and of universal salvation which Saint Paul had so successfully preached in Syria, in Asia Minor, and in Europe, and which, by the time that Matthew wrote his Gospel, were tending to take clear precedence over the more conservative expression of Judaistic Christianity. At the beginning of Paul's ministry, and particularly when he was writing the letter to the Galatians, the great apostle had found himself in the midst of a severe conflict with the "Judaizers" who, speaking as by the authority of the temple of Jerusalem, had maintained that no one could become a Christian until he had first been accepted into Judaism. That had been the situation in Galatia about the year A.D. 50.

But by now a generation or more had passed and Jewish and Gentile Christians had learned to live peacefully together; at any rate they were being taught to do so lest they give offense to the cause of Christ. And it was because of their need of being rightly taught that Matthew now undertook to remind Christians of what, among other things, Jesus had meant when he said: "Take heed that ye despise not one of these little ones...."

[1] Matthew 8:11.

For the Son of man is come to save that which is lost." [2]   To make the truth plain, the Evangelist quotes Jesus as uttering one of the richest of the parables of the Gospel.   It is especially chosen to answer the question: How far beyond Judaism is it God's plan to promote His kingdom through the Christian church?   Its message is, in essence, that of Matthew's Gospel:

> How think ye?   If a man have an hundred sheep, and one of them be gone astray, doth he not leave the ninety and nine, and goeth into the mountains, and seeketh that which is gone astray?   And if so be that he find it, verily I say unto you, he rejoiceth more of that sheep, than of the ninety and nine which went not astray. [3]

Such was the background of this most universal Gospel.   The time had come to heal the breach and to tell the whole story. Its central theme was (1) that the Jews had rejected Jesus, but (2) that through that fact the Christian gospel had been released to the whole world.   And the teaching within the framework of this story was that the kingdom of God was being offered in grace to those who needed and deeply desired it, and that it was immediately at hand for those willing and prepared to assume its special responsibilities.

II

THE GOSPEL AND THE CHRISTIAN CHURCH

Modern scholars are mostly in agreement with Canon Streeter in locating the composition of Matthew in Antioch, and in giving it the date of about A.D. 85.   The reasons, to the gospel historian, are evident.   Antioch had for nearly fifty years been a large and lively center of evangelistic activity.   Peter and Barnabas and Paul had been active there.   It was Jerusalem's first outpost of Christian missions in Syria, and a center of Roman commerce and of Greek culture.   Paul himself had made it the base of his great missionary enterprise in Asia Minor and Europe.   It would, for this reason, be natural for the Christian community there to be in possession of both the oral and the

[2] Matthew 18:10, 11.
[3] Matthew 18:12, 13.

written sources necessary to the composition of Matthew's Gospel. Some Christian traveling to Rome might bring back with him a copy of the Gospel of Mark, together with information of the reverence in which the memory of the apostles Peter and Paul was held there since their martyrdom under Nero twenty years before. And Antioch itself had its own valued collection of the Sayings of Jesus, very probably containing the precious Logia, or nucleus of our Lord's teaching, gathered together by Matthew the Apostle and known to us now by its symbolical name Q. Besides these sources there was the important body of tradition that had been brought up directly from Jerusalem, the citadel of Judaism, and the scene of Jesus' trial and suffering. The Holy City had fallen in A.D. 70, and the temple now lay in ruins; but by as early as A.D. 65 this tradition had been put into writing; and a copy of it lay before the author of Matthew as he began to write.

Thus (1) furnished with this document, now called M, (2) guided in his narrative by Mark, and (3) prepared for his task by the inspiring content of Q, the First Evangelist undertook and completed the writing of his Gospel at some time close to the year 85. His accomplishment was one of the greatest in all Biblical literature: for to this day the Gospel of Matthew has been variously extolled as the Gospel of Jesus the Teacher; the kingly Gospel of Jesus' majesty and passion—and of his divine humility; the Universal Gospel; the Gospel of One World; and the Magna Charta of Christianity.

Viewing Matthew's Gospel in its entirety, one notices at once the four basic elements in it. There is, first, the Markan narrative which it follows almost altogether. After that, as Bishop Dibelius says, there is the Gospel's "program of Christian ethics for all generations of the church." Looking again, we observe the missionary motive in it, compelling the Evangelist to call on the church to hear its Lord's command to go therefore, and make disciples of all nations. Finally, and over all, like "the pillar of a cloud by day and a pillar of fire by night," there is the apocalyptic vision of the Son of man awaiting the end of days to bring all history to fulfilment and to consummate God's plan of His heavenly and ever-enduring kingdom.

The Gospel's central core, we have already said, is the collection of Jesus' teaching. Around it, to preserve this nucleus of truth, is the protective and nourishing tissue of Mark's narrative. And, pressing close to this core of doctrine enclosed in gospel history, acting like the wind and rain on seeded ground, is the world-awakening voice of apocalyptic prophecy. Or, to pursue the further use of our New Testament symbolism, we note, first, the kingdom's unobserved and quiet growth in the parable of the Leaven and the parable of the Mustard Seed. But, following close upon it, there takes place before our eyes the scene of the gathering and burning of the evil tares. So, throughout the Gospel, the truth of the kingdom of God is sown in grace and harvested in judgment.

A further analysis of Matthew shows the Gospel to contain this great central core of teaching, derived from the source Q, in the form of five distinct sections. Each section, or discourse, closed with the formal statement: "And it came to pass when Jesus had ended these sayings (or parables)"; after which the Evangelist returns to Mark's Gospel before him and takes up his version of its narrative at the point where he has left it. This plan, however, is not forced on the material. It works out naturally, not mechanically; and it offers the author of the Gospel the opportunity of giving the discourses a rightful setting in the story of the earthly life of Christ. The five interpolated sections containing the discourses are as follows:

1. Chapters 5-7—The Sermon on the Mount
2. Chapter 10—The Commission to the Twelve Disciples
3. Chapter 13—Seven Parables of the Kingdom of God
4. Chapter 18—Lessons in Christian Discipleship
5. Chapters 23-25—Discourses on the Last Judgment

Although these various discourses are arranged under separate topics and represent diversified themes, they are held together within a pattern of an exact and twofold distinction: first, in the mundane or ethical realm, it is the distinction between the church and the world; second, on the higher eschatological plane, it marks the difference between the dispensations of divine grace and judgment. Corresponding to the five sections

or masses of teaching material, the narrative of the Gospel falls into five intermediate divisions: representing, first, the beginning of Jesus' public ministry; second, his wider ministry throughout Galilee; third, the rising conflict with Judaism; fourth, Jesus' withdrawal from Galilee, and the announcement of his Messiahship; fifth, the journey, through Perea, to Jerusalem. To complete the framework of his narrative, Matthew prefixes a preparatory period; and, after the five sections mentioned above, he incorporates Mark's story of the passion, adding material of his own, and closing with his own account of the Resurrection and Ascension.

Viewed as a whole, Matthew's Gospel, like Mark's, is seen to be divided into two major parts: The first comes to a climax in Chapter 17:1-12 with the Transfiguration; the second culminates at the close of the Gospel in the story of the Resurrection. The first part presents Jesus the Teacher; the second exhibits Jesus as Christ the Messiah. Thus, in this Gospel story, we behold all heavenly wisdom summed up in a manifestation of God Himself in the person of his Son, the savior of the world.

This divine self-revelation is given an especially vivid portrayal in the apocalyptic Chapters 24 and 25 of Matthew's Gospel. Here, in a setting of crisis, the Son of man is presented to us as the Lord of Heaven. And the scene is such as to make the event of Calvary that follows a vindication of the divine judgment on the sin of the world, and so to lift the entire history of Christ from the level of a merely earthly occurrence to the plane of a cosmic event. So exhibited to us, the gospel history is given an ultimate and exalted doctrinal meaning. It is placed in a setting of the conflict between the kingdom of God and the forces of evil—a majestic though hard conflict, in which Christ is represented as Victor, kingly in his divine humiliation, glorious in his resurrection and ascension, and invested with heavenly authority to say:

> Go ye therefore,
> And teach all nations;
> Baptizing them in the name
> Of the Father, and of the Son, and of the Holy Ghost.

And, lo, I am with you alway,
Even unto the end of the world.[4]

One cannot close the reading of Matthew's Gospel without noting particularly the enduring beauty and power of its quotable lines as these are preserved for us in the King James Version of the Bible. They adorn the sermon and survive in the literature of our own time. The following examples justify the Gospel's fame as an extraordinary book:

The voice of one crying in the wilderness.	3:3
Man shall not live by bread alone.	4:4
Blessed are the peacemakers.	5:9
Ye are the salt of the earth.	5:13
Sufficient unto the day is the evil thereof.	3:34
Judge not, that ye be not judged.	7:1
By their fruits ye shall know them.	7:20
The Harvest is plenteous, but the laborers are few.	9:37
Behold, I send you forth as sheep in the midst of wolves.	10:16
He that findeth his life shall lose it; and he that loseth his life for my sake shall find it.	10:39
Come unto me, all ye that labour and are heavy laden, and I will give you rest.	11:28
For my yoke is easy, and my burden is light.	11:30
But many that are first shall be last; and the last shall be first.	19:30
For many are called, but few are chosen.	20:16
For unto every one that hath shall be given.	25:29
I was a stranger, and ye took me in.	25:35
The spirit indeed is willing, but the flesh is weak.	26:41
His blood be on us, and on our children.	27:25
He saved others; himself he cannot save.	27:42
Lo, I am with you alway, even unto the end of the world.	28:20

[4] Matthew 28:19, 20.

Chapter 11

THE GOSPEL OF LUKE

I

The Author's Literary Genius

There is an ancient Roman coin on one side of which is stamped the image of a lowly ox. On the coin's reverse side are seen the emblems of an altar and a plow; and beneath them we read the words: "Prepared for both." The ox is the traditional symbol of Luke's Gospel. It fits the narrative exactly in its suggestion of meekness and self-sacrifice and, more particularly, in the manner in which it associates the person of Christ with the appealing simplicity and obedience natural to life in the creaturely world. Quite directly, the symbol is traceable to Luke's Infant Story. The story is so well told by the Evangelist that it has been repeated countless times and survives, for example, in the legend of Thomas Hardy's poem "The Oxen" where, living the scene of the great birth over again to himself, the poet says:

> Christmas Eve, and twelve of the clock,
> "Now they are all on their knees,"
> An elder said as we sat in a flock
> By the embers in hearthside ease.
>
> We pictured the meek mild creatures where
> They dwelt in their strawy pen,
> Nor did it occur to one of us there
> To doubt they were kneeling then.[1]

That is the picture Saint Luke gives us of the coming of Christ. It is outwardly so vivid and arresting and, beyond that,

[1] From the *Collected Poems of Thomas Hardy*. Used by permission of The Macmillan Co., New York, publishers.

98

so welcome, so appealing to us as to lift altogether from our eyes any enshrouding gloom of doubt. With the ancient shepherds we stand wondering at "this thing which has come to pass" and is the Evangelist's prelude to a life exhibited as a continuous miracle of mercy to waiting and suffering mankind.

And, as we follow through the unfolding story, the attending angels of mercy never leave us. We hear the ministering Spirit of the Lord invoked on Jesus in Nazareth; and we trace the events of his miraculous ministry: first, in eastern and northern Galilee; then, on the journey to Jerusalem; after that, through the week of his passion; and, at last, onward to his resurrection and ascension. Nor, according to Luke's Gospel, does the mission of Christ end there. It continues after the Ascension in the working of the Holy Spirit through the apostles whose story is told in the Book of the Acts—through the ministry of Peter and John and Philip, and principally of Paul, until Christianity is established in Rome and commended to all the world as the way of salvation from tragic human suffering and bondage to sin. The Gospel according to Luke is, in essence, a song of deliverance and of triumph in a dark ancient—and modern—world. To one who reads it simply as literature, its elegiac note of pity is blended and transformed into a concordant hymn of creation in praise of the heavenly Creator. To the Christian it is a message of divine grace, of profound consolation, and of sustained strength and hope.

After a rapid reading of this gospel, we find our interest turning naturally to further information about its author. His identity is almost certainly established. He was evidently either a Greek or the son of a Greek father and a Jewish mother. His knowledge of the Greek language is excellent. He knows its idiom, the picturesqueness and music of its words, their poetical use, and the rich culture they convey. His familiarity with Palestine is no less notable than his at-homeness on the continent of Europe. He knows its very life, in its cities and on the sea. Its lively, volatile temper was in his blood. But he was a Christian convert, and what he had learned from living with others of the new faith had wrought a miracle of transformation in him. For this reason it is assumed that he was almost certainly

the Luke associated with Saint Paul in his missionary journeys
and later at Rome. This fact is borne out by a careful comparison of the Gospel of Luke and the Book of the Acts. Their
identical and good style proves that they were written by the
same person; the same sensitive spirit and missionary purpose
run through both writings; their prefaces are closely alike and
clearly suggest that they were intended by the author to be a
single continuous history.

Further evidence of Luke's authorship is furnished by the
now famous "we" sections to be found in the Acts. There are
four of these sections: (1) 16:10-17; (2) 20:5-15; (3) 21:
1-18; (4) 27:1-28:16. They constitute a diary of Luke's
travels in companionship with Saint Paul. Besides telling us
much of interest on their journeyings, particularly across the
Mediterranean to Rome, the diary is so of one piece with the
rest of Luke-Acts, both in outlook and literary style, that we
must conclude that Luke the Evangelist was here using his own
notes of an earlier date in the final composition of his gospel
history. That the "we" sections were not simply material taken
from another writer's notes, and adapted to his own use by this
gifted Christian historian, becomes clear on further analysis of
Luke's narrative in which, for example, the passages incorporated from the Gospel of Mark show the contrasting signs of
their own original authorship. Mark and Luke did not write
alike. That fact is made evident by a close examination of the
synoptic record. It is thus by their own inner evidence that we
recognize the Third Gospel and the Acts as the work of the same
Luke who about the year 50 joined Saint Paul at Troas, traveled
with him to Philippi, remained there upward of six years and,
after that, joined the Apostle on his journey to Jerusalem and,
following some delay, to Rome. That he was with Paul in
Rome is attested by the Apostle's reference to him, in Colossians
4:14, as Luke the beloved physician, and again, in Philemon 24,
as Paul's faithful fellow laborer.

Of Luke's subsequent years little is known. A tradition
traceable to the third century indicates that he was "by nation
a Syrian of Antioch," and that "he died in Bithynia at the age
of seventy-four, filled with the Holy Ghost." His authorship

of the Gospel, however, was early and widely recognized. Marcion, the heretic, writing in A.D. 140, prepared his own version of it to please himself but did not succeed in discrediting it. Justin Martyr, ten years later, quoted it affectionately and widely. Twenty years after that, Tatian gave it a place in the *Diatessaron,* his harmony of the four Gospels. Late in the second century, Irenaeus held it in highest reverence; and, by the year 200, Tertullian had declared its authenticity to be firmly established.

The date and place of composition of Luke's Gospel are likewise indicated by its content. The situation demands that the time be set somewhere between A.D. 70 and 95. Allowing this broad span of years for its composition presupposes two facts: first, that the temple at Jerusalem had already been destroyed; and second, that the letters of Paul, to which no allusion is made by Luke, had not yet been put into wide circulation. The most suitable date for the Gospel, therefore, is one between A.D. 80 and 85. The place at which it was written may have been Antioch, or Ephesus, or Corinth, or Rome. Scholars today tend to favor Ephesus on the rather good ground that Saint John's Gospel and the Book of Revelation, written about the year 90, seem clearly to reflect Luke's influence.

Of more interest to the modern reader are the person and community to which Luke's Gospel was addressed. Luke himself, in his preface, tells us that he was writing to the "most excellent Theophilus" in order that he might know the "certainty of those things" in which he had already been instructed. Theophilus seems to have been a Roman patrician, perhaps an official, and a man at home in the culture of the Greek world. An atmosphere of cosmopolitanism pervades the entire Gospel, indicating Luke's clear intention of commending the gospel of Christ to men and women everywhere in the empire. Indeed, the Evangelist was not content to state the bare facts of the life of Christ, however dramatic they were, as Mark had done. His sense of history, of order in literary composition and, we may say, of the beauty of the divine plan of the redemption of the world, was too strong to limit him to any kind of simple though vivid chronology. Human imagination and divine in-

spiration worked unitedly in him to present a picture that would both please and move the reader—a picture, at once touching, fascinating, realistic, and vast, of the new Christian faith that was to encompass the earth, affect the common life of men, rich and poor, make all things new and, at last, bring "peace on earth and good will to men." In brief, it was the kind of gospel for which the Roman world, like our own, was longingly and unconsciously waiting.

Every page of the narrative, as we look at it, makes us aware of that fact. So eager is the Evangelist to tell his readers how that longing is to be fulfilled that he cannot wait for the development of the story to its natural climax. He must present the entire drama of redemption in one enveloping vision. Accordingly, at the very beginning of the Gospel, he breaks abruptly into poetry: first, in the song of Mary, called the *Magnificat;* second, in the *Benedictus* of Zacharias; and finally, in the *Nunc Dimittis,* in which the Evangelist sees the just and devout Simeon taking the child Jesus in his arms and blessing God, saying:

> Lord, now lettest thou
> Thy servant depart in peace,
> According to thy word;
> For mine eyes have seen thy salvation,
> Which thou has prepared
> Before the face of all people:
> A light to lighten the Gentiles,
> And the glory of thy people Israel.[2]

II

HIS MASTERLY USE OF THE SOURCES

The mind of Luke broods over his Gospel like a dove over its nest. It is, indeed, in the symbol of the dove that Luke sees the Holy Spirit hover above the birth of the church to invest it with His own life. The Evangelist, writing under the shaping influence of Christian doctrine, pictures the Spirit as one of historic order and heavenly beauty, after the dual pattern

[2] Luke 2:29-32.

of the Creation in Genesis and the Greek concept of the cosmos. It is with obvious joy that he contemplates this work of God, wrought in the history of Christ, through the power of the Holy Spirit—of which his Gospel is the artist's genuine and creative record. True to life, as a work of art must always be, and presented as a story involving time and place, yet as a revelation of the truth that lies beyond time, this Gospel fulfils at once the requirements of trustworthy history, of great literature, and of an interpretation of the meaning of the Christian faith.

Luke's plan, we have said, was to use his sources before him to that significant end. One of his major tasks, ultimately, was to reconsider and to use freely, but not literally, the widely circulated Gospel of Mark. This Gospel, with its note of crisis and its stress on the manner in which Jesus, as the strong Son of God, had endured death on the Cross, offering his life as a ransom for sinful men, was now firmly established. It had grown out of the Christian community's heroic age, sealed by the martyrdom of the apostles Peter and Paul. So much was, by then, the hard and formative framework of gospel history.

The evangelist Matthew, perceiving this fact, had kept his narrative close to the Markan record, interpolating sections of Jesus' teaching from the source Q wherever it seemed to him that the setting of the story approved or required it. We may picture Matthew as looking on this sturdy structural framework of Mark's Gospel and adding to it such material from his other available sources as to give to his own account the architectural design and consecrated dignity of a Gospel of the Christian church. To us who now read it, nothing more nobly ecclesiastical, more like a cathedral, could be imagined than Matthew's narrative with its magnificent detail of the apostles in their saints' niches, Peter holding the keys to the kingdom for which the Gospel stands, and Christ himself securely established as the Rock on which the church is built.

It remained for Luke to look with fresh eyes on the event of the coming of Christ, to evaluate anew the strange mystery of his nature and person, his prophetic preaching, his teaching in parables, his death and resurrection, and to point out, as it

had not been done before, that through his advent a new power had been released to the world—a power at once human and divine, expressing human pity and divine compassion, involving in its program of activity both secular institutions and the hierarchy of heavenly angels, and having as its goal not only the evangelization of Jews and Gentiles but the regeneration of man and of mankind. That Luke owed much of this broad vision of the Christian gospel to Saint Paul is evident; though it was not Paul's mature and majestic theological writings, but his earlier missionary preaching, that influenced Luke in undertaking his composition of Luke-Acts.

To accomplish his task, therefore, Luke needed to go to all the obtainable sources, both old and new. The most primitive source of which he had knowledge was that called Q. Luke's strong leaning toward this source, rather than toward Mark, can be readily explained. He had the historian's respect for primitive sources. Versions of Q were in circulation in Antioch and elsewhere as early as A.D. 50. It was shortly after that time that Luke, traveling with Saint Paul, became acquainted with it, noted with what freshness it preserved the teachings of Jesus, perceived its influence on himself and its Gentile readers, and treasured his own copy of it as a transcript of the first "Gospel" then in existence. And such it was. For it contained, besides the Sayings of Jesus, a strong connective thread of story that was long and firm enough to hold these Sayings together within a simple framework of the earthly life of Christ.

But this was only the beginning of Luke's search for the existing original gospel sources, both written and oral. By about the year A.D. 60, very likely while he was in Caesarea, now again near Saint Paul and awaiting the outcome of the apostle's trial in that city, the Evangelist gathered together the material known to us as the source L. Some of this gospel material existed as oral tradition, having, it is rightly supposed, owed its preservation to Saint Philip's missionary work in Samaria and Caesarea, and presumably also to the memory and interest of his gifted family. But the greater quantity of L, including the famous collection of parables now found in

Courtesy of The Art Institute of Chicago.

3. THE ADORATION OF THE WISE MEN. Albrecht Dürer.

Courtesy of The Art Institute of Chicago.

4. THE BAPTISM OF CHRIST. Martin Schongauer.

Luke 9:51-18:14, was in the form of a document. When, a few years later, as we read in Saint Paul's letter to Philemon (v. 24), Luke was in Rome, he combined the collected material of Q and L into a consecutive narrative of "all that Jesus began both to do and teach"—as he himself tells us in his preface to the Book of the Acts. This combined narrative, since Canon Streeter has given it its name, has been called Proto-Luke.[3]

With the edition of Proto-Luke before him, Luke now turned to an examination of further sources. With the gospel historian's mind fixed on writing a complete and satisfying biography of Jesus, he gave his attention to the tradition of infancy stories then actively current in Palestine. In them, and the songs they now contain, he found an appropriate beginning for the narrative as we have it in the first two chapters of the Gospel. As we read them we note at once how well written they are: song and story intertwine to furnish an earthly setting for the heavenly miracle of the birth of Christ that is the theme of the introduction to the Gospel. The entire section of the two chapters is at once so humanly presented, and so overshadowed by the divine Spirit, that the remaining chapters that follow take the natural form of an exposition of the continuing activity of the Jesus of history who was to become the Lord of the Church's life.

By this time, close to the year 75, Luke was in possession of the complete Gospel story—or of what, till then, he considered to be such. Then, apparently, and perhaps unexpectedly, he came upon his manuscript copy of the Gospel of Mark. Without altering the record of Proto-Luke, composed of the documents Q plus L, he gave room in it to seven sections of material from Mark. These, after careful planning, he fitted into the already established pattern of his own narrative. At the same time he purposely omitted portions of that Gospel,

[3] Scholars today, though sometimes preferring to treat Q and L separately, have generally followed the course of this interpretation. See B. H. Streeter, *The Four Gospels: A Study of Origins* (New York: The Macmillan Co., 1924-1931); B. S. Easton, *The Gospel According to St. Luke* (New York: Charles Scribner's Sons, 1926); F. C. Grant, *The Growth of the Gospels,* (New York: Abingdon-Cokesbury Press, 1933); and Vincent Taylor, *The First Draft of St. Luke's Gospel,* in "Theology Reprints," 1927.

contenting himself, for the sake of the story's continuity, with gathering from them their essential thought—as, for example, from Mark 6:47-8:26, containing the account of Jesus' sojourn in Tyre and Sidon, which was quite certainly approved by Luke but not recorded.

To get a clear picture of the manner in which, finally, Luke combined Mark's Gospel with his own edition of Proto-Luke, or Q and L, we need only look at the following simple chart.[4]

A Sections of Material taken from Mark	B Sections of Material contained in Proto-Luke
	1. Luke 3:1-4:30
2. Luke 4:33-44	
	3. Luke 5:1-11
4. Luke 5:12-6:19	
	5. Luke 6:20-8:3
6. Luke 8:4-9:50	
	7. Luke 9:51-18:14
8. Luke 18:15-43	
	9. Luke 19:1-27
10. Luke 19:28:36	
	11. Luke 19:37:44
12. Luke 19:45-21:33	
	13. Luke 21:34-36
14. Luke 21:37-22:13	
	15. Luke 22:14-24:53

The influence of Luke's Gospel—together with that of the subsequent Acts—is probably unmatched by any other book in the world. Its effect on world thought, literature, and art has been great. But, more specifically and pertinently, it has created such movements as that of world-wide Christian missions. The multitude of "St. Luke's" hospitals is a monument to its distinctive humanitarianism; and the hymns it has inspired are legion. Of the hymns composed within our own time, perhaps none better represents the great Evangelist's word to us than that beginning with "Where Cross the Crowded Ways of Life,"

---

4 This chart is an adaptation of Professor F. C. Grant's outline in his *Growth of the Gospels* (New York: The Abingdon-Cokesbury Press, 1933), p. 174.

in which the Gospel's breathing of the Holy Spirit upon the Christian church is felt in these lines:

> O Master, from the mountain side,
>   Make haste to heal these hearts of pain;
> Among these restless throngs abide,
>   O tread the city's streets again,
> Till sons of men shall learn Thy love
>   And follow where Thy feet have trod;
> Till, glorious from Thy heaven above,
>   Shall come the city of our God![5]

[5] Frank Mason North (1850-1935). Used by permission of the heirs and publishers.

Chapter 12

THE GOSPEL OF JOHN

I

THE GOSPEL'S GENERAL CHARACTER

The poet Browning, in the poem "A Death in the Desert," pictures the aged Saint John in profound thought on the content of his Gospel. He rests in a grotto not far from Ephesus, safe from the emperor Domitian's persecuting reach. There, surrounded by four of his followers, he awakens, as if recalled from death, speaks out strikingly, and says:

> . . . it was so; so I heard and saw,
> . . . I saw, I heard, I knew.

Then, as his outward senses return, and the "retreating soul is forced back upon the ashes of his brain . . . taxing the flesh to one supreme exertion," he thinks of the future. He now lives again; but it is in a far-off time when he, the "John" who was the Apostle who heard and saw, is dead. It is in a decrepit age in a vast wasteland that he finds himself, where men have only enough strength to be skeptical. And, feeling his way through this distant time that only grasps "at facts which snap," he hears men say:

> Was John at all, and did he say he saw?
> Assure us, ere we ask what he might see!

In this picture we see reflected the two contrasting views that have been held by men through history concerning the Fourth Gospel. The one is that of tradition, dating from the time of the church fathers, and extending into the nineteenth century. The other is that of rationalistic and liberalistic criticism, beginning with the middle of the nineteenth century and

brought to the threshold of our time by the so-called "Lives" of Jesus, first introduced and made popular by David Strauss and Ernest Renan.

The first lays stress on the Gospel as divine history; the second shifts the emphasis to the story of the Palestinian Jesus and to the speculative and imaginative things that can be said to interpret his extraordinary life to the world. Between these two views there is, at last, no middle ground of compromise. We who read the Gospel today must either reject or accept what it purports to say.

It is only in recent years that we have come to a more realistic and comprehensive view of the Johannine question. Granting, freely, that we have not yet found its full answer, we may now accept the Gospel in this twofold sense: first, as actual history; and second, as the record of a cumulative and enduring gospel revelation. So accepted, it becomes, to an age that greatly needs it, the Gospel (1) of the eternal Word—or mind and will—of God, (2) of the Word made flesh in the earthly life of Christ, and (3) of that Word, as the mystical presence of Christ, made the sacramental source of life to men for all time to come. For the purpose of our present study, the truth it contains can be expressed in the traditional language of the church in these summarizing words: "Christ became partaker of our humanity that we might become partakers of his divinity."

The Fourth Gospel's general character is easily recognized. The style of the narrative is outwardly simple. The story follows its own course. It traces the events it records with singular attention to time and place, and culminates, as the Synoptic Gospels also do, in a vivid account of Jesus' passion and resurrection. But in and around this simple narrative one perceives the movement of profound thought. It suggests the stately motion of a ship on the deep sea. Sometimes, on its journey, the narrative is overtaken by a storm. Fierce winds of controversy between the church and the synagogue threaten the Gospel's majestic serenity—as, for example, in Chapter 6, after the feeding of the five thousand, when the Jews challenge Jesus with the boast that their fathers in the desert were fed with

manna from heaven; whereupon Jesus answers them: "Your
fathers did eat manna in the wilderness, and are dead." [1] But in
another moment tranquillity is restored when Jesus says: "I
am the bread of life"; and those nearest to him answer: "Lord,
evermore give us this bread." [2]

This controversial element in the Gospel has sometimes been
thought by critics to spoil the structure of an otherwise calm
and philosophic dissertation. Actually it has the effect of tear-
ing away the veil from reality and of helping us to look into
the depth of the meaning of the writer's thoughts and through
them into the mind of Christ. Altogether, the Evangelist's
simple yet profound insight suggests the soaring eagle that,
since as early as the second century, has been the symbol of
the Fourth Gospel. This reasoning sublimity, together with
the writer's sense of history, gives to his narrative what we
may call a vertical as well as a horizontal direction and character. Sometimes, before our very eyes, it takes on another dimension, a third, through its illuminating use of symbolism.
At such times the shadowy things of earth disappear and the
heavens are opened, as they were to the sight of Nathanael, for
example, in the very beginning of the Gospel, when Jesus said
to him: "Because I said unto thee, I saw thee under the fig
tree, believest thou? . . . verily, I say unto you, Hereafter ye
shall see heaven open, and the angels of God ascending and
descending upon the Son of man." [3] Such a Gospel, it is clear,
cannot be fathomed, or comprehended, by any ordinary reading.

That its author meant to rest his account on solid history
cannot be denied. He was, most probably, a Jew. His knowledge of the Old Testament is obvious. It is seen in the passage
we have just quoted, in which Nathanael's experience, yet to
come, is compared to that of Jacob's dream at Bethel where he
beholds a ladder set up on the earth and the angels of God
ascending and descending on it. The Fourth Evangelist's purpose was not to write fiction, or allegory, or a treatise on meta-
physics. He had no desire to establish a new mystery cult, to

[1] John 6:49.
[2] John 6:34.
[3] John 1:50, 51.

incorporate Mithraism into Christianity, or merely to conciliate the Gnostics and write a Hellenized gospel. His aim was to write the *whole history of Christ*. Such a history involved (1) a going back to the first words of Genesis: "In the beginning God . . .," (2) a tracing of the main events of the earthly life of Jesus, from his baptism to his crucifixion, and (3) a forecasting of the continued activity of the risen and living Christ in the life of the Christian believer, in the growth of the church, and in the order and destiny of the world.

Measured by this aim, the writing of the Gospel was indeed a great undertaking. If the Evangelist found it difficult to span in a single narrative all the ages of time, we—reading him at this distance—may rightly stand in interrogating awe of what he meant to say by his use of symbolical language in depicting Christ as the Good Shepherd, the Living Bread and Water, the Vine, the Way, the Resurrection and the Life. Such language is not to be interpreted as an attempt at allegorizing the earthly life of Christ out of existence, as, for example, Origen, the Alexandrian theologian and teacher, was inclined to do. The author of the Fourth Gospel is too Jewish for that. The plain fact is that he is both Semitic and Hellenic. On the one hand, he writes from a background of a close acquaintance with such places, for instance, as Bethesda's Pool and Bethany, and such institutions as the Sanhedrin, the Temple, and the Synagogue. Yet, on the other hand, he addresses himself to Greek-speaking readers who understand the meaning of the terms "the Logos" and "the Paraclete," and who know of the existence, in Asia Minor, of the party of thinkers, or "Intellectuals," called the Gnostics. He hears the Jews' demand for "signs" from heaven, and answers them with an affirmation of the Hebrew "I Am"; but he adds to it a definitely Greek symbolic meaning as he says: "I am the Light of the World."

How the Fourth Evangelist works through the medium, for example, of the Book of Genesis, to convey his gospel message to his Gentile Ephesian readers is vividly illustrated by these words: "Verily, verily, I say unto you: Before Abraham was, I am." Further illustrations suggest themselves to us in almost every chapter of the Gospel. The Evangelist wishes to com-

mend the followers of John the Baptist to the Ephesian church.
They are now no longer rivals but fellow Christians. So he
seals the bond between them by joining the Hebrew concept of
Jehovah's Suffering Servant to the Greek ideal of universality
and records the Baptizer as saying of Jesus: "Behold the Lamb
of God which taketh away the sin of the world!" Similarly,
Mary of Bethany, by anointing Jesus beforehand for his burial,
fills the whole world with the fragrance of her deed.

The Fourth Gospel, therefore, is twofold history: first, of
Jesus' life on earth; and second, of his continued presence in
the lives of his followers and in the world. As literature, likewise, it represents a union of two cultures: the Hebrew and
the Greek. East meets West in this most universal Gospel; and
North meets South. And so, by a unique application of its
own symbolism, it occupies a place in the center of the world.

The Gospel's geographical origin is rightly attributed to
—and symbolized by—the city of Ephesus. Other cities like
Antioch and Rome might lay claim to its place of composition.
Jerusalem could not. Even Alexandria might satisfy the demands of the Gospel's universalism. But the tradition that
the author lived and wrote in Ephesus is sustained by the record's internal evidence. Ephesus was the rich and sumptuous
mistress of the Aegean Sea. Its prestige as a center of commerce and culture was world-wide. It was a Roman imperial
colony; it welcomed philosophers from Athens. But, at heart,
it was Asiatic. Gnosticism, the Mystery Religions, Judaism,
and Christianity alike were strongly represented there. Saint
Paul had made it the base of his missionary activity in Asia
Minor. Its cosmopolitanism, like its wealth, was unquestioned.
So also was its deep-seated hunger for life and—as we read in
John 6—for the bread that satisfied the soul. In a word,
Ephesus typified the world. In it men wandered blindly, searching, groping for the light. They were like lost sheep waiting
for the good shepherd or trying to find the door to the sheep-
fold; they were like famished and thirsty men looking for a
well of pure water.

To such among his readers in Asia, the Evangelist came
with the treasured story of the gospel. It was essentially the

same as that told by the three other Evangelists: the story of the earthly life of Jesus, culminating in the gospel of the Cross, and coming to a climax in the message of the risen Christ. This much was now world history, rooted in Old Testament prophecy and in Palestinian soil. But it was not all there was to record of divine history—of *Heilsgeschichte,* as we have before this time called it. For the history of Christ did not end with his death and resurrection. Rather, in its world-wide outlook, it began there. For the ensuing generation of mankind it began anew in the life and activity of the risen and living Christ. That was, and is today, the message of the Fourth Gospel.

To those to whom the hidden symbolism reveals its meaning, the story of Mary Magdalene, on the first Easter morning, well sums up the Johannine conclusion. With Mary, a pitying, searching world looks into the sepulcher.[4] It sees only the "two angels in white sitting, the one at the head, and the other at the feet, where the body of Jesus had lain." In men's thoughts, so suspended between death and resurrection, the Jesus of history, who lived on earth, is but a memory. To Mary, on that eventful morning, the only living person there among the dead was the gardener. Then the risen Christ, calling her by name, said, "Mary." And Mary answered in the familiar manner of former days, saying, "Master."

II

THE AUTHOR AND HIS MESSAGE

Hitherto we have spoken of the author as the Fourth Evangelist. We may now ask: Who was he? And why is his narrative called the Gospel of Saint John? The answer to the latter question is that Christian tradition, from the second to the nineteenth century, steadfastly held to the opinion that the Gospel was written by John the Apostle who was an eyewitness to the events he recorded and who was reverently referred to as the Beloved Disciple. Among the church fathers, Irenaeus held that the Gospel was written by "John, the disciple of the

---

[4] John 20:11-18.

Lord, who also had leaned upon his breast." Clement of Alexandria, impressed by the manner in which all history tended to become symbolism,[5] was quoted as saying: "John, . . . realizing that the outward facts had been presented in the [first three] Gospels, was persuaded by his disciples and moved by the Holy Spirit to compose a spiritual Gospel." Many others of authority in the ancient church similarly assumed the Gospel's Johannine authorship.

But an examination of the narrative makes it difficult to accept this view. Who was the Beloved Disciple? The Fourth Gospel does not identify him as John. Can he have been John the Apostle, once a Galilean fisherman, who was, it is true, an eyewitness to the events of Christ's earthly life? The absence of John's name, and the general style and tenor of the Gospel, do not tend to sustain this conclusion. The intervening years might of course have changed this "son of thunder," as Jesus called him (Mark 3:17), into the Beloved Disciple who in the Fourth Gospel symbolizes the Christian's intimate spiritual communion with Christ. The question is also complicated by the tradition based on Acts 12:2, that John was one of the church's early martyrs. It was assumed, in years past, that the writer of the Book of Revelation, who calls himself John, was also the author of the Gospel. But the style and message of Revelation are so purely apocalyptic that the book can hardly have been written by the Fourth Evangelist, especially since both writings owe the occasion of their composition to the same historic crisis—that is, to the persecution of the Christians in the reign of Domitian, in about A.D. 95.

The suggestion is offered that the Gospel was indeed written by John, but that he was the John surnamed "The Elder." The reasons underlying this suggestion are two: (1) the author of the three Epistles of John, who is almost certainly the writer of the Fourth Gospel, calls himself "The Elder"; (2) Eusebius, the church historian, quotes Papias as saying that he was acquainted with a certain "John the Elder" whom he carefully

---

[5] Note, in this connection, the famous statement of the poet Goethe: "Alles Natürliche ist nur ein Gleichniss"—Everything in nature is but a *parable*.

distinguished from John the Apostle. From a review of these facts we may conclude that the John who wrote the Fourth Gospel was a Palestinian Jew, now unknown to us, who in his early youth was himself a follower of Jesus, and who, in his old age, living in Ephesus, either wrote the Gospel or composed the document from which it was immediately derived. Recent scholarship, relying on manuscript discoveries of the past few years, tends to favor this view.[6]

It is not the identity of the writer of the Fourth Gospel that accounts for its great appeal to us. It is the Gospel's content. Throughout its moving chapters it is not John, but Christ himself, who is speaking to us. The events are historical. But the echoing overtones of the divine symbolism in them are heard above the occurrences in time, suggesting a significance beyond time. The preaching of John the Baptist, the wedding at Cana, the cleansing of the temple, the visit of Nicodemus, the story of the Samaritan woman, the feeding of the multitudes, the healing of the blind man, the controversy with the Jews, the anointing at Bethany, the washing of the disciples' feet, and the Crucifixion—all these, and others, are actual happenings of which John tells us in careful and minute detail. Their setting in time, place, and definite circumstance impresses them indelibly upon the reader's mind. They belong to Palestine, unmistakably: for example, to Jerusalem, Samaria, Galilee, or Bethany. The Fourth Gospel's historicity, like that of the Synoptics, is amply confirmed. But, as an able writer has recently said: "All four Gospels are interpretations." [7] That is, they are more than factual records or itemized chronology. It is the typical and the topical use of the events that stands out in them all, and more especially in the Gospel of John. Here we see what the gospel intends and means. It dramatizes the "Good News" that Christ is the light and life of men.

As we turn the pages of John's Gospel we are moved by the manner in which this truth is made plain. We note how

---

[6] In this connection, and for a good introduction to the Gospel, read Ernest F. Scott, *Varieties of New Testament Teaching* (New York: Chas. Scribner's Sons, 1944), pp. 251-82.

[7] Chester Warren Quimby, *John, The Universal Gospel* (New York: The Macmillan Co., 1947), p. 75.

the Evangelist has selected his material. Mark's Gospel is evidently open before him. Of his other sources, we know only that they are original with him. They are his own. And he draws on them with an artist's skill put to the highest Christian use. We observe how his mind gradually penetrates, by an ascending scale, into the nature and character of Christ. From a viewpoint that suggests Dante's vision in the *Paradise,* John sees Christ's glory manifested in story-pictures of ever-widening dimension and meaning: first, in John the Baptist's proclamation of Jesus as the Lamb of God; then, in a series of signs representing him as the New Wine, the New Temple, and the New Kingdom; after that, in his offer of himself as the Living Water and the Bread of Heaven; thereafter, in the more exalted acknowledgment of him as the Great Physician and Good Shepherd of Souls; and, at last, in the transcendent declaration that he is the Light of the World and the Resurrection and the Life.

All this takes place in the Gospel's first eleven chapters and in an atmosphere of controversy which has the effect of heightening the tension of the story and so giving the reader a glimpse into the mystery of Jesus' divine origin and person. But his humanity is not forgotten. At the climax of his first great Act of self-revelation, at the grave of Lazarus, Jesus is represented as saying:

> ... he that believeth in me,
> Though he were dead, yet shall he live:
> And whosoever liveth and believeth in me
> Shall never die.[8]

And the Evangelist adds that when Jesus saw the people's tenderness and sorrow, and Mary weeping, he groaned in the spirit and wept. Confronted with such proof of his human nature, even the disputing Jews relented and said: "Behold how he loved him!"

In Chapters 12 to 17, which comprise the second general section of the Gospel, the story of the great manifestation of Christ is, so to speak, told over again. But this time—after the dramatic interval of Jesus' "hour of glory," in which he said:

---

[8] John 11:25, 26.

"And I, if I be lifted up from the earth, will draw all men unto me"—it is told, as a more intimate revelation, to the disciples, and for the strengthening of their faith. The preliminary act is the anointing of Jesus. Like the preaching of John the Baptist, Mary's deed signalizes the importance of the coming events. The odor of her good deed will fill the whole world with its fragrance. Only now the mind of the Evangelist is on the glory of the death of Christ. This glory is revealed, first of all, in his self-humiliation. He becomes the Great Servant as he takes water and a towel and washes the disciples' feet. Then, in the parable of the vine and the branches, he indicates how the disciples are to be inseparably united to him: in life, through communion and growth; in death, through the crushing of the grape and the pouring out of the wine of his life. The section comes to an exalted close with (1) the discourse on the Holy Spirit as the Comforter, and (2) the prayer of Jesus as the great High Priest.

The passion story is told in the Fourth Evangelist's characteristic way. Jesus' death is not martyrdom, nor suffering innocence moving us to pity, nor sovereignty affronted and despised. It is the sacrifice of the Lamb of God for the sin of the world. The prophecy of John the Baptist is fulfilled. The earthly life of Christ is ended. But it is not the end of gospel history. Jesus is alive and has shown himself to Mary; he has revealed himself to Thomas, tangibly and beyond doubt. So Christ lives on and his work of self-revelation continues. Peter and all the other disciples after him are to be good shepherds; multitudes are to be gathered together in intimate Christian fellowship until men everywhere, through his love awakened in them, are to be united in one family and one fold. That is the Gospel's final goal. Though Chapter 21 is a later editor's work, it confirms and seals the promise of all the four Gospels as with a holy seal.

The final interpretation of the Fourth Gospel—though placed at the beginning, as it should be—is the Prologue. Its meaning is best made clear to us by first reading the Gospel. It is best read as a hymn, having the solemnity that adoration adds to high reasoning. In it Christian doctrine becomes liturgy, ele-

vating the truth of what is believed into the mystery of what is revealed. Here the Hebrew psalmist and the Greek philosopher are joined, and surpassed, by the Johannine theologian and saint, as he writes, first, of the deity of Christ, second, of his humanity, and third, of his divine mission. The Prologue has come to us in words worthy to be set to music in a Bach choral and to be sung in a Gothic cathedral. Repeating after John, we join the church of the centuries, confessing its faith, and saying,

> In the beginning was the Word,
> And the Word was with God,
> And the Word was God.
> The same was in the beginning with God....

> And the Word was made flesh,
> And dwelt among us,
> And we beheld his glory,
> The glory as of the only begotten of the Father,
> Full of grace and truth....

> And, as many as received him,
> To them gave he power to become the sons of God,
> Even to them that believe on his name:
> Which were born, not of blood,
> Nor of the will of the flesh,
> Nor of the will of man,
> But of God.[9]

[9] John 1:1-14.

PART III

THE EARTHLY LIFE OF CHRIST

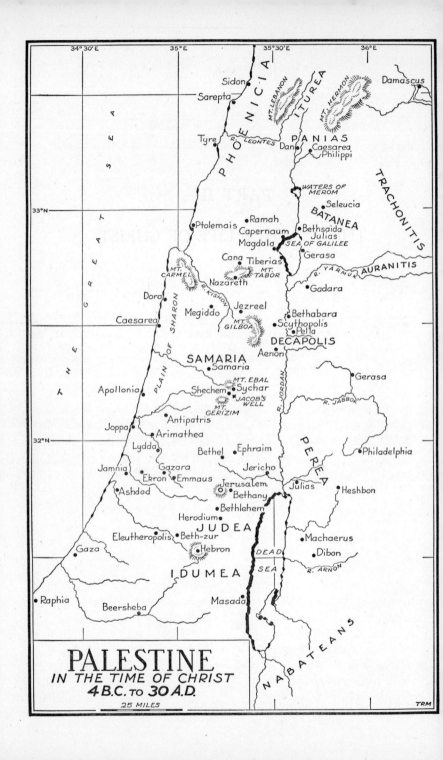

PALESTINE
IN THE TIME OF CHRIST
4 B.C. TO 30 A.D.

25 MILES

Chapter 13

LOOKING AT THE LIFE OF JESUS

I

STATING THE PROBLEM

A modern writer, setting out to write a biography, would not begin, as for example the Evangelist Mark did, by calling his narrative "the gospel of . . . the Son of God." He would be content to portray a man, to describe his character and habits, to indicate his success or failure, and perhaps to praise or blame whatever he might find. A biographer does not write about a man as if he were a supernatural revelation. He senses, as indeed we all do, that biography has to do with persons whose natural talents, individual aspirations, and private fortunes are of unusual and so of general public interest. The Gospels, though they are narratives, do not belong to this category.

Essentially, the life of Christ is history. It is the history of God's mighty work in the world. It therefore belongs to the history of the Christian faith, and first of all to the history of the faith of the early Christian community. To tell the story of the earthly life of Jesus is, as it has always been, possible. But in order to do so we must keep clearly in sight, just as the Evangelists never forgot, that what he taught and did is to be interpreted as being, first, in fulfilment of Old Testament prophecy, and, second, for our eternal salvation. To separate the life of Jesus from this context is to ignore the fact that he was Christ the Messiah, as Matthew undertook to show, and to which Luke also agreed by announcing him as the savior of the world.

Such a separation of the history of Jesus from its theological context—that is, from the life and faith of the early Christian community to which the earthly ministry, the death, and the resurrection of Christ had this distinct meaning—has frequently

been attempted, especially within the last century. Scores of times the life of Christ, popular, critical, or both, has been written since the time of David Strauss and Ernest Renan; and written in order, it has been supposed, "to free the historical Jesus from the shackles of a traditional dogmatic theology." The result has been a stress on the "human" Jesus that is altogether different from the historic gospel teaching of the humanity of Christ.

What has happened has been an attempt to bring the Jesus of the Gospels "down to earth," not as in the doctrine of the divine incarnation but in accordance with the social demands of the modern day. Jesus the honest carpenter, the patriotic Nazarene, the Good Teacher, the ideal man: these have been the humanitarian biographer's names for him. Sometimes, where the recorded gospel facts have been too hard and unyielding or the individual details lacking, the imaginative narrator has simply substituted or added the desired information. The product has been a "life of Jesus" that has been either a scholar's rationalized interpretation or an author's creative work of fiction. One noted critic says of the most famous of these "lives," Renan's *Vie de Jésus:* "The gentle Jesus, the beautiful Maries, the fair Galilean women who form the escort of the 'charming carpenter,' might have simply stepped out of the windows of one of the ecclesiastical art shops on the Place Saint-Sulpice." [1] Another New Testament historian, after quoting these words, adds: "Jesus is presented as a kind of gentle dreamer who wanders through the countryside of Galilee, smiling at life, whom his followers draw into a sombre drama which turns him into a wonder-worker, and a candidate for the Messiahship, and brings him to his death." [2]

As we should expect, this bland humanization of the life of Jesus was found to be untrue to the nature and person of Christ as he is represented to us in the Gospels. By an inevitable reaction, it led to the opposite extreme. Accordingly, there were those who, seeing the Christ of revelation so separated from the

[1] Albert Schweitzer, *The Quest of the Historical Jesus,* (New York: The Macmillan Co., 1910), p. 182. English translation.
[2] Maurice Goguel, *The Life of Jesus* (New York: The Macmillan Co., 1933), p. 51-52.

Jesus of history, turned toward philosophical speculation for an answer to the question which, Matthew tells us, Jesus himself asked the Pharisees: "What think ye of Christ? Whose son is he?" If Christ was Lord, what mattered whose earthly son he was? It was enough that there were once—and still are—Christians believing in him. Quoting Saint Paul, but not comprehending his true position, they cared to know nothing of Jesus "after the flesh." The tendency was to stress the Christology of the Gospels without a due regard for their historicity. Men who held this view talked freely of the cosmic and timeless Christ, associating him all too easily with the universal deity of other ancient faiths, and the worship of him, for example, with that of Mithraism, Platonism, and the Mystery cults of the East. Into the place of the Biblical emphasis on divine revelation through history there was put the tantalizing and transcendent concept of Jesus the Holy One.

The underlying basis of this view is Asiatic; its speculative framework, or pattern, is Hellenic. If the danger of the popular biographer has been to lose himself in fiction, that of the speculative Christological philosopher has been to see the historic figure of Christ melt away before him into a theosophic myth.

It is therefore with renewed assurance that we turn to the solid facts of gospel history. Biblical scholarship today unitedly affirms the historicity of Jesus. That he lived in Palestine, preached the gospel of the Kingdom in Galilee, healed the sick and demented, brought forgiveness and hope to sinful souls, called and taught his disciples, accepted the role of Messiah, was involved in open conflict, first with the scribes and Pharisees, then with the Herodians, and finally with the chief priests in Jerusalem, was condemned to death by them, giving himself up willingly to be crucified and so completing his mission of Messiahship are now undisputed facts. The record of the Evangelists, which affirms that God wrought mightily in and through his person, that his Messianic consciousness was fully attested by his words and deeds, that he worked miracles, and that after his death he revealed himself alive to his disciples is in accord with this verified history. Contemporary Palestinian, Syrian,

and Roman life, in the judgment of those who have made a detailed study of its character and setting, tends to corroborate both the story of Jesus and the early church's faith in him as the living and redeeming Christ. Thus the twofold problem of approaching and understanding the life of Christ—first, that of history, and second, that of religion—has been successfully met and reasonably solved. The facts, even those involving the miracles of Jesus, are no longer denied, however they may be explained; and it is granted that no explanation that is negative can claim to be scientific and at the same time final.[3]

Nevertheless it is to be acknowledged that the tradition of the early church—which is by us always to be thought of as of one piece with the earlier history of the Old Testament—directed the general course of the Gospel narrative. The generation of time that elapsed between the death of Christ and the composition of Mark's Gospel was, in its religious character, at once strongly retentive and formative. Those among the apostles and missionaries who remembered the acts and sayings of Jesus would be expected to hold fast to them, to treasure them literally, make them the texts of their evangelistic preaching, instruct their converts in their exact meaning, and exhort all faithful believers to live by them. Many of Jesus' prophetic utterances, aphorisms, and parables, spoken in the terse and rhythmic Aramaic tongue, certainly clung to the memory and went straight to the heart of those who heard the wonderful story. We who now read through certain sections of the augmented and edited Gospel narrative can easily detect some of these sayings by the direct aim and swift wing of their lines of poetry; and we are therefore strongly supported in saying that they represent the very words of Christ. Among such—and

[3] Maurice Goguel, *The Life of Jesus, op. cit.,* p. 216-17 states the position of the modern theologian in these words: "The a priori denial of the possibility of certain facts is an unlawful prejudice . . . and is in reality non-scientific. In natural science, no seeker would systematically deny a fact simply and solely because he was unable to explain it by the laws which he knows. . . . Gospel historians have sometimes adopted an attitude towards the question of miracle which can be explained from the philosophical point of view rather than from that of considerations of method. . . . Their position would have been stronger if they had remained upon the ground of facts, and had simply tried to register those which seemed to be established without trying to explain them all."

especially among those whose setting in the Gospels gives to them the note of surprise that is an added mark of their authenticity—are utterances like these:

> Suffer the little children to come unto me,
> And forbid them not;
> For of such is the kingdom of God.[4]

> And I say unto you,
> That many shall come from the east and the west
> And shall sit down
> With Abraham, and Isaac, and Jacob,
> In the kingdom of heaven.[5]

But another generation was to pass before all four of the Gospels, as we know them, were finally written. It was during these years, between A.D. 70 and 100, that the tradition of the early church exercised its most formative influence on the literary composition of the narratives of Matthew, Luke, and John. The two main sources of outside influence during this period were the church's contact with the Jewish synagogue and its acquaintance with Hellenism. Next in importance were the Asiatic Mystery cults and the prophetic movement of the followers of John the Baptist. It is clear that certain passages in the Gospel narratives reflect these contacts. But it is also noticeable that a strong tension existed between the Christian message and these alien influences. There was more often open hostility between them than friendship; and it is therefore reasonable to suppose that the Gospel writers sought, wherever they could, to keep their records free of the taint of all such alien and subversive teaching. The presumption that they did so is certainly in their favor, even though the church must have desired through the Gospels to win converts among the people of the outlying Roman colonies.

We must not forget that the Christian church was, from the beginning, a strongly separatist movement. The first Christians went out into the world to win followers for Christ among all men. But as believers in Christ they kept themselves apart from

4 Mark 10:14.
5 Matthew 8:11.

the world, both in fellowship and in doctrine—so Luke tells us
in the Book of the Acts. Saint Paul's stress, too, in declaring
that he had "kept the faith," and the repeated advice he gave to
Timothy to "hold fast to the form of sound words," [6] indicated
the resolute desire of the early church not to stray from the
purity of the original apostolic teaching. At the end of the age,
close to the year 100 when the Book of Revelation was written
and the temptation to apostasy was real and strong, this twofold
word of invitation and of warning was given to the Christians
then living:

> The Spirit and the bride say, Come;
> And let him that heareth say, Come;
> And let him that is athirst come.
> And whosoever will,
> Let him take of the water of life freely. . . .

If any man shall add unto these things, God shall add unto him
the plagues that are written in this book; and if any man shall
take away from the words of the book of this prophecy, God shall
take away his part out of the book of life.[7]

From such recorded evidence as this we note the solemnity
with which the command to hold fast to the letter of the "new
law" was regarded by the Christians of the time. Apparently,
as with the keeping of the old law, every jot and tittle was desired to be preserved. The divine authority which the Evangelists attached to the words and works of Jesus carried with
it the positive charge to keep the tradition committed to them
in sacred trust against any arbitrary change.

II

Outlining the Method

As the Gospel tradition crystallized into the present narrative, the Evangelists faced a further task. It was to fit together
the documentary and orally transmitted material in their possession in such a manner as, first, to give it a chronological and

[6] II Timothy 1:13.
[7] Revelation 22:17-19.

geographical framework, and, after that, to find the right situation in the record for the expression of the inner thought and life of Jesus.

Such a task, we must infer, was not an easy one. Yet, as we have before said, the document called Q, which had taken shape very early, had already provided Matthew and Luke with the broad outline of such a framework; and, besides, the passion story had itself by then assumed the character of an orderly narrative. That there had been a rather prolonged Galilean ministry of Jesus was, on examination of the various episodes, also evident. The town of Capernaum and the Lake of Galilee, for instance, had been too intimately associated with the recorded events to separate them from these places. Like the flowers and bushes that grew there, many of the parables and discourses of Jesus were native to that region; and the Gospel writers would entertain no thought of uprooting and transplanting them, let us say, to the more somber region of Judea.

As we open Mark's Gospel we read that Jesus' "fame spread abroad throughout all the region of Galilee," centered in Capernaum, and came to a particular focus in Peter's house when "all the city was gathered together" at his door. The radius of Jesus' early Galilean activity is here unmistakably indicated. Similarly, when, in Chapters 5-7, Matthew gathers together the sayings and teachings of the Sermon on the Mount, he does so as if he were gleaning the fields for flowers that grew along the roads between the villages of Galilee. He has cut the flowers from their stems; but everyone knows that they have their roots in the region roundabout. This fact is substantiated by what we see in Luke. Here the sayings of Matthew 5-7 are scattered throughout four sections of the Gospel; the time limit between the sections is extended; but all four of them have their setting in the region of greater Galilee.

There are obvious geographical and chronological problems to be met in outlining a Galilean and Judean ministry of Christ. It is as useless to minimize these problems as it is unwise to magnify them. All that we can do is to give the *pericopae,* or preaching units, that make up the main body of the gospel tradition the setting that best suits them; and that is what the

Synoptic Evangelists themselves attempted to do. There is, in consideration of these facts, little advantage in assuming that we can accomplish this task better than they did; and it is agreed that nothing appreciable is gained by simply plucking these units from their present setting and letting them lie, like wilting flowers, where we may drop them.

The difficulty of shaping the gospel material into a coherent narrative is a very real one. Matthew's and Luke's independent setting for many of the sayings and parables of Jesus is, we have said, evident. Moreover, the wide difference, in both content and chronology, between John and the Synoptics must be recognized and noted. Not only does the Fourth Gospel add much new source material, but the stories of the events are given their own setting in a chronological pattern that allows close to three years for the history of Jesus' earthly life, in contrast to the Synoptic Gospels which require but one year. And we must add, besides, the opinion of recent Johannine scholars that the Fourth Gospel is not simply to be regarded as a theological treatise but as a genuine Gospel. This fact means that it is also history, and that the events in it follow a chronological pattern which the modern historian tends to find, in certain parts, more acceptable than that of Luke. Yet in the presence of these problems that vex the scholar but do not disturb the believer, one great heartening fact presents itself to us: the historicity of Jesus remains unshaken. Thanks to a generation of sound scholarship, that rock has been closely examined, and it now stands established and firm. The truth is that Jesus lived, and that his life is, as ever, the solid foundation of our faith.

Lately, another task has challenged the attention of the reader who looks penetratingly at the earthly life of Christ. It is that of attempting to adjust the inner life and thought of Jesus to the outer details of this historical pattern. Much of the space of the Gospel narrative is occupied with what is called the Messianic consciousness of Jesus. Here the problem, in so far as it involves the critical study of the record, is psychological. It consists of finding in the history of the events some ground and occasion toward helping us to understand the mind of Christ as the Evangelist uncovers it to us in such significant

accounts of Jesus' experience as those of the Temptation, the Transfiguration, the decision to go to Jerusalem, the Agony in Gethsemane, and the Seven Words on the Cross. Taken by themselves alone, these events are among the most precious in the treasury of Gospel literature. They belong to that perennial history by which the gospel renews itself in the world, century after century; that is, they are religious history, the bond of connection between Jesus' experience and our own. Do the outer circumstances of history in the Gospels provide a natural setting for these events? An examination of the record will, we believe, indicate that they do. The connection between them and the historical circumstances of the narrative is one of crisis; and the outward facts of gospel history that offer a setting for these apparent crises are mainly those associated with the prophetic ministry of John the Baptist, the political ambitions of Herod, and the growing hostility of the scribes and chief priests of Judaism.

It should here be noted that the Gospel writers, in telling the story of the life of Christ, were careful to indicate that the external facts of history did not actually determine the inner course of Jesus' thoughts and the decisions into which they crystallized. The religious experience of Jesus was not simply the result of the outward circumstances. The social environment did not create either the gospel tradition or the written Gospels. Nor did the enmity of Judaism, of itself, force on Jesus the role of the martyred Messiah. The situation, it is true, was furnished by history; yet it was but the stage set for the great and divine Act—the stage set by the providence of God, and in fulfilment of Holy Scripture. The decision to be the Messiah was wholly the act of Jesus himself. Such is the Gospels' verdict, for the sake of which the narratives were written.

We can see, from these facts, how important it was that the collected and recorded events of the life of Christ should be wrought into a complete narrative. For the gospel was from the beginning a whole and integrated story, the story of mankind's redemption through the Messiahship of Jesus. That this truth came to be recognized and firmly held immediately after

the events of Jesus' earthly life had transpired is shown by the early composition of the complete account of the passion. It could only be a matter of time until all the events whose record was available would take this historic form. For in order to bring out the meaning of Jesus' Messiahship, it was necessary for the early church to have this whole history. It has already been said that the gospel preached before the four Gospels were written consisted of groups of sayings of and about Jesus that served as texts for Christian evangelism and teaching. But behind them lay the great expanse of Old Testament history whose prophetic force was, so to speak, propelling the gospel message forward into the course and pattern it was to take. And it was therefore inevitable that the life of Christ should assume the character of the consummation of this history.

The history of Jesus, like that of ancient prophecy before him, was one of crisis. As we should expect, it was in times of Israel's great crises that the voices of the prophets were heard: Isaiah's, during the siege of Jerusalem; Jeremiah's, when the kingdom of Judah fell; Ezekiel's and the Second Isaiah's, during the Exile. These times of crisis, it is known, made Israel's history; and what happened in them, by reason of the fact that the word of God was spoken, now, in our own time, constitutes Scriptural history. The outward or secular events furnished the stage for the decisive acts of God. Yet these outward events also were providential history. God himself set the stage in the world for his mighty deeds.

It was even so with the earthly history of Jesus. The inner crises in his life, notably those associated with his conversations with the disciples in Caesarea Philippi, his departure for Jerusalem, and his trial and death have their outward counterpart and setting in the hostile aggression of Antipas, the guileful interrogations of the scribes and Pharisees, and the murderous designs of the Sanhedrin. It is in terms of such decisive events as these that we may sketch, in broad outline, the main periods of Jesus' earthly ministry.

Here, we conclude, we have the basis for an orderly narrative of the life of Christ. It will not involve a chronology of all the events. But in it there will be place and time enough to

indicate clearly the following facts: (1) that Jesus underwent a significant period of preparation for his public appearance; (2) that he entered upon his Galilean ministry with popular favor, centering his activity mainly in Capernaum; (3) that, after an intervening crisis, his second period of activity in the north of Palestine was continued under threat of Herod's ensnaring hostility and was therefore "not one of itinerating but of wandering" in and out of Galilee; (4) that, as he saw his work accomplished in the north—and the signs of God's will being done in and through him—he set out for Judea, journeying through the borderland of Perea, resuming his public teaching, and now assuming his appointed office of Messiah; (5) that, upon his entry into Jerusalem, his open Messianic presentation of himself was fiercely and summarily rejected; and (6) that, after days of retirement among his friends and a farewell message to his disciples, he surrendered to the august Sanhedrin, was betrayed, tried, and put to death.

Into such an outline it will be possible to place a sufficient amount of the assembled tradition, representing the things Jesus said and did, and offering us, first, a true historic portrait of him and, second, an insight into the meaning of his earthly life and mission. To succeed in our undertaking, we shall need to be aware of a twofold obligation: (1) to stress an attentive search for the historic facts; (2) to adopt the religious attitude of approach appropriate to our study. For in this as in all history, the discoverable facts do not all lie on the surface. Some are partly, others wholly, hidden from the casual observer's sight. He who would find the treasured deposit of Christian truth underlying the story of the life of Jesus of Nazareth must, above all else, work with a sensitive spirit—a spirit able to detect the depth as well as to trace the onward course of the narrative before him. In a word, the history of Jesus cannot be written without a knowledge of its implied meaning to our Christian faith. To the historian this presents a problem in psychology; to the believing Christian it offers an ever deepening and widening prospect of religious insight.

Our critical task and its required attitude are well summed up in this statement of a contemporary New Testament scholar:

"In order to understand the thought of Jesus we must have, or we must acquire, the spirit of a Christian. Erudition is indispensable, but where there is nothing else, an essential element is lacking. The Jesus whom it will paint will not be the real Jesus. As Wernle says, in order to understand Jesus, the historian ought to have in himself something that is like Jesus— *etwas Jesuähnliches.*" [8] Such an attitude is not easily acquired. It is, we must admit, a gift of grace. Without the intuitive insight it implies, the most critical exposition of the life of Christ is of necessity fruitless. What is required, besides and beyond an examination of the essential facts of that life, is the will to bring our thoughts wholly to a focus on the story's great meaning. So, looking on the events, with meditative rather than quizzical minds, we may—with Edmund Spenser,

> Beginne from first, where He encradled was
> In simple cratch, wrapt in a wad of hay,
> Betweene the toylefull oxe and humble asse,
> And in what rags, and in how base aray,
> The glory of our heavenly riches lay. . . .
> From thence reade on the storie of his life,
> His humble carriage, his unfaulty wayes,
> His cancred foes, his fights, his toyle, his strife. . . .
> And looke, at last, how of most wretched wights
> He taken was, betrayd, and false accused; . . .
> How scourgd, how crownd, how buffeted, how bruised;
> And lastly, how twixt robbers crucifyde,
> With bitter wounds through hands, through feet, and syde. . . .
> And let thy soule, whose sins his sorrows wrought,
> Melt into teares, and grone in grieved thought.[9]

Accepting this timely advice, we shall pursue our course of the study of the life of Christ in observance of these considerations: (1) that, when Matthew, Mark, and Luke record the same events, Mark's early account containing the oral tradition attributed to Peter is to be regarded as a trustworthy guide; (2) that, when Matthew and Luke record the same sayings, those of Matthew may be given priority as standing nearest to

8 Goguel, *The Life of Jesus, op. cit.,* p. 215.
9 The hymn, "Of Heavenly Love."

the Logia preserved in the source called Q; (3) that, when the account directs our particular attention to Palestinian history, Luke, the historian, may be expected to present us with a clear picture of what actually transpired; (4) that, when we endeavor, from time to time, to walk close to the borderland of verified history—while still remaining within history's domain —in order to get glimpses of Jesus' inmost thoughts, we shall go to the Evangelist John to whom the words of Jesus were as windows letting out the light of eternal truth emanating from God.

Chapter 14

THE VOICE OF ANCIENT PROPHECY

I

PROPHECY AND THE GOSPEL

If Jesus had been simply an itinerant Galilean teacher who acquainted himself with the Hebrew Scriptures and passed the time reciting the traditional *midrash,* or interpretations, about them, men in his day would not have needed to go far out of that hill country to account for him and for what he said and did. The town of Capernaum and the synagogue in it might have composed a circle large enough to encompass his life and enshrine his memory. But such is not the story the Gospel writers tell of him. They boldly call him Christ the Messiah; and they glean the richest pages of the Old Testament to explain his coming and doing. He stands, for them, at the center of the entire story of Biblical revelation. Whenever, therefore, the voice of prophecy is heard, indicating that a new age in Israel's history has come to life, it points directly to the cry of John the Baptist, uttered as though it were a cry in the wilderness of our modern world, saying:

> Prepare ye the way of the Lord,
> Make his paths straight....
> Repent ye:
> For the kingdom of heaven is at hand.[1]

Old Testament prophecy has, of course, its own national and geographical setting. The history of the Hebrew people is itself a part of authentic world history. Outwardly, the nation, like all nations, has its political crises, its social and economic problems, its moral and spiritual rise and fall. But it is the use the prophets make of this history that is now of especial interest to

[1] Matthew 3:3,2.

us. To them the nation's history was a continuous and living sign of God's will and plan to redeem His people, and through it to save the world. Often, also, it was the sign of the human effort to escape God's will, and of the futility of such an effort. The typical example of this futility—and its hidden blessedness —is found in the story of Jonah who, representing the children of Israel in the time of the Exile, cried out of "the belly of hell," and was heard.

The prophetic message is the same from first to last: Moses, hidden in the cloud on Mount Sinai, writing the Ten Commandments; Samuel, ruling as judge in Israel, and anointing Saul to be the savior of his people; Isaiah, looking beyond the nation's conflicts to the coronation of its Prince of Peace; Amos, preaching divine righteousness and social justice; Hosea, likening God to a loving husband, forgiving and tenderly restoring his once unfaithful wife; Jeremiah, picturing God as the great Potter reshaping the shattered nation with His own hands; Ezekiel, comforting the exiled remnant of Judah with a vision of a glorious future; and the great Unknown Prophet of the Exile, picturing Israel as the Servant of God chosen, through its humiliation and suffering, to redeem the world. These men, and the lesser prophets with them, stand as so many sentinels on the Old Testament highway to the city of salvation in the New Testament kingdom of God.

To the Christian apostles and evangelists, the history of Israel offers the providential setting for the triumphant entry of Christ the king into his kingdom. The prophets are the proclaimers, first, of the judgment, second, of the glad tidings associated with his coming. It is the same story from the beginning to the end, from Isaiah's announcement that "the government shall be upon his shoulder," to Zechariah's exultation, two centuries later:

> Behold, thy King cometh unto thee:
> He is just, and having salvation;
> Lowly, and riding upon an ass....
> And he shall speak peace unto the heathen;
> And his dominion shall be from sea to sea.[2]

[2] Zechariah 10:9, 10.

The "Yahwist" historian holds this same prophetic view when he undertakes to interpret the story of Genesis. The curse of sin and the mark of the finger of God are on Cain's forehead; and the first epoch of Biblical history ends in the judgment of the Flood in which only Noah, the prototype of the redeemed remnant, is saved. And the writer of the New Testament letter to the Hebrews, looking back upon the bygone centuries and seeing the meaning of Israel's history at its dawn, interprets it aright when he says that Abraham, journeying by faith, "looked for a city . . . whose builder and maker is God"; and he adds the inference that the divine plan by which Abraham was called out of ancient Ur of Chaldea is perfected in the establishment of the community of Christian believers to be known, in the future, as the church. In a similar manner, the story of Moses, the giver of the law, is written to exhibit its distinctly prophetic character. As if to show how clearly the Gospel writers understood this fact, John the Evangelist, thinking of Israel's danger of perishing in the wilderness, records these strikingly relevant words of Christ:

> As Moses lifted up the serpent in the wilderness,
> Even so must the Son of man be lifted up;
> That whosoever believeth in him should not perish,
> But have eternal life.[3]

It was natural, in the course of time, that not only a prophetic but a symbolical interpretation should be given to the events in Hebrew history. Such a step was inevitable if the true meaning of this history was to be discovered. For it was only through such symbols, for instance, as those of water, bread, and wine, and most important of all, that of the Cross, that these events which could but once have their setting in history, that is, their occurrence in time, could be given a recurring and perpetual meaning and so be timeless. That is why the Fourth Gospel, whose genuine history can no longer be questioned, is, besides this fact, so rich and perennially applicable to Christian living through its use of such symbols, in referring to the person of

3 John 3:14, 15.

Christ, as the Good Shepherd, the Bread of Heaven, the Vine, and the Resurrection, and the Life.

The parables found in our Synoptic Gospels serve a similar purpose. They lift the great truths contained in them above the barriers that separate us from an ancient time and present what they teach to us on the level of its ageless content. However, in their use no problem of historicity is involved. For the parables are not assumed to be history. They are simply illustrative stories. When, accordingly, some of the church fathers, notably Origen and Clement, of the Alexandrian school, took the liberty to turn Old Testament history to allegorical use in order to interpret the Gospels, they were acting wholly within their own rights. Only, in doing so, they were treading on the borderland between history and philosophy, between the earthly story of Jesus and its heavenly meaning, where, unless great care were taken to keep a solid footing on the facts of gospel history, they might easily fall into merely speculative and therefore erroneous conclusions. Generally speaking, we may say that this danger was avoided by the deep reverence and discriminating judgment of the men who thus undertook to apply a symbolical meaning to the range of Old Testament history.

A classical example of such discretion, and of the way in which through it the history of ancient Bible times was elevated to the status of Holy Scripture, is to be found in Psalm 114:

> When Israel went out of Egypt,
> The house of Jacob
> From a people of strange language;
> Judah was his sanctuary,
> And Israel his dominion.

on which the poet Dante makes this comment:

If we look at the letter alone the departure of the children of Israel from Egypt in the time of Moses is indicated to us; if to the allegory, our redemption accomplished by Christ is indicated to us; if to the moral sense, the conversion of the soul from the woe and misery of sin to a state of grace is indicated to us; if to the anagogical sense, the departure of the consecrated soul from the slavery of this corruption to the liberty of eternal glory is

indicated. And though these mystic senses may be called by various names, they can all generally be spoken of as allegorical, since they are diverse from the literal or historical.[4]

It was with the rise of Samuel that prophetic history actually began. As Moses had heard the voice of God in the burning bush, so Samuel now heard it in the holy tabernacle, the institution which Moses himself had established. Like Moses, he was called to lead and to judge Israel. But now that Israel desired to be a world power, the people wanted a king to rule the land and to represent them; and Samuel was commissioned to anoint him. As the vial of oil was poured upon Saul's head, "God gave him another heart." He was filled with the Spirit; and the question was rumored through the land: "Is Saul also among the prophets?" Instead, however, he became a warrior and died forsaken and by his own sword.

Nevertheless the historian reminds us that the Lord had not wholly forsaken Saul. God had chosen him to make history: not secular history merely, but divine history; and to this end a personal or political or military failure might serve as well as a success. For God Himself was to turn this failure of Saul into success through the rise and kingship of David. In him that political kingdom was to be established which was to be the symbol of the greater kingdom of God that was to follow. Jerusalem was to become the holy city, the sign and citadel of the reign of divine righteousness and everlasting peace. David himself was to be the great prototype of Christ the King of kings. That is the picture that runs through all prophetic history: a king like unto David is to rise; the government of the nations is to be on his shoulders; and of his kingdom there is to be no end. To a waiting world, and to an expectant Israel, this was good news. It was an event to be proclaimed with rejoicing. There was, indeed, first to be much suffering—likened by the prophet to the suffering of a woman in travail when her son is born. But the very intensity of the tribulation, when it came, heightened the prophet's vision of that joyous day when

[4] Translation by A. H. Gilbert, *Literary Criticism: Plato to Dryden* (New York: American Book Co., 1940), p. 202.

Israel, delivered out of the Exile, newly born, and grown to strong manhood, was to go forth to fulfil his mission:

> How beautiful upon the mountains
> Are the feet of him
> That bringeth good tidings,
> That publisheth peace;
> That bringeth good tidings of good,
> That publisheth salvation;
> That sayeth unto Zion:
> Thy God reigneth! [5]

Accordingly, with the establishment of the united kingdom of Israel, we see in David the pattern of the king who is to rule the world after God's own heart.   He exemplifies the essential nobility of soul that later prophecy is to associate with Israel's preparation for the role of Messiah.   Even his fall into sin, followed by his genuine self-humiliation and his exaltation to divine favor, served in the course of redemptive history to exemplify the frail nature of humanity fallen from its kingly state and so placed under the judgment of God, but thereby made penitent and offered the special benefits of divine forgiveness and grace.   It is hardly possible for us, today, to read Saint Luke's Parable of the Lost Sheep without this association of it with the penitential Psalms of David; or to listen to the Fourth Gospel and not to hear in its discourse on the Good Shepherd a clear echo of the Twenty-third Psalm.   And when, at last, the Great Birth is proclaimed, it is in fulfilment of prophecy that the angel is heard to say:

> Fear not; for, behold,
> I bring you good tidings of great joy,
> Which shall be to all people.
> For unto you is born this day, in the city of David,
> A Saviour, which is Christ the Lord. [6]

[5] Isaiah 52:7.
[6] Luke 2:10, 11.

II

THE PROPHETIC VIEW OF HISTORY

The author, or editor, of the book of Kings, too, belonged to the school of the prophets. He clearly saw the hand of God in Israel's history, (1) holding together the breaking pieces of the Hebrew kingdom, and (2) letting them fall apart at His will in order to show those who lived in it that the house of Israel, like the Temple, was His possession, to build and to destroy.

Again and again the prophetic historian declared that as the Lord had called Solomon and given him the wisdom to make peace and to build the Temple, so in the end He had also called Nebuchadnezzar to lay siege to Jerusalem to lay it waste and to take Jehoiachin captive with him to Babylon. At the book's close, in II Kings 24:13, we read that Nebuchadnezzar "carried out thence all the treasures of the house of the Lord, and the treasures of the king's house, and cut in pieces all the vessels of gold which Solomon king of Israel had made in the temple of the Lord, *as the Lord had said.*" The author's inference is that the making and the breaking of nations, alike, was God's work. It was not to be supposed that human freedom of action was thereby impaired. Man's freedom was to be interpreted within this framework of the divine plan. Israel and Judah were enjoined to keep the commandments of Moses and to walk in the way prepared for them by the Lord Jehovah. But the writer assumed that they were a stiff-necked and sinful people desiring rather to follow the way of all nations. Yet God had called Israel to a special task not yet fully revealed to it; and it must therefore walk by faith and so fulfil its divine destiny.

Such is the pattern that Old Testament history takes to prophetic eyes. In it two factors unite to form the thread of thought that is to run through all future prophecy. They are (1) Israel's consciousness of sin and (2) its sense of mission. Between them, in time there develops a fateful tension that is to characterize the entire story of the Bible and is to come to a climax in the Gospel offered for man's and mankind's redemption. By this tension, between the prophet's sense of unworthi-

ness and his divine call, a situation develops involving the facts of challenge and response. It is the challenge of the divine world order to the natural human will.

A typical instance of such a situation is presented to us in the story of the prophet's commission in Isaiah 6. The prophet Isaiah is called to holiness, but his vision makes him aware of his sinfulness; he wishes to bring deliverance to his people, but he can only call the nation to judgment. Standing between the divine call and his response to it, he faces a dilemma. It is in his acceptance of God's will that he finds the solution. Reading the short dramatic chapter, we note the compression of the divine argument and the gradual release of tension that follows the prophet's response to the plan and will of God:

THE SERAPHIM	Holy, holy, holy is the Lord of hosts: The whole earth is full of his glory.
THE PROPHET	Woe is me! for I am undone; ... I am a man of unclean lips, And I dwell in the midst of a people of Unclean lips.
THE SERAPHIM	Thine iniquity is taken away, And thy sin purged....
THE VOICE OF THE LORD	Whom shall I send, And who will go for us?
THE PROPHET	Here am I; send me.
THE VOICE OF THE LORD	Go, tell this people.... Shut their eyes; Lest they see ... And be healed.
THE PROPHET	Lord, how long?
THE VOICE OF THE LORD	Until the cities be wasted ... And there be a great forsaking in the midst of the land.... Yet in it shall be a tenth; And it shall ... be ... the holy seed.

It is in exactly such a setting that the earlier prophets Elijah and Elisha appear on the historic scene. Outwardly their mission is concerned with the maintenance of Israel's national religion. But within this framework the two prophets are pictured as the protagonists of the soul's conflict to reach a higher and purer conception of God. The scene on Mount Carmel enacts the perennial drama of the struggle between a national and a revealed religion. The contest between Baal, the god of the earth's fertility, and Jehovah who answers by fire from heaven, is re-enacted in the ministry of John the Baptist who is regarded by the expectant people of his time as Elijah returned to earth to usher in the coming Messianic age. The close association of Old Testament prophecy and the Gospel is strikingly brought to our attention when Elijah's fiery countenance and Moses' shining face appear together at the scene of Jesus' transfiguration. The history of divine revelation, we are reminded again, is of one piece; it is continuous, having one purpose, one end; to bring mankind to a knowledge of the nature and will of God. That His nature is that of a heavenly Father, and His will the expression of redemptive love, is at this early time not yet made clear. But the promise of the harvest is in the seed that, in this early time, is being sown on little-cultivated but good ground.

We have just indicated how the transcendence of God, together with His immanence in history, is vividly demonstrated in the prophetic movement beginning with Isaiah. Clearly here the picture is one of the death of an old and the birth of a new Israel. What is taking place is best described by a word that, in the fulfilment of time, is continually on the lips of Saint Paul. It is the word "regeneration." Outwardly the body or nation of Israel, which is the present temple of its soul, is daily decaying; but its inward life—to use the language of Paul—is, through the activity of divine judgment and grace, in the process of being completely renewed. Out of this renewed Israel, this "rod of the stem of Jesse," as the prophet calls it in Isaiah 11 ; 1, this "remnant" of His people, God will build up a kingdom in which His righteousness is to reign and peace is to prevail, and in which men

> ... shall not hurt or destroy
> In all my holy mountain
> For the earth shall be full
> Of the knowledge of the Lord,
> As the waters cover the sea.[7]

But Isaiah goes a step further. He asks: "How shall this be? Who shall bring it to pass?" The present situation, certainly, is not promising. The people will not listen to divine reasoning, with its promise that

> Though your sins be as scarlet,
> They shall be as white as snow;
> Though they be red like crimson,
> They shall be as wool.[8]

Judah is disputatious but unrepentant. The prophet marvels as he says: "Except the Lord of hosts had left unto us a very small remnant, we should have been as Sodom, and we should have been like unto Gomorrah." Then on the verge of disaster, his vision expands. It becomes Messianic. Looking to the region "beyond Jordan, in Galilee of the nations," he delivers his oracle:

> The people that walked in darkness
> Have seen a great light;
> They that dwell in the land of the shadow of death,
> Upon them hath the light shined. ...
> For unto us a child is born,
> Unto us a son is given:
> And the government shall be upon his shoulder:
> And his name shall be called ... Prince of Peace.
> Of the increase of his government ...
> There shall be no end.[9]

From then onward a new note of Messianism is heard in Hebrew prophecy. It is not immediately discernible in the messages of Amos and Hosea; it is muted by sobs of pity for Israel in the words of Jeremiah; but it emerges as a trumpet in C

[7] Isaiah 11:9.
[8] Isaiah 1:18.
[9] Isaiah 9:2, 6, 7.

major in the announcement of Zechariah: "Behold, thy King cometh." After that it proceeds to the movement of an adagio of brooding hope in the passage on the Suffering Servant of Jehovah in the fifty-third chapter of Second Isaiah; and, at last, finishes its course through Old Testament history in a triumphant celebration of the coming of the Son of man with the angels of heaven in the apocalyptic book of Daniel. After that it is but a historic moment until John the Baptist is heard at the river Jordan, saying,

> Prepare ye the way of the Lord,
> Make his paths straight....
> Repent ye:
> For the kingdom of heaven is at hand.[10]

[10] Matthew 3:3, 2.

Chapter 15

THE MESSIANIC VISION

I

THE CHOSEN COMMUNITY

We have noted how the sensitive recording hand of the prophetic writer was laid on the events of Israel's history. Outwardly, what happened in Palestine was, very much like elsewhere in the world, a succession of transpiring occurrences. But there was here a special meaning in what was taking place. God himself was behind the curtain of the stage of history, directing the course of the drama toward a particular end. Side by side with the moral of the great play, there was its divine argument leading to the climax of God's self-revelation; and this divine self-revelation was expressed in the developing doctrine of the coming of the Messiah. The whole of Hebrew history pointed to this end, to the drama's last act, the mighty act of God in sending His Son, as presented to us in the story of the Gospels. Toward this end, too, all world history converged. All nations, empires, and kingdoms were to play their part in the establishment of the Kingdom of God, of which Christ was to be the Saviour-King, and to whom, as Saint Paul later said,

> Every knee should bow,
> Of things in heaven, and things in earth, and things
>   under the earth;
> And that every tongue should confess
> That Jesus Christ is Lord,
> To the glory of God the Father.[1]

But for a further perspective of the relevancy of the prophetic message to the study of the Gospels we must return to

[1] Philippians 2:10-11.

Amos and Hosea. Having long been regarded as a teacher of
social justice, Amos is looked upon as the most "modern" of the
prophets. But what is really essential about him is the fact that
his idea of the moral law is deep-rooted in his conception of divine justice. He announces that social oppression is sin against
God, an offense against the corporate nature of humanity, which
is God's family. The encircling thunder of Jehovah's judgment
on Damascus, Gaza, Tyre, and Edom, with its lightning bolt of
the oracle, "For three transgressions of Israel, and for four, I
will not turn away the punishment," sounds to our ears like a
familiar prelude to the dire judgment pronounced by Jesus upon
all offenders of little children. It is the voice of judgment and
warning that has echoed down the ages to our own time. A
modern version of it may be translated into these words of
William Blake:

> A robin redbreast in a cage
> Puts all Heaven in a rage....
> He who shall teach the child to doubt
> The rotting grave shall ne'er get out....
> The harlot's cry from street to street
> Shall weave old England's winding sheet.

If Amos is the prophet of divine judgment, Hosea is the
messenger of divine grace. Both are prototypes of the gospel
which is offered to the world in mercy, in a seedtime and rain
of grace, and whose fruit is required of it in a harvest of win-
nowing judgment. Hosea is the prophet of the redemptive love
of God. His message comes to him in a parable taken from his
own domestic life. His argument rests on his own inner experience, his God-consciousness. Gomer, his wife, has proved
unfaithful to him. Yet he loves and redeems her from a life of
sin. So God loves Israel; He will not let her go. She is His
betrothed people. An unbreakable bond exists between them, a
bond that is to continue everlastingly. This is the word by
which Jehovah tenders His assurance:

> And I will betroth thee unto me forever;...
> I will betroth thee unto me...in judgment...and in mercies,
> I will even betroth thee unto me in faithfulness;

And thou shalt know the Lord. . . .
And I will say unto [you] : my people;
And they shalt say: My God.[2]

Hosea witnesses the betrothal. It is in the New Testament
that we read of the consummated union of Christ and his
church. The marriage is announced; the wedding feast is prepared; the Spirit and the Bride say, "Come!" The Wise Virgins
are there with their lighted lamps; the servants have gone out
on the highways and invited all who would come. The wine of
life is on the Bridegroom's lips; the bread to be broken is in his
hands. It is the appointed time, the *end* of time, when Christ
and the redeemed are at last gathered together at the banqueting
table in the everlasting kingdom of God. That is the picture
with which, in its own language, the gospel story completes the
prophet's parable and vision.

In the character of Jeremiah a new element is added to the
prophetic message. The prophet identifies himself with his people in suffering and in hope. In his own shrinking from his
calling, his personal disappointment, and his exposure to persecution, he sees the hand of God upon him. In agony of spirit
he looks on the contemporary scene. God is making history in
a most mysterious way. The Deuteronomic reformation, under the good king Josiah, in 621 B.C., has come and gone, leaving little lasting effect. It has been good. But there has been no
rending of the soul, no piercing of the nation's marrow and
bone. Judah remains proud, like a stalk of corn, though Nebuchadnezzar, the worm of Babylon, even now crawling up out
of the Euphrates, will soon devour its root. Moved with pity
as he sees his people's impending ruin, Jeremiah exclaims: "Can
the Ethiopian change his skin, or the leopard his spots?" Judah,
holding up its head, is saying "Peace, peace" when there is no
peace. Like a sick man condemned to die, and not knowing it,
Jerusalem decks itself in royal finery, parading its pride, saying
all is well. But the prophet, seeing the deadly cancer devouring
the flesh, cries out: "Is there no balm in Gilead, is there no
physician there?" Judah's condition seems hopeless. The fall

[2] Hosea 2:19-23.

of Jerusalem seems an utter tragedy. But Jeremiah does not despair. He pins his hope on the faithful remnant; he rests his faith in God. No prophet, in his personal experience, comes so close to a foreknowledge of the meaning of Calvary. His mission is clearly a prelude to the Messianic prophecy to follow. When again its voice is distinctly heard, the time is near to 550 B.C., and the prophet who speaks is the great Second Isaiah of the Babylonian exile.

But before this poet and seer can accomplish his task, the prophet Ezekiel must appear on the scene. He must furnish the setting for the new Israel that is to be established after the downfall of the nation. Ezekiel is sometimes understood to have been a legalist and therefore the representative of a reactionary trend in the prophetic movement. To hold this view is to misconceive his important mission. Like all prophets, he was an advocate of Israel's law. The great tradition of Moses underlay his work among the exiles then living in Babylon. He remembered the good intent of the Deuteronomic reform of a half century before his time. For, together with the prophet's zeal and imagination, he had the aristocrat's orderly and scholarly mind, taking delight in whatever was chaste and disciplined and formal in art and architecture; and the ceremony and liturgy of worship once associated with the Jerusalem temple greatly interested him. It was natural, therefore, that his thoughts should turn toward the communal and sacramental aspects of his people's faith: that is, toward that which (1) bound together those who remained faithful into a community of believers, and (2) gave to this bond of their union, or life together, the character of a covenant with God.

This stress on the priestly ministry of a prophet of God was unique with Ezekiel. It made him the notable example of the modern minister of the gospel who must be both a priest and a prophet to his people. For the distinction today, as then, is clear: as a prophet, the minister represents the revelation of God's will and word to man; as a priest, he is the bearer of man's and mankind's offering to God.

In summary, Ezekiel's vision of the holiness of God and his

farseeing emphasis on the sacramental life of the Jewish community—by which was meant a communal life dedicated to God
in a covenant of holiness—can be seen to have a direct bearing
both on the primitive message of the gospel and on the doctrine
and life of the Christian church through the ages. This relevancy is pointed out to us today, for example, by the poet T. S.
Eliot who, likening our time to that of the Exile, in his poem
"Ash Wednesday," hears again the question asked long ago in
Ezekiel 37:3, "Can these bones live?" and answers, with the
prophet, "O Lord God, thou knowest." And, sensing how like
a valley of dry bones our world is—how near death, yet not
dead, but torpid and waiting—Eliot sums up the almost ironic
justice of our present state in these lines:

> Under the juniper-tree the bones sang, scattered and shining.
> We are glad to be scattered, we did little good to each other,
> Under a tree in the cool of the day, with the blessing of sand,
> Forgetting themselves and each other, united
> In the quiet of the desert. This is the land which ye
> Shall divide by lot. And neither division nor unity
> Matters. This is the land. We have our inheritance.[3]

It is of the community of exiles in Babylon that Second
Isaiah is thinking when he introduces us to his vision of the
Suffering Servant of Jehovah. Here is the story of Israel's
mission foretold in new language. God has chosen His people
to be the deliverer of mankind from its burden of oppression
and sin. The cry of the world's woe has reached the prophet's
ear and penetrated his heart. A chastened Israel is pictured as
answering this cry, as offering itself up in sacrifice, willing to
be despised, in meek resignation, meek and still as a sheep under
the knee of the shearer, as a lamb that is brought to the place of
slaughter. Before such a picture the world would stand in
touched stillness and awe. It could not, and would not, withhold its compassionate response. In their high moments of insight men would be moved to say with the prophet, "It was for
us the Suffering Servant did this deed":

[3] *Collected Poems of T. S. Eliot,* "Ash Wednesday." (New York: Harcourt, Brace & Co., 1935.) Used by permission of the publishers.

> He was wounded for our transgressions,
> He was bruised for our iniquities:
> The chastisement of our peace was upon him;
> And with his stripes we are healed.[4]

Behind the veil of this climactic scene of Old Testament prophecy the Christian reader can clearly picture the meaning of the Cross. Saint Paul saw it and, under its amazing compulsion, wrote the letter to the Romans in which he said, "God commendeth His love toward us, in that, while we were yet sinners, Christ died for us." [5] The apostle Peter made it the theme of his evangelistic message, reminding the first Christians that they had been redeemed from slavery and death, not through the payment of silver and gold, but "with the precious blood of Christ, as of a lamb without blemish and without spot." [6] And the evangelist Mark expressly indicates that Jesus, having already assumed the role of the "Son of man," as outlined in the Book of Daniel, added to it, at the moment of high crisis in his earthly ministry, his acceptance of the mission of Second Isaiah's "servant of Jehovah"—as we read in these words, in Mark 10:45, which may be called the golden text of that Gospel: "For even the Son of man came not to be ministered unto, but to minister, and to give his life a ransom for many." [7]

Such is the atmosphere of Isaiah 40-55. It is a book of prophecies fragrant with the incense of self-sacrifice. In it one comes upon passage after passage that, pressed together, yield their odor of "herbs of grace." Their equal is found elsewhere only in the passion narrative of the Gospels.

II

THE GREAT APOCALYPSE

But we should misread the prophets if we did not detect also another element in them. The recognition of it arrests us. It

[4] Isaiah 53:5.
[5] Romans 5:8.
[6] I Peter 1:19.
[7] It should be remembered that the title the "Son of man," as used in the book of Daniel, was originally collective and applied to the people of God— that is, to the faithful remnant of Israel.

lightens—and in turn darkens—the page of prophetic history
by its flash from heaven and authoritative voice of the word of
God. Its favorite images, or literary symbols, are those of
wind and fire. It is the heavenly word that creates and destroys,
that judges and regenerates the world. It is also the *Word* that
ends all words, all plans and devices of men, and covers them
over with the majestic utterance: "Thine is the kingdom, and
the power, and the glory, forever. Amen." Signs and manifestations of this supernatural sovereignty are to be found in
Israel's early history: the anger of Moses on Mount Sinai; the
trumpet of Joshua at the walls of Jericho; the sword of Gideon;
Elijah's fiery chariot. And we note how this sovereign power
is put to strange use as God commands the land of Israel to be
overrun by an army of Assyrians, a terrorizing horde of Scy-
thians, or a devouring cloud of locusts.

These pictures, selected at random, illustrate the kind of
prophecy that has come to be associated with the term *apocalyptic*. Its keynote is the announcement that God rules the world.
The compelling thing about it is that it implies a great religious
conception, or philosophy, of history. Through it the prophets,
and later the Synoptic Gospels, indicated (1) that the destinies
of men and nations are in divine hands, (2) that history is not
an endless cycle of merely contiguous events, (3) that nature,
or the order of created things, is also involved in God's plan
of redemption, and (4) that the souls of the faithful survive
a natural death and live on in a blissful fellowship with God
Himself throughout eternity.

Whatever its historic origin—whether or not we today see
elements in it that suggest the active influence of the Eastern
religions of Egypt or Persia or of the Mysteries of Asia Minor
—this apocalyptic view did two things for the people living in
Palestine during the centuries between the rise of Alexander the
Great in 333 B.C. and the end of the apostolic age in A.D. 100.
It gave them a faith based, first, in a realistic outlook on the
world, and second, on a conception of a divine order equally
above nationalism, naturalism, and moralism, yet active in the
affairs of men. In summary, the world and life in it were given
a meaning and a goal, and men could look forward to a con-

summation of God's purpose in all things. That such a view pervaded the principal writings of the New Testament is now increasingly evident. It dominated the thinking of Saint Paul; it guided Mark in the composition of his Gospel; and it became the outstanding thesis of the Book of Revelation.

Apocalyptic prophecy is generally regarded as having begun with Zephaniah (*circa* 625 B.C.) and come to a climax in the Book of Daniel (*circa* 165 B.C.). Thereafter, and particularly during the Roman rule of Palestine, it continued in the more subdued and ardent mood reflected in the apocryphal Book of Enoch. Throughout this long span of centuries, Israel was forced to face one calamity after another at the hands of despotic nations until its faith in the moral order of history was put to the severest test. History, it was seen, always involved an element of human tragedy; it was never, in and of itself, a demonstration of justice; everything unfulfilled in human experience had always to wait until some tomorrow that never came. Life, for men individually and for the community, seemed doomed to futility; hope seemed but destined to despair. The expectation of Israel's waiting saints ebbed into a cry: "O Lord, how long!"

It was then that certain prophets realized that God would one day put an end to this cycle of ageless recurrence. For, as history had a beginning, so it would also have an end. This end, or goal, would be an event beyond time. But its attainment would come within the compass of God's ordered plan of human redemption; that is, it would belong to what we have previously called *Heilsgeschichte,* or "salvation history," but not any longer to *Weltgeschichte,* or world history. Stated more concretely, it meant that this event would be history's supreme climax; its great Day of Doom—and of felicity: of doom for the wicked of the world; of felicity for the blessed saints. To moderns addicted to the dual cult of relativity and perpetual progress, such a view may seem ancient and strange. But in that day it offered—and it still offers—an eschatological view of history by giving to it a goal and a meaning. Most important of all, it was this view, with its interpretation of Old Testament his-

tory, that furnished the background for the story of the life
of Christ as presented to us in the Synoptic Gospels.

It is therefore with much interest that we turn to the prophetic Book of Zephaniah [8] to hear the first strains of the magnificent but direful hymn of judgment that, centuries later, was
to fill the choirs of the Gothic churches of Europe, sounding out
the words of the *Dies Irae:*

> Day of wrath! O day of mourning!
> See fulfilled the prophets' warning,
> Heav'n and earth in ashes burning!
>
> King of Majesty tremendous,
> Who doth free salvation send us,
> Fount of pity, then befriend us!
>
> Think, good Jesu, my salvation
> Cost Thy wondrous Incarnation;
> Leave me not to reprobation!

Then, with the scope of a knowledge of the intervening ages,
we come to the Book of Daniel. Jerusalem had fallen; the long
years of the Exile had slowly worn away; the remnant of faithful Jews had tried to rebuild the city. Time passed, measured
in long silences between the inspired words of the prophets.
While working to rebuild the city's walls, and worshiping at the
re-established temple altar, the people had waited and grown
weary. History, to them, had begun to mean an unending sub-
jugation to alien heathen powers and one long cry for deliverance. It came, temporarily, in the period of the Maccabean
revolt when Judas and his sons set the colony free from the yoke
of Antiochus Epiphanes; and, with that new breath of freedom,
the voice of the prophet was heard again in the land.

The vision of the prophet is recorded, in essence, in the
seventh chapter of the Book of Daniel. In it we see the four
beasts, representing the four major heathen kingdoms, rising before us in their evil fury: Babylon, as a winged lion; Media, as
a ravenous bear; Persia, as a four-headed leopard; and Greece,
as the unnamed monster having iron teeth and ten horns. It is

[8] See Zephaniah 1:14-15.

then that we behold, with the apocalyptic prophet's vision, the Ancient of days sitting in world judgment on these powers. The prophet describes Him in this symbolical manner:

> Whose garment was white as snow,
> And the hair of his head like the pure wool.
> His throne was like the fiery flame,
> And his wheels as burning fire.[9]

When the unnamed monster has been judged guilty and slain, there intervenes, as the prophet says, "a season and a time." The exact events are hidden in the future's uprolled scroll. They are mostly tragic events in which the Jewish state is again to lose its freedom, this time to the rising empire of Rome. But no cloud of tyranny can dim the prophet's vision; and what he foresees finds its New Testament counterpart in the apocalyptic sections of the Gospels, in some of the most notable passages of the letters of Saint Paul, and, summarily, in the Book of Revelation—as Daniel writes:

> And behold,
> One like the Son of man
> Came with the clouds of heaven,
> And came to the Ancient of days,
> And they brought him near before him.
> And there was given him dominion, and glory,
> And a *kingdom,*
> That all people, nations, and languages
> Should serve him:
> His dominion is an everlasting dominion,
> Which shall not pass away,
> And his kingdom that
> Which shall not be destroyed.[10]

The rest of the way between the two Testaments was one of weary traveling and waiting. After Pompey had taken over Palestine and Herod had become king of the Jews, the yoke of empire on them was galling and the burden was heavy. The aristocratic Sadducees were easily satisfied, profiting by the

[9] Daniel 7:9.
[10] Daniel 7:13-14.

power given to them to live on the toil of the people. The Pharisees sought refuge in an intenser piety and a stricter keeping of the Mosaic law. The uprisings of the Zealots were easily suppressed, and with terrifying results, as trees of crosses were exhibited on the Roman roads leading from Judea to Galilee. The voice of prophecy was all but stilled.

Only a little group of "redemptionists" kept the flame of hope from flickering out in Israel. Among them were two persons, mentioned in Luke 2 :25-38. They were Simeon and Anna, born before the dark shadow of Rome fell upon the land. They had lived their youth in the time of Israel's free state, and now they hoped ardently for the redemption and consolation of God's people. And in that dawn that was to break into a glorious day, they were in the temple—just at the time, Luke tells us, when Mary brought in her first-born child. The vision that came to Simeon, and the expression of it found in the *Nunc Dimittis,* appropriately ended the old dispensation and began the new :

> Lord, now lettest thou
> Thy servant depart in peace,
> According to thy word :
> For mine eyes
> Have seen thy salvation,
> Which thou hast prepared
> Before the face of all people;
> A light to lighten the Gentiles,
> And the glory of thy people Israel.[11]

[11] Luke 2 :29-32.

Chapter 16

THE RECORD OF BEGINNINGS

The Stories of Matthew and Luke

According to the record of the Gospels, five things may be said of the birth of Christ: (1) that it was a historic fact; (2) that it had its setting in an order of natural circumstances; (3) that it was a providential occurrence in fulfilment of ancient prophecy; (4) that it was regarded as an event of supernatural origin and significance; (5) that the early Christian church saw in it a deep religious and universal meaning.

What these facts, and the truths they contain, mean to us today is a matter of genuine concern. But it is well for us to remember that our attitude toward them is, by its very subsequent nature, secondary to the reported event. We may therefore take it or leave it, believe it or not, and so exercise our personal privilege and accept the responsibility it implies. But we cannot, by what we think or say, erase what has been written. The record of the Evangelists stands for us to judge—and, at last, to be judged by. If, to many living in our generation, the story has little meaning—that is to say, if Christ to them remains unborn and the Word continues to remain unspoken— the reasons for their attitude are likely to be found to lie deeper than any difficulties the criticism of the text or the study of gospel history may offer. It is to this deeper cause of our dryness and deafness of soul that the story of the Great Birth, told in the Gospels of Matthew and Luke, must once more make its urgent appeal.

If, in looking for the deeper meaning of these birth stories, we are told that their literary composition points to an element in them that seems to be legendary, there is no reason to be disturbed. For what is important in them is that they reflect the

sound reason underlying the faith of the early Christians; and this faith is indisputable history. In them we have recorded the dawn of a great day that, when the Evangelists wrote of it, was in the light of its full glory. Memory had hallowed that blessed dawn to the first disciples, just as it had darkened the sky above Calvary. The history of the event had assumed the significance of the enduring: to Matthew it was prophecy fulfilled; to Luke it was the poetry that linked heaven to earth in a song of man's salvation.

It is always so with important history, after the mind has long been focused on it in search of its meaning. The acts of Lincoln, for example, are surrounded with legend: his Gettysburg address is now widely inscribed in stone as poetry; and he himself occupies a place above the events once used by some of his critics to account for and explain him. Similarly, but now to divine ends, the birth stories enshrine what was known and believed about Jesus' heavenly and earthly origin, crystallizing it into poetry and legend in a manner consistent with his entire life, his ministry, his passion, and his resurrection. It is within this pattern which makes these stories of one seamless piece with the entire Gospel account—like Jesus' robe "woven from the top throughout," as the Fourth Evangelist tells us—that we must seek to trace and understand their divergent narrative threads and so to credit the entire record with the authenticity that belongs to it.

Looking at Matthew 1-2, we note, first of all, the chapters' strongly Davidic character. Jesus is born in Bethlehem, the city of David. He is of royal lineage. His genealogy is traced through forty-two generations to Abraham. Behind him lies the vast and glorious region of Old Testament history. The voice of that history is its prophecy; the consummation of the prophetic message is the Messianic kingdom; and Jesus is heralded as Christ the Messiah. The revelation of his coming is given to Joseph in a dream; and the meaning of the event is disclosed in the name "Emmanuel," which is, "God with us." It was he for whom the world had been waiting, a world wandering in dreariness and darkness until then. His advent was indeed a theme worthy of the harp of David: for out of Israel's

sorrow there had been born a great new hope; and the Evangelist Matthew, seeing this hope realized, could record the angel of the Lord as saying:

> Joseph, thou son of David, fear not to take unto thee Mary thy wife; for that which is conceived in her is of the Holy Ghost. And she shall bring forth a son, and thou shalt call his name JESUS: for he shall save his people from their sins.[1]

But, with the second chapter of the Gospel, a new note mingles with that of the first. It presages the opposition that is to come. For the people of Judea already have a king. He is Herod the Great, founder of a dynasty of Herods, a tyrant, jealous, popular with Rome, an astute ruthless politician with no desire to relinquish his power. He has fortified himself in the east of Palestine, at Machaerus, where later John the Baptist is to be imprisoned, and in the west at Gaza and Caesarea; he has rebuilt the temple at Jerusalem; and everywhere, to please himself, he has built palaces with underground vaults and theaters of imposing architecture, and, on the Mediterranean coast, a magnificent amphitheater overlooking the sea. But Herod is now old. His frustrated pride has turned to hate, and he resolves to kill the newborn king. Thus, as the First Gospel points out, the world is turned against Jesus from the start.

Warned in a dream, Joseph takes flight, with the child and his mother, into Egypt. What will the future bring? Let the stillness of the desert answer. We, too, who live today, await the final answer in another desert stillness. Louis Untermeyer has expressed the age-old anguish that here grips Matthew's story, in a sonnet called "The Pilgrimage," in which as Joseph and Mary make their journey onward,

> Suddenly something looms; the infant starts
> And cries with terror, kicks, and will not rest.
> A wave of anguish strikes three quivering hearts
> Until she soothes him with her magic breast.
> And so they pause, while little Jesus drinks
> Beneath the eyes of an ironic Sphinx.[2]

[1] Matthew 1:20, 21.
[2] Used by permission of the author and Harcourt, Brace & Co., Inc., New York, publishers.

King Herod is furious against Bethlehem; he slays the children in it and "in all the coasts thereof." But in the end he is mocked not only by the Wise Men but by the little town itself which, by the word of the prophet, is to be known as the birthplace of the new Prince. The king's fury is stilled by the simple eloquence of Matthew's statement: "when Herod was dead." Yet the hatred of Herod is a portentous sign, and the child Jesus is not returned to Bethlehem but is taken by his parents to Nazareth in Galilee. Thus the birth story, as told by the First Evangelist, clearly foreshadows what is to follow throughout the entire Gospel: the Prince of Peace and the prince of this world are in open conflict; the Hebrew nation has rejected its Messiah; but God in His wisdom rules the world, and it is His will that through the coming of Christ the world should be saved.

To this account Matthew now adds the story of the visit of the Magi. These kings of the Orient, representing the wisdom of the world empires, are led by a star to Bethlehem, to the cradle of the Christ child. In them an old world finds a new hope; and they bring with them their gifts of gold, frankincense, and myrrh. In humble grandeur they acknowledge Jesus as King of kings. The obvious thought behind the story is that it is the will of heaven that old dynasties and dispensations will some day yield their thrones to the kingdom of Christ the Lord. It is not to be assumed that this end will be attained by any easy road of natural progress. For the kings of this world do not willingly give up their wealth, their glory, and their very way of life, for the vision of a star. But it is just this sacrifice that we see the Wise Men making, as Matthew's story proceeds. Even the bitter myrrh, signifying the death of their kingdoms, is offered up to the new king. Thus, in the story of the Magi, the facts of birth and death are brought into that close juxtaposition in which we see them as we read the Gospel through to the end.

We do well to note this fact at the very outset of our study of the life of Christ. For we shall miss the First Gospel's central teaching if we fail to see it in the setting of this pattern: (1) that the kingdom of God is a new creation; (2) that entrance into it is by a rebirth out of death to life. The death of

their old kingdoms is the life of this new Kingdom: that is
what the Wise Men know as they return from their worship of
the young Christ child. And this is the conclusion to which one
of them—it must have been he who brought the gift of myrrh—
comes when, in T. S. Eliot's poem "Journey of the Magi," he
says:

> Were we lead all that way for
> Birth or Death? There was a Birth, certainly,
> We had evidence and no doubt. I had seen birth and death,
> But had thought they were different; this Birth was
> Hard and bitter agony for us, like Death, our death.
> We returned to our places, these Kingdoms,
> With an alien people clutching their gods.
> I shall be glad of another death.[3]

Luke's story of the birth of Christ is simple, familiar, beautiful. It seems domestic and private by the side of Matthew's
display of the benignant grandeur of the newborn king. The
account in Luke 1-2 centers in Mary, the mother, and her child.
Joseph is the guardian of the little household, the awed onlooker
and worshiper at the scene; Mary's is the secret of the great
divine-human mystery. The story's keynote is our blessed humanity: God has been gracious to us and visited us with His
offer of salvation. The earth is almost a strange place; yet the
Christ child is at home in it. It is, we are aware, the *first
Christmas*. The whole atmosphere in Luke's narrative is festive,
yet with an overtone of high seriousness. We observe that the
wonder in Mary's eyes is compounded of mingled joy and sorrow; for Luke, like Matthew, is looking backward as he writes
his Gospel. He sees the end in the beginning, and the beginning
in the end. The whole drama of the earthly life of Christ is
re-enacted before him. For, in a sense, it is Mary's story he is
writing. Bowed down in sorrow at the Cross, she seems again
to remember the words of Simeon, spoken in the temple, as he
took the child in his arms and said: "This child is set for the
fall and rising again of many . . . and, yea, a sword shall pierce
through thy own soul also." [4]

---

[3] *Collected Poems*, 1936. Used by permission of Harcourt, Brace & Co.,
Inc., New York, publishers.
[4] Luke 2:34, 35.

It is a mistake to treat Luke's birth story as though it were unrelated to the main body of the Gospel. It, too, is a part of gospel history, even if its source in the tradition is taken to be legendary; for, in this as in any carefully compiled record, the outward events do not tell the whole story. A divine purpose runs through them which is itself making history. And it is with this unique history of the early church, and of the primitive Christian faith, that we are here concerned, and not merely with the bare incidents as they are reported to have occurred in Palestine under Roman rule in the first century.

It must be evident to us that every historian, as he writes, reads both forward and backward. His mind moves as a weaver's shuttle between the first and last of all that he composes. Events, he observes, do not occur in isolation; they are parts of a pattern—like words which, only when someone discriminately puts them together, give forth their meaning. The analytical method of reducing history to an exclusive attention to individual facts is a fetish of rationalism. By presupposing, erroneously, that events yield up their meaning apart from their context and the thought which the historian must give to them, it attempts to write a history that does not exist. Knowledge comes to us through the process of composition: facts are loose stones until they are placed together; and, when they are designedly placed together, the resultant structure is more than the gathered stones.

The infant and childhood story of Jesus, as Luke tells it, is a part of such a complete historical structure. It is less episodic than Matthew's; it exhibits style in composition and reveals its close reliance on sources. The six main sections in it are held together by a common theme, as if they were parts of a moving tone poem, variations in the prelude of a great symphony of world redemption. The Annunciation, in Luke 1:26-35, prefaced by the announcement of the birth of John the Baptist, is followed by the *Magnificat,* in verses 46-55; after that, in verses 68-79, we come to Zacharias' prophecy known as the *Benedictus,* with its reference to the "dayspring from on high"; then, after such an overture of predictive strains from the choicest parts of the Old Testament, the Evangelist tells the story of the Great

Birth. The scene is Bethlehem; the child lies in a manger because there is no room for him in the inn; the shepherds are in the field watching over their flock: they do better by their fold than the city of David does by its Saviour. It is night. But, suddenly, the voice of angels is heard, saying, "Glory to God in the highest, and on earth peace, good will toward men." It is so: Christ is come; the shepherds come to wonder and worship; and, while they come and go, Mary remembers the Annunciation and ponders in her heart all this that has happened to her and to the world.

> Blessed with a joy that only she
> Of all alive shall ever know,
> She wears a proud humility
> For what it was that willed it so.[5]

That is Luke's story. And when, later, the child is presented in the temple and Simeon blesses it, saying in the *Nunc Dimittis,* "Now lettest thou thy servant depart in peace . . . for mine eyes have seen thy salvation," we know that the writer's intent has been achieved. The kingdom of God is come. After that there is little more to report. The Evangelist's silence is briefly interrupted when, at the age of twelve, the boy Jesus is found in the temple among the doctors. It is the sign that he is beginning to be about his "Father's business."

There has been much speculation on two questions in connection with the birth stories found in Matthew and Luke. The first has centered in the question of their source; the second, in the doctrine of the Virgin Birth. Matthew's special source, according to Canon Streeter's theory now generally called M, is obviously Palestinian; so also is Luke's, similarly called L. But there is a difference between them: M is strongly Messianic, with its stress on the kingship of Jesus; L, in contrast, is marked by a universalism that has its wide application in the rebirth, not of Israel in the form of Christ's kingdom, his *Ecclesia,* that is, the church on earth, but of man and mankind. It is for this reason that M is generally regarded as having had its origin in Jerusalem or nearby, while L is believed to reflect the influence

[5] Edwin Arlington Robinson, "Gift of God," from *Collected Poems,* 1929. Used by permission of The Macmillan Co., New York, publishers.

of such a cosmopolitan place as Caesarea. Some modern scholars of the Gospel are inclined to attribute it to Joanna, the wife of Herod's steward, and certain other women who, according to Luke 8 :3, supported Jesus during his earthly ministry.

The doctrine of the Virgin Birth must be regarded as something more than a mere legendary addition to the record. The Evangelists Matthew and Luke, looking backward to an earlier time, saw in the tradition from which this doctrine grew a deeper meaning than that of a natural birth; they saw in it the birth of a new world and a new humanity by the act of God. This birth was indeed a natural birth; but it was God's doing, not man's; though in Matthew's eyes, Israel, and in Luke's eyes, Mary, was the chosen means of the miraculous event. Our insistent rationalistic attempts at explaining the great miracle are therefore without real meaning. They are intended to satisfy us with an explanation which is destined to be unsatisfactory. It is better to rest our conclusions on the record than to give vent to "scientific" speculations about it. The Evangelists record the Virgin Birth as a mystery, that is, as a revelation of the hidden will and plan of God; and it is in this context that it must be interpreted. So regarded, it becomes an integral part of the greater miracle of the Incarnation. It witnesses to the fact that God the Creator is nature's Lord: that He is not limited by anything He has created, but limits Himself, takes on flesh, humbles Himself for our sake, becoming like us and partaking of our humanity, in order that, through Christ's resurrection—which brings to an end what was begun by His incarnation—we also may rise to lordship over nature and become partakers of His divinity.

II

MARK'S AND JOHN'S VIEWPOINTS

What the Evangelists Mark and John imply by their omission of the birth story can be treated briefly. But it cannot be dismissed lightly. Mark's silence may be accounted for on the ground, first, of what he knew, and second, of what he wished

to do. We must assume from Luke's Preface,[6] as well as from a further analysis of the four Gospels, that not any one of the Evangelists had access to all the gospel tradition. Versions of it were current everywhere in Palestine and throughout greater Syria. Most of them, either oral or written, in the course of time became the possession of the leaders of the early church. But to gather them up into a complete narrative remained the task of such skilled historians as the writers of the Gospels of Matthew and Luke.

The Evangelist Mark was not such a skilful author. He was, indeed, a forceful writer, an impassioned and a dramatic one; he knew what he had set himself to do; his source of information was original, coming mainly from Peter himself, and from the tradition generally current in Rome. What he wrote down was realistic and authentic and had been tested in the crucible of Christian martyrdom. In it the reader could find the essence of the gospel message to the early church. But it was a limited record. Absent from it, for example, was most, if not all, of what was contained in the important other source called Q. The birth story, likewise important, was not accessible to him.

In the interest of comprehensiveness, this fact was regrettable. For the fact, together with the circumstances, of Christ's birth could not have seemed inconsequential to him. But for the achievement of his practical aim, he saw, in that early time, no necessity for including them in his account. For Mark, under the urgency of the now stilled voices of the apostles Peter and Paul, was writing what was in immediate need of being written. It was that the kingdom of God was come; that the gospel of Christ was being proclaimed and attested by the heroism of the martyrs; that the present was a time of further testing, of expectancy, and of the need for a fortitude that faith alone could give. Accordingly, Mark's thought was centered on the heroic life of Christ, on his mighty works which were the acts of God, on the imminence of the establishment of God's kingdom, and on the story of Jesus' passion.

Altogether, Mark was looking forward to the consummation

[6] Luke I:1-4.

of all that was to be accomplished through the life of Christ, and not backward to its earthly beginning. But if the Evangelist was silent about the birth of Christ, he was eloquent about his coming. Indeed, we may gather up the burden of his message in these brief words : the Son of God has come to earth; the kingdom of God is now at hand.

The Fourth Gospel also omits the birth story. Writing late as he does, and with a theological aim, the author's elevated discourses may seem to us to be far removed from such a simple and almost idyllic story as that of Luke. And so they are. The Gospel is indeed so far removed, or advanced, in time and thought that some Johannine scholars think it has no biographical value. The narrative, it is supposed, serves only as an outline to which to attach the writer's polemical views, and so to present his symbolical interpretation of what Jesus Christ meant to him and to his Hellenistic associates. But, more lately, much has been written both to indicate the intense Jewishness of the Gospel and to establish its historicity. But—whatever may be said of his larger cultural background—of this fact the Fourth Evangelist himself assures us : he is interested in the origin of Jesus, and in the beginning of a gospel that goes beyond the birth of Christ and his earthly ancestry, and beyond time, to the eternal mind and plan of God. He is, in a strict sense, the true gospel historian, having the knowledge that divine history has its beginning in the Word made flesh.[7] It is in the thought of John, and in his doctrine of the Incarnation, that the story of the birth of Christ ultimately completes itself and finds its full meaning.

The Fourth Gospel and the synoptic narrative, it is true, cannot be either verbally or chronologically integrated. They are different in their literary structure and general plan. Yet they supplement one another—as do, by way of comparison, the cultures of the East and the West. When, for instance, John writes that in Christ "was life, and the life was the light of men," [8] he is saying nothing with which Matthew, Mark, and Luke do not agree. But John is even more directly concerned

[7] John 1 :14.
[8] John 1 :4.

with what we may call the Great Birth. For to him Christ is the life of those who are "born, not of blood, nor of the will of the flesh, nor of the will of man, but of God." [9] And we remember here the words of Jesus to Nicodemus: "Verily, verily, I say unto thee, Except a man be born again, he cannot see the kingdom of God." [10] What we commonly call the birth of the church is of one piece with the birth of Christ; and both are linked together, in the entire record of Scripture, with the rebirth of Israel through its release from the Exile and, still further back, with the birth of the Hebrew nation and, at the beginning, with the creation of the world and of man.

The doctrine of the Incarnation is therefore not to be regarded as an alien philosophical concept that later attached itself to the simple Palestinian story of the birth of Jesus. It stands as one of the two great pillars that bridge the distance between the beginning and the end, or goal, of divine revelation. The other pillar is the doctrine of the Resurrection. Between them, and beneath the span of this bridge, in the valley below, is the road of Christ's humiliation, of Jesus' earthly life, beginning with his lowly but kingly birth and leading him, by stages, toward the *via dolorosa,* ending at the Cross.

It is with this perspective, offered to us at the beginning of our study, that we shall now try to pursue our course through the remaining chapters of the life of Christ. While giving our attention to the recorded events before us, we shall be invited also to fathom some areas of their intended deeper meaning. Perhaps, with our best insight and outlook directed toward this history, we may get glimpses of the great truth as the seventeenth-century poet Robert Herrick expressed it, when he wrote:

> Christ took our nature on Him, not that He
> 'Bove all things lov'd it, for the puritie.
> No, but He drest Him with our humane trim,
> Because our flesh stood most in need of Him.

[9] John 1:13.
[10] John 3:3.

Chapter 17

DAYS OF PREPARATION

I

JESUS AND JOHN THE BAPTIST

In a "Negro Sermon" called *The Creation,* James Weldon Johnson pictures God as stepping out into space and saying, *"I'm lonely*—I'll make me a world." Continuing, the poet says,

> Then God smiled,
> And the light broke,
> And the darkness rolled up on one side,
> And the light stood shining on the other,
> And God said, *That's good!* [1]

But, as human history indicates, the world did not remain good. Something happened that the prophetic historian, writing in the Book of Genesis, called man's fall; and the result was the long Old Testament story of Israel's sin. In a later time, when the nation's culture was at its highest and the ruling Ahab and Jezebel lived like the Florentine bankers, the Medici, in splendor and vice, the prophet Elijah came out of the desert with a message of wind and fire, calling Israel to repentance and to judgment. Other prophets followed—Isaiah, Amos, and Hosea, Jeremiah, Ezekiel, and the Second Isaiah and Daniel—suiting their messages to the trying times. And after the last of them had spoken, there was a prolonged century of silence. The word of God, often spoken, lingered in the waste places around about Palestine where, suddenly, it found a voice in the preaching of John the Baptist. It came, as Mark tells us, as "the voice of one crying in the wilderness: Prepare ye the way of the Lord,

[1] From *God's Trombones.* Copyright, 1927, by Viking Press, Inc., New York. Used by permission of the publishers.

make his paths straight." The Evangelist then goes on to say that John baptized in the Jordan those who followed him. To them this baptism was the symbol of two things: first, of purification from moral stain and sin; second, of their admission into the community of John's disciples.

In writing of John the Baptist, scholars have long felt themselves to be on solid historical ground. Not only do all three of the Synoptic Evangelists record the story, but the historian Josephus tells of it; though there is in his *Antiquities* no note made of John's association with Jesus; nor does he mention the Baptist's Messianic preaching. The convincing reason to be inferred is that Josephus, as usual, carefully avoids getting himself involved with the scrutinizing authority of Rome. But the historian voluntarily says this of John:

> Herod slew him, who was a good man, and commanded the Jews to exercise virtue: both as to righteousness toward one another, and piety towards God; and so to unite themselves together in baptism. For he held that the washing with water would be acceptable to him, if they made use of it, not only in order to serve toward the putting away, or the remission, of certain sins, but for the purification also of the body.... Now, when many others came in crowds about him—for they were greatly moved, or pleased, by hearing his words—Herod feared lest the great influence John had over the people might put it into his power and inclination to raise a rebellion.... Accordingly, John was sent a prisoner to Machaerus, the fortress I before mentioned, and was there put to death.[2]

It has been held by some scholars that John was a Nazarite who stressed the rite of purification; by others, that he was a zealot concerned with political freedom; by still others, that his way of life most closely resembled that of the Essenes. Klausner, an authority on the life of Judaism in the first century, says that John was both like and unlike the Essenes—like Banus, the teacher of Josephus, "who lived in the wilderness, clothed himself in a garment made of leaves, ate only wild fruit, and bathed day and night in cold water, for the purpose of purification."

[2] *Antiquities of the Jews,* XVII:5. Whitson-Burder translation (1880), revised.

But, unlike the Essenes, he gathered disciples around him and proclaimed the coming of Messiah. John, like Elijah, was a "preacher and reprover." [3] Whatever resemblance he may have shown to members of these parties, he was a man of original genius and striking personality whose strength lay in the divine Spirit which, like wind and fire, swept through him and possessed him. He was a *voice* in this world's wilderness, suggesting, as did the ancient prophet Amos, a roaring lion coming out of his den at the dusk of day.

The four Evangelists, all of whom tell John's story, do not literally agree in their interpretation of it. As we should expect, their accounts reflect the Christian tradition current in the time and place in which they were written. Their testimonies vary according to the point of view of each; but the scene before them is vivid and compelling. Here is a man with a message. He comes as though he were armed with an axe to cut down a fruitless tree; or, as a thresher of that ancient time, with a flail in his hand to beat the chaff from the wheat on the granary floor. But he is a destroyer only of what is evil; the good tree he spares and the pure wheat he garners up unto the forthcoming harvest.

John's message may be summed up in these four statements: (1) it was a call for the purification and cleansing of the soul; (2) it was a declaration that the regenerated life of the believer must be lived in community; (3) it was an announcement of the coming of Messiah; (4) it was a reaffirmation of the prophetic promise of divine judgment and grace. But above all, it was a call for decision in a time of crisis. "The day of the Lord is at hand," cried John: "Repent; believe; be baptized; be prepared." For us moderns the urgency of this message is strikingly translated in these words of William Blake who, like John, was impelled by the vision of Elijah:

> Bring me my bow of burning gold:
> Bring me my arrows of desire:
> Bring me my spear. O clouds, unfold!
> Bring me my chariot of fire.

[3] J. Klausner, *Jesus of Nazareth* (New York: The Macmillan Co., 1929), p. 245.

The Evangelists tell us that John was baptizing in the Jordan when Jesus came upon the scene. Mark's account says, briefly, that Jesus, being baptized, saw the heavens opened and the Spirit descending on him like a dove, and heard a voice from heaven, saying, "Thou art my beloved Son, in whom I am well pleased." Matthew adds that John hesitated to baptize Jesus, thinking that he ought rather to be baptized by him. Luke follows Mark, adding only that Jesus prayed and that the Holy Ghost descended "in a *bodily* shape like a dove upon him." The Fourth Evangelist gives us his later version of the story in which the Baptist, as a divinely appointed witness to the coming of Christ, exclaims: "Behold the Lamb of God which taketh away the sin of the world."

It is clear that by the end of the first century the story had reached its farthest bounds. Its outward motion resembled the waves on a pool into which a stone is dropped. At the center is the event. Surrounding it, within the widening circle of its influence, we find the interpretations of the event's meaning, first, to Jesus himself, and second, to the early Christian church. At the outer boundary of the narrative we read its meaning for John in the words, in John 3:30, "He must increase, but I must decrease." Here, in the language of the Fourth Evangelist, was the gospel's significance for all time to come. All who came before Christ were but the heralds of his advent; he was the One for whom the world was waiting; there was no need now to look for another. He was the Messiah. In the more meaningful and proved words of apostolic faith, he was the Bridegroom who had come to join the bride, his church. Luke sums up the early Christian tradition in these words. "The law and the prophets were until John; since that time the kingdom of God is preached, and every man presseth into it."[4] What he means is that the new dispensation has begun. The Father has sent His Son; and, through the ministry of the Holy Spirit,

> The world is charged with the grandeur of God....
>   There lives the dearest freshness deep down things;
> And though the last lights off the black West went
>   Oh, mornings, at the brown brink eastward, springs—

[4] Luke 16:16.

Because the Holy Ghost over the bent
  World broods with warm breast and with ah! bright wings.[5]

II

THE STORY OF JESUS' TEMPTATION

The account of Jesus' baptism is inseparable from that of his
temptation. Both relate to events of his inner life and experience. To interpret them requires, besides historical research, a
sympathetic imagination and individual insight. To treat wisely
of the fact of the consciousness of Jesus is a difficult task. But
it is not one for which the historical or the psychological expert
alone is qualified. Their specialized skills may properly be
brought to bear upon the subject. But the answers to the questions we ask about what happened within the area of the inner
thought-life of Jesus must, at last, be found in ourselves, in
something "Jesus-like" in us, and in an understanding of what
is actually implied in the Gospels by membership in the kingdom
of God. The words of Christ that "the kingdom of God cometh
not with observation," and "is within you," have here a particular application. We must acknowledge that, at this distance
from the scene, our clearest outlook upon the facts is "through
a glass darkly." There is for us, at last, but one way of insight
into Holy Scripture: it is the way opened to us by the aid of the
Holy Spirit.

All three of the Synoptic Gospels preserve the account of
the temptation. Scholars are in disagreement as to its documentary source. Some of them attribute it to Mark; others, to
Q, holding, however, that Mark was somehow acquainted with
it. The form critics quite generally regard the account as a
purely legendary strand of the oral tradition. Those of the
social, or environmental, school of criticism hold it to be the
product of the thought of the early Christian church and of its
attempt to explain the sinless human character of Jesus.

What is, of course, important is that the sinless life of Christ
was an accepted fact and needed to be explained. The most

[5] Gerald Manley Hopkins, "God's Grandeur," from *Poems of G. M.
Hopkins*, 1919. Used by permission of the Oxford University Press, New
York.

natural explanation is that Jesus himself, in his intimate association with the inner circle of disciples, was here giving expression to the thoughts which occupied his mind at the outset of his public ministry. We can easily see how, during the closing months of his earthly life, surrounded by the Twelve, and living in daily anticipation of the Cross, he would be moved to talk to them of the theme of the temptation and its bearing on his Messianic consciousness. This theme bore directly on the fact of sin and evil in the world, from a knowledge of whose power he could not have been exempt, since by his sense of vocation he felt himself called to be its conqueror.

Matthew the Evangelist tells us that Jesus was "led up of the Spirit into the wilderness to be tempted of the devil." The Book of Job may perhaps suggest to us how the inner drama took outward form.[6] The voice at the baptism had said: "Thou art my beloved Son." The devil, whom Mark calls Satan, now says to him: "If thou be the Son of God, command that these stones be made bread."[7] Matthew and Luke tell us that Jesus had been in the desert for forty days and had fasted; Mark completes the picture by noting that he was "with the wild beasts" and that "the angels ministered unto him." Wild beasts were popularly believed to be inhabited by demons, and so symbolized the powers of evil. Wandering between angels and demons, the Son of God, clothed in our humanity, sharing our creatureliness, is to us an arresting figure. Remembering Israel's experience in the wilderness, we can readily imagine Jesus in retrospect living through the days of his people's suffering, and—in the very beginning of his earthly ministry—preparing to take upon himself the burden of its sin, according to the law as set forth in Leviticus 16—

> And ever with Him went,
> Of all His wanderings
> Comrade, with ragged coat,
> Gaunt ribs—poor innocent—
> Bleeding foot, burning throat,

[6] See Job, 1-2.
[7] Matthew 4:3.

The guileless old scapegoat;
For forty nights and days
Followed in Jesus' ways,
Sure guard behind Him kept,
Tears like a lover wept.[8]

The three temptations are depicted by Saint Matthew on an ascending scale of severity. The first is at the common level of the world's daily need of bread. It corresponds to the economic demand for physical well-being and security. To feed the hungry, clothe the naked, and relieve the suffering of the poor: could there be a more worthy task even for the Son of God than this? It is interesting to note that this thought suggested itself favorably to Jesus. Yet the suggestion was an evil one; for man is more than an animal and he cannot feed his soul on corn. That was what Jesus later said in the parable recorded in Luke 12:13-21. We can easily enough detect in this temptation the age-old struggle of the church against the engulfing materialism of which Saint Paul wrote, in Philippians 3:18-19, saying: "For many walk ... that are the enemies of the cross of Christ: whose God is their belly, and ... who mind earthly things."

The second temptation was of another order. It appealed to the higher faculty of man's belief in the supernatural and rested on the sound assumption that God will take care of His own. Was it not on a sign from heaven for which earth's children, even at that moment, were waiting? "If thou art the Son of God," the tempter said, "then show the people a sign that they may believe. Yonder, in Jerusalem, is the temple; cast yourself down from its pinnacle. Is it not written in Holy Scripture: 'He shall give his angels charge over thee, to keep thee: and in their hands they shall bear thee up, lest at any time thou dash thy foot against a stone'?" [9]

Jesus put the tempter to silence with the answer: "Thou shalt not tempt the Lord thy God." It is an evil thing for the human creature to demand a proof of the Creator's care of him—an

[8] Robert Graves, "In the Wilderness," from *Poems*. Used by permission of Doubleday & Co., Inc., New York, publishers.
[9] Luke 4:10-11.

indication of distrust, of disbelief.   It is a heathen thing to
think that man has made God and can judge Him.   Jesus drew
strength from the words in Deuteronomy 6:16—as certainly as
God lives, He will not forsake His children.   What is this cry
that is heard in the world: "Show us a sign"? Man's first duty
is to obey God, unqualifiedly, unquestioningly.

The third temptation was less subtle, but more terrifying.
With brazen aggressiveness the tempter now suggested to Jesus
a view of "all the kingdoms of the world and the glory of them,"
and said: "All these things will I give thee if thou will fall
down and worship me."   To be a prince of this world—a Herod
or a Hitler—was not that reward enough for having lived? But
Jesus' rejection of the offer was prompt and final; "Get thee
hence, Satan; for it is written: Thou shalt worship the Lord
thy God, and him only shalt thou serve."   It will not escape
our notice that the devil is both a liar and a tyrant.   For the
kingdoms of this world do not by right belong to him but to
God.   Satan is a usurper and a villain.   Besides, by his code of
base politics, all earthly princes are necessarily his slaves: they
must fall down and worship him.

Jesus regarded such a view of the world with deserved repug-
nance.   So also did the early Christian church which, when the
temptation story was written, found itself in the midst of a
conflict between two philosophies of world history: (1) that
symbolized by Rome and the late tyrant Nero; and (2) that to
which Saint Paul and the Gospel writers after him were fully
committed—the assurance that the kingdoms of this world
would one day become the kingdom of Christ the Lord.

But it was to be noted that, until that time came, the kingdom
of God would "suffer violence."   Countless numbers of Christians would become martyrs; the cause of Christ would be put
in great jeopardy; many would prove unfaithful and—as Pliny,
writing to the emperor Trajan, said—would "curse Christ and
worship the image of Caesar."   The times would wax worse:
great tribulations would ensue; "false Christs and false prophets" would appear.   After that, in one great conflict which the
writer of the Book of Revelation was to call Armageddon, the
final issue would be resolved.   Babylon, symbolizing the king-

dom of Satan, would crumble to dust. The evil beast would
fall before the might of the Lamb of God. Then joy would
reign at the marriage feast of Christ and his bride, the church;
and the new Jerusalem, the holy city of God, would descend
from heaven to be established on earth.

Such was the background of the apocalyptic-Messianic hope
against which the Synoptic Evangelists recorded the story of
Jesus' temptation. In it we see reflected the temptations which
confronted the early church—and which confront us in our
time. The story signalizes the fact that the church today—as
its history through the centuries has also shown—can withstand
the evil tempter only by the gracious help of God. The poet
Milton, living in a time of bitter conflict between the church
and the world, pictures Christ as the mighty victor in the epic
poem *Paradise Regained,* in which he says:

> So Satan fell and straight a fiery globe
> Of angels on full sail of wing flew nigh,
> Who on their plumy vans received Him soft
> From his uneasy station, and upbore
> As on a floating couch through the blithe air,
> Then in a flowery valley set him down
> On a green bank, and set before him spread
> A table of celestial food, divine,
> Ambrosial fruits fetched from the Tree of Life,
> And from the Fount of Life ambrosial drink,
> That soon refreshed him wearied, and repaired
> What hunger, if aught hunger had impaired,
> Or thirst, and as he fed, angelic choirs
> Sang heavenly anthems of his victory
> Over temptation and the Tempter proud.

Chapter 18

PREACHING AND HEALING IN CAPERNAUM

I

PROCLAMATION OF THE KINGDOM

A noteworthy mark of difference existed between the first Christians who lived about A.D. 35 and those who followed them a generation later. The early disciples, after Jesus' death and resurrection, looked forward to his immediate return to effect the consummation of his kingdom. The later apostles, especially those living after the destruction of Jerusalem in A.D. 70, had for some time now also been looking backward upon the earthly life of Christ; and they had begun to lay stress on his ethical teaching and to adapt it to the then established historic church. The story of Christ's passion, we know, had from the beginning been the nucleus of this history. Next to it in importance had been the account of his resurrection, his ascension, and his anticipated coming again to judge and rule the world. After that, to give the history completion and meaning, the gospel tradition had included an emphasis on Jesus' heavenly and earthly origin.

This, in outline, was the first "history" of Christ. That history, as we have said,[1] was (1) Christological and (2) eschatological—that is, it contained what in the beginning had come to be believed about the divine person and redemptive work of Christ, and it set forth the plan of how this work was to be brought to a definite conclusion in the world. What we are now called upon to note, as we proceed with our study, is this primitive history's doctrinal character. It had, from the start, to do with Jesus Christ the Son of God, who was of divine birth, who suffered under Pontius Pilate, was crucified, raised

[1] See pp. 121ff.

from the dead, and was now at the right hand of God, waiting to come again in his heavenly glory to be the savior of men and the lord of life.   It is clear that we have here the essence of what was later in the church's history to be summed up in the text of the Apostles' Creed.

But this is not the whole history of which the Gospels tell us. The events of Jesus' public ministry are also a part of it. They, too, belong to the accumulated tradition of the early apostolic preaching whose vital core was the gospel of the mighty words and acts of Christ the Lord.   Of the authenticity and trustworthiness of this tradition the life of the church through the ages and the summarized verdict of Biblical scholarship, alike, furnish the convincing proof.   It now remains for us to trace the progress of this history in greater detail.

The Synoptic Gospels record that Jesus' public ministry began in Capernaum.   The town on the northwestern shore of the Lake of Galilee, and still recognizable today, was well suited to the missionary enterprise.   It was on the Roman highway leading to the Mediterranean Sea.   Travelers, and people of all sorts, were to be found there, and in the neighboring towns of Chorazin and Bethsaida.   But Jews predominated.   And there was a synagogue in the village, in the ruins of which still lie some gathered stones that speak of the place where Jesus preached.   A little distance inland, among the steep hills, lay Nazareth; and by the lake, with its harbor of sailboats, was Magdala.

Galilee was rich in Old Testament history.   But its inhabitants were a frontier and freedom-loving people whom distance from Jerusalem and contact with the outside world had especially prepared to be the first to hear and welcome the Christian gospel.   We do not find it difficult, therefore, to picture Jesus in the synagogue, or in Simon Peter's house, or by the lakeside in Capernaum, preaching, teaching, and healing the people that come to him, as the Gospels record.   If, in this distant time, there are those among us who, listening to the waters of that far-off lake, still sometimes hear in them a Voice whose music "soothes all sorrows and drives away all fears," we moderns of

less imagination may well stand in respect of them as they repeat, with Whittier:

> O Sabbath rest by Galilee!
> O calm of hills above,
> Where Jesus knelt to share with thee
> The silence of eternity,
> Interpreted by love!

Everywhere in Galilee there were devout Jews who were stirred by a great hope. Outwardly, conditions in Palestine promoted it. The yoke of Rome was galling. Caesar and Herod, alike, oppressed the people. Matthew the Publican, at the tollgate on the Roman road in Capernaum, symbolized the unearned riches that were gathered by the alien overlord to keep the people in poverty. The Galileans were of a volatile temper; and there were Zealots among them who favored the overthrow of the tyrant and any vigorous attempt to establish a free Jewish state. Such was the general feeling in the land.

But the ground of the great hope by which the more thoughtful among the people were moved lay deeper. It was historical; and it was profoundly religious. In it, centuries before, the faith of Messianism had taken root; and, though beginning as a tender plant in a dry ground, this faith had grown mightily and was now a flourishing tree spreading its branches widely over Palestine. The growth of this Messianic hope was particularly vigorous in Galilee. For there it was nourished by the established synagogue in which—and this was a very important fact —the sacred Scriptures were read on the Sabbath. Particular and urgent stress was laid on those passages of prophecy which gave expression to the coming of the great Deliverer who was pictured before them after the pattern of one or another of these three controlling historic concepts: (1) as the Davidic king, spoken of by the prophet Isaiah; (2) as the Suffering Servant, written of by the great Unknown Prophet of the Exile; (3) as the heavenly Son of man, referred to in the apocryphal Book of Enoch and in the prophecy of Daniel.[2]

Here, in the vision of the coming Day, there was fuel

[2] See (1) Isaiah 9:1-7; (2) Isaiah 53:1-12; (3) Daniel 7:1-28.

enough to fan the flame of hope.   Jerusalem might have its imposing temple where the priests, after the tradition of Levi,
kept their vigil over Israel's religious heritage and offered daily
sacrifice for her past sins.   There the Sadducees, content with
their aristocratic ties with the ruling political powers, might
live in august serenity, skeptical of Messianism, condescending
toward the common people's piety, and declaring their disbelief
in the Resurrection.   There, too, the scribes and Pharisees could
pursue their ardent and painstaking study of the law; honorable
men, most of them, dutiful, patient, interested in the education
of the people, ascetic formal pietists, seekers after the truth—
not the truth yet to be revealed, but the truth already written
down by wise men and seers, on the scrolls of sacred Scripture.

But in Galilee there were only the synagogues.   In them the
people met freely to worship, to be taught, and sometimes simply to talk.   It was natural that Jesus, himself brought up under
the shadow of the synagogue in Nazareth, should choose such
an appropriate place to begin his preaching in Capernaum; and
that he should, not long thereafter, bring his activity to a climax
in that region by returning to Nazareth, going to the synagogue
on the Sabbath day, "as his custom was," and reading aloud,
to those gathered there, these significant words of the prophet
Isaiah:

> The Spirit of the Lord is upon me,
> Because he hath anointed me
> To *preach* the gospel to the poor;
> He hath sent me to heal the brokenhearted,
> To *preach* deliverance to the captives,
> And recovering of sight to the blind,
> To set at liberty them that are bruised,
> To *preach* the acceptable year of the Lord.[3]

We do not have preserved for us the assembled content of
Jesus' first preaching in Capernaum.   To find it we must go to
the entire Gospel record and glean from it those passages, or
sayings, which best fit the setting of this early stage of Christ's
ministry—passages which, like the one we have just quoted,
announce the Good News that the Messianic kingdom is at hand,

[3] Luke 4:18, 19.

that its coming is to be attended by signs from heaven and deeds of wonder, and that it is to bring peace and consolation to waiting Israel. But the Synoptic Evangelists, in the early chapters of their narrative, are not silent about the circumstances and the effect of Jesus' message. According to the apostolic tradition, certain definite things are to be said about it: (1) that Jesus' hearers were astonished and won to him; (2) that he spoke with the authority of one who not only gave expression to, but *revealed,* the word of God; (3) that, as Luke records it,[4] Jesus' message was described as having both doctrine and power; (4) that men who felt themselves held in the grip of evil spirits recognized his power and authority over them and cried out against him—and yet implored help from him; (5) that the multitudes, in their physical infirmities, came to him to be helped and healed; (6) that he gave evidence of having the divine power to forgive sins; and (7) that, before long, his influence among the people aroused the opposition, first, of the observing Pharisees and, later, of Herod Antipas, the tetrarch of Galilee.

The essence of Jesus' early preaching is contained in what F. C. Burkitt has called the message of "the good time to come." It differed, as we have indicated, from that of John the Baptist, in its stress on the healing, the pardon, and the consolation which the imminent advent of the heavenly kingdom was to offer. One notes with interest Luke's reference to "the gracious words" which came from Jesus' lips, in contrast to the fiery challenge of John through whose message a "generation of vipers" was seeking to escape from "the wrath to come." Words of judgment, too, were later to be spoken by Jesus; but their time was not yet come. This was, for him, the seedtime of the Good News. All too soon, in his public ministry, he would find himself driven toward the harvest day of judgment. When that day came, the enemies of the new kingdom, who themselves refused his invitation and forbade others to accept it, would be forced to hear condemnation enough.

But this was now the time of his dispensation—and their

---

[4] See Luke 4:32.

day—of grace. And why should it not be such when the kingdom of God, even then so urgently at hand, was to be ushered
in supernaturally by the mighty act of God? Its coming, we
are compelled to note again, was not to be by any gradual or
evolutionary process of nature. It was to come from above.
It was, by its own definition, not a natural phenomenon : it was
something different, something miraculous, not merely other-
worldly—for it had something to do with this world—but other
than worldly, a phenomenon of the visiting divine Spirit, supra-
historical, and therefore belonging not simply to world history
but to the history of redemption. In a word, the nature of the
kingdom was eschatological. It pointed to the goal of history,
to the end and ultimate meaning of all things.

Jesus himself looked forward with eager anticipation to its
arrival, carrying the secret of his Messiahship, as it must by
then have been revealed to him, deeply secure in his own consciousness. The kingdom of heaven was to him indeed a
secret and a mystery, "a dogmatic idea" which, as Schweitzer
tells us, wholly possessed his thought.[5] It was regarded by him
as something not to be earned, but to which men were called;
and it was to this fact that he owed the consciousness of his
own office which, in the first stage of his public ministry, was
to call people to an attitude of willingness and readiness to enter
into the kingdom. His early preaching in Capernaum was,
therefore, the work of a Sower who, as in the parable in Matthew 13:1-23, went forth to sow. The seed was the divine
mystery of the kingdom; it was to be sown everywhere : by the
wayside; on stony soil; among thorns; and into good ground.
The time of the harvest was yet to come. That time, too, with
its song of ingathering and chant of doom, its oncoming rush
of wind and flame of fire, was a secret, and was in God's hands.
Jesus, at the beginning, was thinking only of the sowing.

[5] Albert Schweitzer, *The Quest of the Historical Jesus, op. cit.,* pp. 351-53.

II
Signs of God's Mighty Work

The Gospel of Mark is our chief source of information on both Jesus' early preaching and healing. Matthew and Luke who, besides following Mark, drew upon the source called Q, add one important story to complete the scene. It is the story of the healing of the Centurion's servant, found jointly in Matthew 8:5-13 and Luke 7:1-10. The fact that the events to be reviewed here are closely associated with the life of Peter, whose memoirs are contained in Mark's narrative, assures us of their genuineness as gospel history. And our assurance is further confirmed (1) by the story's simple and realistic setting, and (2) by the Evangelist's straightforward and dramatic style of writing.

We are well advised, in approaching the miracles of Jesus, to look at them with newly opened eyes; not prejudicially, nor credulously, but in the light of what they assume. Their assumption is the belief that God exists, that it is in His nature to do mighty works, and that His acts are miracles, whether or not we can explain them. The Gospel writers assume that we cannot clearly understand God's ways among us. They are generally hidden from us, "too wonderful" for us, and "past finding out." The suggestion, fundamentally, is that our true nature and destiny are concealed from us by the fact of sin. Our insight into life, though not destroyed, is dimmed. We do not *know* ourselves, or one another, or God; we err, are lost, confused. But God Himself has sought and found us: the life of Christ is the demonstration of that fact; and the miracles of Jesus are the reported signs and acts of God by means of which this truth breaks through to us.

It must be clear, therefore, that any attempt we may make to explain the Gospel miracles naturalistically—that is, with an eye to seeing how they must look when exposed to the laws of nature—assumes a position that is altogether contrary to the intent of Holy Scripture. The Biblical writers did not aim to accommodate divine events to natural laws, but simply to ac-

knowledge and record these events wherever they occurred.   In common justice, the miracles must be judged by what the Evangelists claimed them to be, namely, signs of God's power and approval, witnessing to the divine person and work of Christ on earth.   To the Evangelists, the Gospel was itself a miracle—a demonstration of both the inner hidden mystery and the outwardly transpiring history of the divine plan of salvation.   It should be added that these men who wrote the Gospels did not share, or anticipate, our modern scientific view of the world. To them, no great gulf existed between the natural and the supernatural; all nature was subject to the activity of the divine Spirit; and every thoughtful man's view of natural phenomena, in that time, was theological.   Atheism as we know it, for example, with its presumptuous rationalistic attitude toward the external world, would have been unthinkable to him.   Everything worthy of being called an event in nature and history was the act of an imminent yet transcendent power.   It is with a recognition of this more profound insight that our interpretation of the miracles must begin.

The Gospel writers, we have said, found the occurrence of miracles natural.   They discovered in them a revelation of God and a witness to the Messiahship of Jesus.   Miracles were not impossibilities to them, but invitations and challenges to faith. There was, for example, in Jesus' driving of demons out of diseased men, nothing contrary to reason.   Demons, the assumed cause of human ills, were subject to him.   Knowing that by the word "demons" they were but giving a name to the fact of sin and evil in the world, can we say, today, that they were wrong? No doubt it stretched their reason to believe such a power belonged to Jesus.   But they did not doubt that it belonged to God.   We who are so ready to extol natural law, and to subject God to it, have forgotten how to think theologically—that is, to reason from first causes.   We need, in our age, to step out of this bondage to the rule of syllogism, our prisonhouse of sense perception, and to ask our reason to follow the course which, for example, the seventeenth-century physician and metaphysical writer, Sir Thomas Browne, outlined for himself when he said:

I love to lose myself in a mystery; to pursue my reason to an *O altitudo!* 'Tis my solitary recreation to pose my apprehension with those involved enigmas and riddles of the Trinity—Incarnation and Resurrection.... Where there is an obscurity too deep for our reason, 'tis good to sit down with a description, periphrasis, or adumbration; for, by acquainting our reason how unable it is to display the visible and obvious effects of nature, it becomes more humble and submissive unto the subtleties of faith; and thus I teach my haggard and unreclaimed reason to stoop unto the lure of faith.[6]

Let us now return to the story of Jesus' healing in Capernaum. We note that he is preaching the news of "the good time to come," when the multitudes begin to crowd about him: first, in the synagogue; then, in Simon Peter's house; and, after that, at the open seaside. They have been amazed at his outspoken authority; now they are to see the outward demonstration of his divine power. A man whose unclean spirit cries out against him is healed. The evil demon is driven out of him. It is a sign that Jesus' power is supernatural. He has authority over demons, over the realm of evil—answering by his own act, for the first time, the petition in the prayer he is later to teach his disciples: "Deliver us from evil; for thine is the kingdom."

Clearly, according to Mark's story, it is not simply a case of human pity that here confronts us.[7] It is a picture of divine compassion; and the whole incident is a drama confined to the celestial sphere; it includes earthly concerns, private ones, men's domestic lives: it takes into its scope, we are told, all the city that is "gathered together at the door of Peter's house." Here, then, at the beginning of the Gospel narrative, we see exhibited the sign that, in the earthly life of Christ, the will of God is even now being "done on earth as it is done in heaven."

We must not fail to note how, at the very beginning of Jesus' earthly ministry, the seeds of conflict were germinating in the varying soils of Palestine. Galilee was good ground for the preaching of the gospel of the new kingdom; but Jesus' sudden popularity there began to stimulate to growth a crop of

[6] *Religio Medici* (1643).
[7] Mark 1:23-27.

tares threatening to choke the good seed. The synagogue, where the sacred law was taught, was an excellent institution; but its scribes and Pharisees were even then showing signs of becoming the enemies of the gospel. Finally, the deliverance from evil which Jesus' coming was especially to make possible, and which was indeed the greatest good and need of mankind, was providing his opponents with an opportunity to array their strength against him, to destroy him if they could. This last, most ominous cause of opposition was slow in growing. But Jesus' early experience in Nazareth, recorded in Luke 4:16-30, and his almost immediate encounter with the scribes who, according to Mark 3:22, dared to say that he was casting out devils by the prince of devils, and therefore had an unclean spirit, were evidence enough of what was soon to come. But the seeds of this conflict were still only germinating; and Jesus, if we read the Gospels aright, must have thought that, before the tares could spring up to their full growth, the great day of harvest in the new kingdom would be at hand and the work of the Evil One would be destroyed in the fires of the last great judgment. Such was the apocalyptic atmosphere of hope in which he began to preach and to heal.

Jesus' healing, then, had a greater than humanitarian end. Both his pity and his power were demonstrations of God's compassion for suffering and sinful humanity. As he had the authority over demons, so he had the right and power to forgive the sins of those who suffered under the tyranny of evil, as well as to help those whom the curse of sin had afflicted with physical infirmities and diseases and with the pain of natural death. The healing of men's bodies, minds, and souls, accordingly, was of one piece with his preaching. It was the sign, the great inference, of what would happen when the Kingdom, now at hand, was fully come. It was this, indeed, that the miracles of Jesus demonstrated: they signalized and were prophetic of what would happen when sin and sorrow and pain would be no more. They represented moments in history when, by the uplifted "finger of God," [8] the common order of things was interrupted: the blind saw; the lame walked; the demon of evil was cast out;

[8] Luke 11:20; Matthew 12:28.

and, for a time, life on earth was as it should be, altogether natural, as at the first creation—a little space of Eden restored in a world of sin. Only now the order was reversed. The kingdom of God was a forward-looking event. Its direction was eschatological, pulling all history with it toward its great end. Everything was pressing toward that End. The day of Judgment was impending. If it was delayed, it was by God's mercy—a time of forgiveness and of grace. Healings were the marks of grace; the Kingdom's coming was the all-embracing event.

In this allotted time of grace, to preach, to teach, to heal the deep hurt of the world: this was the task assigned to Jesus, as the Son of God, by the Father. The early Christian community for this reason knew and remembered this underlying fact of the gospel story, cherished the great truth it contained, and circulated it freely in the centers where the church had begun to grow. And because it was the truth as represented in the accumulated gospel tradition, and preserved by the primitive church, this writing finally became Sacred Scripture. The words and work of Christ had been tested in the crucible of the church's historic experience and confirmed.

It did not matter then, nor does it now, that the world in which the early Christians lived, together with all its reported happenings, was an ancient one. Their knowledge of the world's evil and of man's sin was real and right. They knew that evil was something much more than psychological, or environmental; that its cause, and its curse, lay deeper; and that the problem it presented was somehow bound up with a concept of the universe. Men in that age, battling with sin, saw themselves waylaid by an evil power. They did not call it "nerves," as many moderns do; nor the fault of institutions, as the romantic humanitarians still think of it; nor a vestige of primitive superstition; but "demons," that is, a hostile evil Spirit that only God could conquer. So recognized and overcome, it left a man, as Mark the Evangelist put it, "clothed and in his right mind." It is little wonder that the demonstration of such healing was said to be a marvel to men's eyes. It always is—as the poet Vachel Lindsay, for instance, pictures it:

Jesus came from out the courthouse door,
Stretched his hands above the passing poor....
The lame were straightened, withered limbs uncurled,
And blind eyes opened on a new, sweet world.[9]

[9] From the poem "General William Booth Enters into Heaven," 1913.
Used by permission of The Macmillan Co., publishers.

Chapter 19

JESUS AMONG SCRIBES AND SINNERS

I

THE GOSPEL OF FORGIVENESS

One cannot read far into Mark's Gospel and escape the urgency of it. Something extraordinary begins to move in the first chapter, and nothing can stop it until its expenditure of strength is cut off abruptly by the Gospel's last missing page. This urgent note cannot be attributed simply to Mark's literary style, or to the energetic temper of Peter, his principal narrator. It is inherent in the gospel message and in Jesus' relationship to it. So impelling is this gospel, so mighty its power, and so near at hand its victorious days, that Jesus is himself drawn along with it as by a magnet whose pole is the irresistible and loving will of God.

And the people, too, are drawn along with him. They follow him to Peter's house, crowding into the dooryard after sunset. After that, before the dawn comes to sleeping Capernaum, Jesus goes to a solitary place to pray. Only in prayer is the compulsive tension released, as the Son rests his wearied mind in the thought of doing the Father's will. At that moment the picture changes; a strange "otherness" than our fallen humanity characterizes him in the prayer scenes, as the Gospels jointly depict them. The poet Henry Vaughan expresses what they portray in these words:

> Early, while yet the dark was gay
> And gilt with stars, more trim than day,
> Heaven's lily, and the earth's chaste rose,
> The green immortal branch, arose,
> And in a solitary place
> Bowed to his Father his blest face.

We can see, as we read the first two or three chapters of Mark, that the Evangelist is not trying to be simply or precisely chronological. He finds some order necessary; but his use of his material, like that of the other Evangelists after him, is essentially topical. Capernaum and the nearby towns represent Galilee, where Jesus began and continued his ministry; and we are able to get a closer view of him, and of what he did, by noting what happened on a typical day in his earthly life. Mark usually helps us by summing up his impression of the day's events in some terse statement such as this, for example, addressed to Jesus by one of his early followers: "All men seek for thee." [1]

One such typical day occurred in Capernaum after an apparent interval of Jesus' absence. Again, Mark tells us, Jesus is preaching, probably in Peter's house, when four men carrying a paralytic on their shoulders arrive, ascend the stairway to the roof, remove the layers of tile, and let down the palsied man into the room where Jesus is standing. The episode is obviously authentic. Peter, we can imagine, must have been a little shocked. But, impulsive though he was, he did not cry out, in natural indignation: "Stop! Why this vandalism? This is my house!" But Peter remembered the incident. When Jesus beheld the paralytic, he said an astonishing thing: "Son, thy sins be forgiven thee." That utterance started a disturbance and proposed a problem. The scribes, "sitting there," as Mark puts it, were not slow to take it up. They called Jesus' utterance blasphemous. "Who can forgive sins but God only?" they asked; and by that question the gospel's offer of forgiveness was announced to the world. Mark's comment on the incident is also typical. When the paralytic is healed and forgiven, we are told that all who witnessed the miracle were amazed, and glorified God, saying: "We never saw it on this fashion."

Both Matthew and Luke record the event, indicating by that fact that Mark is their source of information. Neither Matthew nor Luke here changes Mark's order of sequence, except to interpolate certain desired material from other sources: Matthew going to Q to include the Sermon on the Mount; Luke

[1] Mark 1:37.

inserting only the story of the Miracle of the Fishes from a source exclusively his own.[2] We may therefore regard the event as of singular historical, as well as topical, importance. It will help us to get a clearer view of the whole picture before us if we are careful to remember that, at the time the Gospels were written, the Christian church had already been established, and that therefore faith in the grace and power of Christ to forgive sins had by then become an accepted fact. Saint Paul, whose evangelistic preaching and theological writings antedated Mark's Gospel by considerably more than a decade, had declared it to be the peculiar glory of the gospel that Christ forgave sinners.

The power to forgive sins was not merely attributed to Jesus because of his natural kindness toward people—as though he were willing to overlook the faults of publicans and sinners because they acted "naturally," as persons should, and did not wear the masks of hypocrites. Rather, it was a power resident in him by the plan and will of God, and demonstrated in gospel history by his death on the Cross. Saint Paul had given the death of Christ the central place in his extended missionary career by calling the gospel he preached the Gospel of the Cross. Peter the apostle, to whom Mark owed much of his narrative, had held the same view—if we may attribute to him the epistle of *First Peter,* bearing his name. The Cross had come to stand —as it stands today—for the forgiveness of the sin of the world. That, clearly, was the reason why the story of Jesus' passion and resurrection occupied, from the first, the primary attention of the early Christian evangelists and teachers, and so became the nucleus of the oral tradition upon which the later Gospel writers depended for their literary compositions.

When, accordingly, the Gospel Evangelists depict Jesus as the friend of publicans and sinners, their assertion has a weightier meaning than is generally given to it. For behind it lies the offer of divine redemption to publicans and sinners everywhere and for all time to come; and the doctrine of the Cross is the symbol by which this gracious offer is given its enduring significance and form. The Evangelists—let us note this fact carefully—saw in Jesus' life, as he had lived it, a fore-

2 Matthew, Chs. 5-7 and Luke 5:1-11.

shadowing of his death; and the sinners who came to him typified those who, in time to come, were to find deliverance from evil and rest for their souls. More particularly, they were the types of those persons who freely and openly acknowledged themselves to be sinners in the sight of God, and were therefore in a position of readiness to respond to Christ's invitation to enter the newly prepared kingdom of heaven. The unforgivable sin was the denial of mankind's universal sinfulness; or, in the language of the Fourth Gospel, the great sin of the world was its rejection of Jesus Christ, the world's savior from sin.

It is little wonder that, as Mark says, the scribes, "sitting there," began to "reason in their hearts," asking: "How can this man forgive sins?" It has been, we can see at once, the typical question of the inquisitive scribes of all time. Saint Paul, writing for the early church, answers them by saying that this, precisely, is the hidden mystery of the Gospel, now openly revealed to mankind as the power of God: that Christ came into the world to forgive and to save sinners.[3]

The synoptic Evangelists, as historians, simply record that Jesus himself, during his earthly life, gave ample and concrete demonstration of that fact. He forgave sinners, and they were forgiven. The act was God's doing. The people were amazed. They believed and rejoiced. Such forgiveness was a sign of heavenly grace pouring out on mankind, like a river refreshing the dry land. The "good time to come" was indeed near. The onlooking Pharisees might stand aloof, pleased with themselves, with their fasting "twice a week," their tithing of everything they earned—how righteously they earned and deserved their yearly income! But there were the publicans. In them the poor, sinful world could see itself symbolized. Despised by the self-righteous, shamed by his own unworthiness, the publican could only strike his breast and say: "O God, be merciful to me a sinner!"[4] But by his repentance he demonstrated that the kingdom of God had come. It was his ready response to the divine challenge to enter the kingdom.

It is of interest to note, in this close connection, the call of

[3] I Corinthians 1:18-24.
[4] Luke 18:10-14.

Levi, thereafter called Matthew, one of the twelve disciples and the traditional author of the First Gospel. All three Synoptists place the incident after the healing of the paralytic; and Luke adds that Levi was a publican. The episode is briefly recorded. But the inference is clear. Jesus said to him: "Follow me"; and the publican arose and followed him. We observe the spontaneity of his act, his readiness to enter the kingdom. The news of the "good time to come" is for him: tired of his sinful extortioner's life, he responds.

Luke, we have just observed, is particularly interested in the way in which sinful people attracted Jesus and were attracted to him. He shows, also, that Jesus did not despise or shun the company of the better Pharisees. In Luke 7:36-50, we read that he was invited to dinner in the house of one Simon the Pharisee. Jesus accepted the invitation, and the conversation was no doubt proceeding satisfactorily on the good points of the Jewish law when a woman whose life was known to be sinful entered the house, fell at Jesus' feet, and began to wash them with her tears and to anoint his feet and his head with a precious ointment. Here, if we merely interpret the story naturally and socially, was simply an embarrassing situation. But Jesus saw only the sinful woman's—and the world's—hunger to be forgiven and to live a new life. Simon, the good Pharisee, was taught a lesson on forgiveness; the woman, type of sinful but repentant mankind, was forgiven and blest.

Later, through the use of parables to illustrate the mystery of the kingdom and how men may enter into it, Luke further elucidates this great theme. Among them, the most familiar are the two parables of the Lost Sheep and the Prodigal Son. The refrain of the first, announcing that "joy shall be in heaven over one sinner that repenteth," sums up the gospel of forgiveness completely; and, of the countless writers of commentaries on the second, hardly anyone has put the truth more simply and in sweeter strains than has George Gascoigne, the Elizabethan poet:

> Thou delight'st not to see a sinner fall;
> Thou hark'nest first before we come to call;

Thine ears are set wide open evermore;
Before we knock thou comest to the door.

II

THE LAW AND ITS TRADITION

Now, according to the narrative, all this that happened did not pass unnoticed in high ecclesiastical circles. Nor was it viewed with indifference by Herod Antipas whose political ambitions were beginning to be put in jeopardy by the strength of Jesus' following—but to this threat of opposition, so crucial when it came, the Gospels will call our later attention. It is enough, at this moment, to observe that resistance against Jesus, when it arose, came from two centers: Jerusalem and Rome. The powers represented by them were themselves opposite in character: that of Jerusalem was the power of patriotism and religion, of conscience and the moral law; that of Rome was the power of a vast empire, of military strength, of a sense of civil justice and of stoical pagan morality. The attitude of Rome was that of a conqueror; self-confident, patronizing, indifferent to minor disturbances. The feeling of the Jews in Jerusalem, and indeed everywhere in greater Palestine, was that of a conquered people: proud, humiliated, passionately hopeful of deliverance, jealous of a great tradition, intent on cultivating domestic virtue, and devoted to a literal and deeply religious reading of the Mosaic law.

There could be little doubt that, in the natural order of events, it would one day be the fate of Jesus to be caught and crushed between these two opposing forces, as between two millstones—the upper stone, the revolving physical strength of the Roman empire; the lower stone, the immovable burning spirit of Palestinian Judaism. That Jesus, from the beginning of his public ministry, was aware of this impending danger, is to be assumed. How soon—again, speaking only of the natural course of human events—he would be crushed in this slowly grinding mill, he did not know. But he was certain—guided by a divine assurance—that, before then, he would have time to finish his appointed earthly task. Perhaps—and this appears to

have been his most ardent hope during his early period of preaching in Galilee—before that fateful day could come, the hour of divine history's clock would strike, the Ancient of days would call time at an end, and the Son of man would be seen coming in the clouds of heaven to establish his everlasting kingdom.

If such was his hope, the time was yet distant when Jesus was himself to assume the office of the Son of man. The day of that assumption was altogether in the Father's hands. When, at last and by the Father's will, it came, Jesus' Messiahship was not, at once, to be one of suddenly manifested glory—except as the apostles, later looking backward, were to see how this glory was actually and wondrously manifested on the Cross. The role of Messiah was, instead, to be that of the self-humiliating and Suffering Servant of God, who, in the words of Mark's Gospel, was "to give his life as a ransom for many." [5]

To tell how all this was to come to pass was the main reason why the Evangelists undertook to write their Gospel narratives. We shall see how, in the story of the Transfiguration, Jesus does appear in a cloud of glory, together with Moses and Elias, and how, according to Mark 9:1-13, the Son of man is identified with the Messiah. But we must note that the Gospel narrator is looking backward as he writes, and seeing each event he records in the light of the culmination of them all. This culminating event was the passion and, following it, the death and the resurrection of Christ. For Jesus, at this early time, the "overshadowing cloud" had not yet come into view. It awaited him at Caesarea Philippi which was to mark the final crisis of his Galilean ministry. [6] Until then he must continue his evangelistic mission: to heal the sick; to exercise authority over demons by the might of Him who sent him; to invite sinners to accept the forgiveness of a loving heavenly Father; and, above all, to preach the Good News of the kingdom to those who, with him, looked for the consolation of Israel.

We have thus far stressed Israel's—and the world's—hope because it was uppermost in Jesus' mind. But, besides its hope, Israel had its law. We have already indicated, in an earlier

---

[5] Mark 10:45 and Matthew 20:28.
[6] Mark 8:27-38.

chapter, how for the Jewish people the Law and the Prophets were the two axes on which its life revolved. As time passed, the message of the prophets resolved itself into an utterance of the great Messianic hope; while the daily life of the Jewish community was kept intact by a close observance of the Levitical, traditionally ceremonial, law. Of this law the scribes were the learned doctors and the Pharisees the pious and faithful observers. These men were rabbis: that is, teachers, careful readers of the Old Testament and of the commentaries on it, as these were represented chiefly by the schools of Hillel and Shammai, then at the height of their influence in Judea.

To the more friendly of the Pharisees, the less strict ones of Galilee, Jesus was a familiarly known rabbi. They saw in him, at first, nothing revolutionary. He had, like them, been brought up under the free teaching of the synagogue in the north country. Like most of them, too, he had acquired no formal education in the niceties of the law. After all, he was but teaching the people as he believed they should be taught; only his emphasis was not on the law of Israel, but on the promise, by the prophets, of the coming of the Deliverer. Perhaps, the liberal Pharisees thought, Jesus was more a prophet than a rabbi. And so, for a time, they let him continue his work undisturbed. One of them, called Simon the Pharisee, mentioned in Luke 7:40, invited him to a banquet in his house. The incident, at the dinner, proved to be a trying one for Simon; but, apparently, he let the matter pass. Jesus had used a parable—an interesting and appealing form of object lesson—to convince him that persons who have much forgiven them, greatly love those who forgive. Besides all this, any Pharisee, even one in unacademic Galilee, liked a good discussion.

But the case was different when, as we may infer from the account in Mark 7:1, certain scribes and Pharisees came up from Jerusalem to look into the situation. They had been informed that, by slow degrees, Jesus had broken the Jewish law. The first instance had occurred in the house of Levi, later known as Matthew the Disciple.[7] There had been the usual banquet at which Levi had entertained his former fellow publicans.

[7] Mark 2:14-22.

Other guests, called "sinners," had been present; and Jesus and the disciples had been invited to share the feast. The occasion —we are reminded in Mark 2:19—had been like a wedding, a time of much merrymaking. Jesus' presence at a feast had suggested a manner of life so different, for example, from that of John the Baptist and his disciples, who were ascetics, that the Galilean Pharisees had questioned him about it. And Jesus had answered them with a little pronouncement parable, saying that the friends of the bridegroom could not fast so long as the bridegroom was with them. Then, perhaps wistfully, and looking about him at his followers, he had said: "But the days will come when the bridegroom shall be taken away from them, and then shall they fast." [8] It is interesting to be told that, according to Jewish law, the persons nearest to the bridegroom were exempt from ceremonial restrictions during the seven days of the wedding feast.[9] But what is important here is that Jesus had turned a point of ceremonial law into an occasion of announcing the Messianic feast that was even now made ready for them through his coming.

Later there had arisen the question of the Sabbath. Why had Jesus' disciples, walking through the fields on the Sabbath day, stopped to pluck ripe grains of wheat and eaten them? Jesus, again referring to the Messianic kingdom rather than to the Mosaic law, had answered: "The Son of man is Lord even of the sabbath day." [10]

But when, after a time, the scribes and Pharisees came up from Jerusalem, armed, as we read, with "the tradition of the elders," Jesus did not answer them with a Messianic invitation. He met them on their own ground, which was the Jewish law.[11] But his approach differed from theirs. They were concerned with the tradition of ceremonial purification; he was interested in the commandment of Moses. They insisted on the frequent washing of the hands; he answered by saying that God demanded of them a clean heart. It was evident that, even with the deep reverence Jesus shared with the Pharisees for the

[8] Matthew 9:15.
[9] See Klausner. *Jesus of Nazareth, op. cit.,* p. 274.
[10] Matthew 12:8.
[11] Mark 7:1-23.

teaching of the Old Testament, there was little possibility of an agreement between them. The incident also made plain the fact that Jesus' work in Galilee was approaching its anticipated crisis.

The separation between Jesus and the Pharisees was inevitable. It was not, as might be supposed, simply the result of a difference of human temperament or of an individual point of view. Jesus understood people; he knew the hearts of men: their hardness, tenderness, sinfulness; their unquenchable longing for deliverance from evil, and for God. To Simon the Pharisee, whose guest he was, Jesus said with the utmost freedom, "Simon, I have somewhat to say to thee"; and Simon answered with the same freedom: "Master, say on." The view often expressed that the differences between Jesus and the Pharisees were purely matters of personal opinion is superficial and untenable. The Law and the Gospel, indeed, belonged together. Both, as Saint Paul said clearly, were ordained of God. But they belonged to two different dispensations in the history of divine revelation. The Law was *first;* but the Gospel was *final.*[12] The great apostle, very early in the establishment of the Christian church, summed up the relation between them when he said: "The law was our schoolmaster to bring us unto Christ, that we might be justified by faith."[13] Jesus himself said: "Think not that I am come to destroy the law, or the prophets: I am not come to destroy but to fulfil."[14]

The early church was itself witness to this fact. Jesus, by his word and deed, was the fulfilment of the law. He was Messiah. The belief, indeed, of all devout people within Judaism had been that, when Messiah came, all bondage to sin would end and men and nations alike would learn to live in permanent peace.

Nevertheless, what Jesus had to say as a teacher and leader of men during his life on earth was important to the early church. The tradition in which his "mighty works" and "sayings" were placed together and carefully preserved was, as we have learned, given its earliest documentary form in the Gospel

[12] See Ephesians 1:10 and 3:2; Colossians 1:25.
[13] Galatians 3:24.
[14] Matthew 5:17.

of Mark and in the source called Q.   It was principally in Q that the sayings were incorporated.   In the course of time they became known as the teachings of Jesus, containing, in large part, the material underlying the so-called "ethics" of the gospel of the kingdom.

The summary of the earliest of these teachings is to be found in Matthew 5-7, and is known as the Sermon on the Mount.   In it the new law of the kingdom—which is not something added to the gospel of the kingdom but is identical with it—is clearly set forth.   What that law is, in its full content, and inseparable from the gospel, we shall see in a later chapter.   Meanwhile, as a guide to what is to follow, we may place against the tradition of the scribes and Pharisees this impressive summary of Jesus' "interim" ethical teaching :

> To love our God with all our strength and will;
> To covet nothing; to devise no ill
> Against our neighbors; to procure or do
> Nothing to others which we would not to
> Our very selves; not to revenge our wrong;
> To be content with little; not to long
> For wealth and greatness; to despise or jeer
> No man, and, if we be despised, to bear;
> To feed the hungry; to hold fast our crown;
> To take from others nought; to give our own,—
> These are the precepts, and, alas, in these
> What is so hard but *faith* can do with ease? [15]

[15] From the collected poems of Henry Vaughan.

Chapter 20

EVANGELISM IN GALILEE

I

THE CALL FOR DISCIPLES

By now the wave of Jesus' popularity was sweeping over Galilee. It had become true, as Mark had said, that all men sought after him. Demonstrations of his power at Capernaum and by the seaside had captivated the throngs of people, and he had sought to escape them by crossing over to the other side of the lake, not because he had no compassion on the multitudes but because he did not wish simply to be known as a popular healer. His aim, now more than ever, was to proclaim the Good News of the kingdom, to announce that it was immediately at hand, that prophecy was being fulfilled, and that the Son of man was soon to come in his glory to usher in the awaited Messianic age.

To this end he had already gathered around him certain men who were to accompany him in his mission. Among the first of them had been two brothers, Simon Peter and Andrew, both of them fishermen. To them Jesus had said, "Come ye after me, and I will make you to become fishers of men."[1] Almost immediately after that he had found two other men, also brothers and fishermen. They were James and John, the sons of Zebedee who owned a ship and hired his own servants. With these four companions Jesus had begun his ministry of preaching and healing. His first appearances, as we have learned, had been in the synagogue in Capernaum. But soon he had found himself teaching the people publicly, either in Peter's house or from Zebedee's boat by the edge of the lake. This latter place had given him a larger public contact and personal freedom from

[1] Mark 1:17.

the curious pressing crowds. Then, as we read, when the investigating scribes had also come to look in upon the scene, Jesus, walking by the gate of customs on the Roman road that led through Capernaum, had seen Levi the Publican, seated at the customs desk, and had said to him, "Follow me." And Mark records simply that Levi, later to be called Matthew, arose and followed Jesus.

With these five men by his side, Jesus now began his larger ministry. People came from near and far to hear him: some, Mark says,[2] from as far as Tyre and Sidon; others from Jerusalem; some to be healed and to praise God; others, in the "hardness of their hearts," to hinder those who would be helped and to plot against him. Altogether, besides the little company of disciples and friends, there were three groups of onlookers and hearers of what Jesus was saying: (1) the people; (2) the Pharisees and scribes; (3) the Herodians. Each group, we should observe, had its own motive for coming and listening.

But what was most important—at this period of respite, before the opposition to him, now begun, could take an aggressive form—was that the eager multitudes came. The three Synoptists agree to this fact and stress it; and their record reads like authentic history. All Galilee was stirred; great hope was awakened in the minds and hearts of men; the sick, as never before, were being healed; those possessed of evil demons —that is, the demented—were restored to sanity; and it now appeared that the ardent hope of all true Messianists was soon to be fulfilled. And Jesus, as we have seen, himself shared this hope. The signs of the new age were everywhere at hand. An urgency greater than that which had possessed John the Baptist moved Jesus to greater activity, even against—rather, more truly, because of—a noticeably gathering opposition.

Besides the five—Andrew, Peter, James, John, and Matthew —other men were now added to the circle of intimate disciples until it numbered twelve—symbolical of the twelve tribes of Israel over which the twelve apostles were one day to rule in the new dispensation of the realized kingdom of God.[3] The most

2 Mark 3 :8.
3 Matthew 19 :28.

important of them were Philip, Bartholomew, and Thomas; and, after them, the man who was later to be the notorious traitor, Judas Iscariot. The Twelve may conveniently be listed in three groups of four: (1) Peter, James, John, and Andrew; (2) Matthew, Philip, Thomas, and Bartholomew; (3) James, the son of Alphaeus, Thaddaeus, Simon Zelotes and Judas Iscariot.

The Fourth Gospel, drawing for its information on an independent source, mentions also Nathanael, and adds that Philip found him and brought him to Jesus.[4] This Gospel then says that Andrew, who until that time had been a disciple of John the Baptist, sought out Peter, and that the two brothers thereafter followed Jesus. The records here, as elsewhere in the Gospel narratives, differ; but their general agreement, we note, is most remarkable. It attests to the historicity of the Palestinian record that here outlines the greater divine history of which the Gospels are the special revelation.

How this divine history may be seen breaking in upon the Palestinian scene before us—and how intimately thereby the four Gospels are related to one another—is at this point well illustrated in the Fourth Gospel's account of Jesus' words to Nathanael: "Verily, verily, I say unto you: Hereafter ye shall see heaven open, and the angels of God ascending and descending upon the Son of man."[5] The reference to the Son of man is obviously apocalyptic in its original meaning. Can the Fourth Evangelist, like Matthew and Luke, have had access to Mark's Gospel? If so, the Gospel of John, different as its narrative is from that of the Synoptists, is to be regarded as in close touch with the most primitive Christian tradition. That fact, as we have noted,[6] seems to be borne out by the Gospel's intense Jewishness, even though Greek ideas are freely used by the Evangelist to interpret his profound Christian teaching.

But a second question, at this stage of our study, presses for an answer. If Andrew, and possibly Peter, were originally John's disciples, did not Jesus begin his ministry in Judea where

4 John 1:35-51.
5 John 1:51.
6 See Chapter 12.

the Baptist preached? That is the impression the Fourth Gospel
clearly gives us; and we must therefore reckon with this circumstance. It seems to imply that Jesus, for a short time after
his baptism, remained in the region close to John before going
to Galilee to begin his own ministry there. And we should
assume that to have been a very natural thing for him to do in
consideration of the fact that he owed much to the occasion,
even if not to the content, of the message of that great prophet.
The difference between the preaching of Jesus and that of John
has already been pointed out.[7] In another Chapter we shall see
that just as John's preaching prompted the beginning of Jesus'
public ministry, so the Baptist's death precipitated its final Galilean crisis. In their earthly course their careers were strangely
united. The recording Evangelists were well aware of that
fact. There is therefore little cause for surprise that the Galileans were sometimes confused about their separate missions.
But that the early church, after all the events had transpired,
clearly saw the difference between the work of Jesus and that
of John is shown in the account of Matthew, who reports Jesus
as saying: "Among them that are born of women there hath
risen not a greater than John the Baptist; notwithstanding he
that is least in the kingdom of heaven is greater than he." [8]

Matthew, completing Mark's account, and viewing the events
from a later day, gives four distinct reasons why Jesus chose
his twelve disciples: (1) that they might be his companions in
his earthly ministry; (2) that they might be witnesses to God's
mighty work being wrought through him; (3) that they might
be given his power over "unclean spirits," and his authority to
heal the sick; (4) that they might be sent forth to the lost sons
of the house of Israel and preach to them, saying: "The kingdom of heaven is at hand." [9]

Having chosen the disciples, he now proceeds to instruct
them. The Evangelist sums up certain striking things Jesus
says to them: (1) that the command to preach the Good News
is urgent, the time short—the field is ripe unto the harvest;

[7] See Chapter 17.
[8] Matthew 11:11.
[9] Matthew 10.

(2) that they are to make no lengthy preparation, but to go, saying to the people of any house into which they enter, "Peace be in this house"; (3) that they will be ill received by many; it will be as though sheep were going out to persuade wolves; (4) that they are to be wise, harmless, not courting martyrdom, but expecting persecution; (5) that they are to go without fear —Did not God keep watch over the little sparrow in the field?

But Matthew's account of the sending forth of the Twelve does not end there. He writes as one who sees the beginning from the end. The whole picture is before him, both of what then occurred and of what was further anticipated. The great expectation, he recalls, was that the Son of man would come in his glory even before the disciples had completed their mission. Mark's brief report states the fact with dramatic brevity: the day of judgment was at hand for those who hearkened not, and believed not; they would be destroyed, as were Sodom and Gomorrha.[10] But Matthew looks first at what actually transpired during the earthly life of Christ; then at the life of the Christian community from the death of Christ to his own time; and finally, also down the years yet unknown to him, when the Christian church would face its long and severe encounter with the world.

The setting of the story, in Matthew 10, reflects the task which the Christian disciples and evangelists were facing in the apostolic age. Matthew's perspective is accurate and clear. He retains Mark's eschatological focus; the apocalyptic picture does not fade away before him; rather, it is intensified by these words of Jesus: "Ye shall not have gone over the cities of Israel, till the Son of man be come." And what is equally if not more important is his use of the symbolism of the Suffering Servant in his reference to the Cross when he quotes Jesus as saying: "He that taketh not his cross, and followeth after me, is not worthy of me. . . . He that loseth his life for my sake shall find it."[11] The Son of man is the Suffering Servant, even in this early passage in Matthew's narrative; and Christian dis-

[10] See Genesis 19:1-28, Matthew 10:15.
[11] Matthew 10:38, 39.

cipleship is defined by him in these terms.[12] "The disciple is
not above his master": these are the words of the conditions
under which Jesus has called the Twelve to be near him. He
says to them, "Follow me," only to command them saying:
"Go ye"; "Fear not"; "He that loseth his life shall find it"; "He
that receiveth you receiveth me."

> For he who follows Christ must not respect
> Promotion, money, glory, ease, delight;
> But poverty, reproof, and self-neglect,
> Disgrace, tears, hunger, cold, thirst, scorn, despite;
> Friends, father, mother, brethren, children, wife,
> Must be forgone, yea, lands and goods and life.[13]

II

THE URGENCY OF THE MESSAGE

But the test of discipleship was yet to come. The training
for it lay yet in the future. When that time came, Jesus would
be going to Jerusalem to face the indignation of the Jews, the
sophistry of the scribes, the evil plotting of the chief priests,
the agony of Gethsemane, the betrayal of Judas, and death on the
Cross. After the crisis in Galilee, and under the shadow of the
Cross, the conception these humble fishermen and followers of
Jesus were to get of what it meant to be a disciple of Christ was
to undergo a change. It would take on new depth as visions of
new heights appeared—like a mountain landscape in which, in
the late afternoon, the cliffs fill the ravines with darkness, while
their crests are radiant in the sunlight. In those days to come,
filled half with the disciples' foolish questioning and half with
their solemn wonder, Jesus would ask them: "Are ye able to
drink of the cup that I shall drink of?" and they would answer:
"We are able." As Matthew the Apostle later recorded the
sayings of Jesus, he must have thought of this rash promise and
of the martyrdom of Peter and James. But of all this that was
to come, the Twelve, when they were sent out, were unaware.
Mark tells us that "they went out, and preached that men should

---

[12] Matthew 10:38-40.
[13] Author unknown. Poem signed *I.F.* (1613).

repent; and they cast out many devils, and anointed with oil many that were sick, and healed them." [14]

It is pertinent to note that Luke, supplementing his version of Mark's account, adds the statement that, a little later, Jesus sent out seventy followers, in pairs, to go "into every city and place whither he himself would come," saying to them: "The harvest truly is great, but the laborers are few: pray ye therefore the Lord of the Harvest that he would send forth laborers into the harvest." [15] It is obvious, from a close look at them, that the accounts are related to one another and to those of Matthew and Mark. We have here an instance of a very early and trustworthy tradition. This tradition was, in all likelihood, current in a number of versions which were then being orally transmitted. We note how it abounds in the paradigms, or striking pronouncements of Jesus, that served as timely texts for primitive apostolic preaching. Good quotable examples of them are these: Luke 10:2, "The harvest is great . . . the laborers are few"; Luke 10:7, "The laborer is worthy of his hire"; Luke 10:20, "Rejoice, because your names are written in heaven"; Luke 10:23, "Blessed are the eyes which see the things ye see." Such sayings, from the beginning crystallized into their present form, are evidence first of the tradition's historic authenticity, and second, also of its eschatological character.

Luke records Jesus as saying twice, in two verses found close together, that the "kingdom of God is come nigh unto you," and as adding significantly: "Be ye sure of this." The Seventy return. They are overjoyed that "even the devils are subject" unto them. Jesus replies, convincingly, "I beheld Satan as lightning fall from heaven." Then, in words that invite us to a glimpse into the inner consciousness of Jesus, his assurance that God's will was being fulfilled in him, the Evangelist adds, in Luke 10:21-22, that Jesus "rejoiced in spirit." The "Messianic secret"—that is, the hidden mystery of God's will and plan for his life—was truly revealed to him. It was the secret hidden from the wise of the world, but known to him, as a little child knows the loving care of his father. After that there follows

---

[14] Mark 6:12-13.
[15] *Cf.* Luke 9:1-6 and 10:1-24.

this declaration which, with what immediately follows it, well sums up Jesus' own knowledge of the aim and end of his entire earthly ministry:[16]

> All things are delivered to me of my Father:
> And no man knoweth who the Son is but the Father;
> And who the Father is but the Son,
> And he to whom the Son will reveal him.

Mark records, in Chapters 4:35-5:43, four so-called "mighty works" of Jesus which, in Matthew 8:23-9:26, precede the sending forth of the Twelve. They are the stilling of the storm; the curing of the Gadarene demoniac; the healing of the afflicted woman; and the raising of Jairus' daughter. In them, as never before, the disciples are represented as witnessing a demonstration of Jesus' power: (1) over "the wind and the sea"; (2) over the unclean spirit which called itself "Legion"; (3) over sickness, cured by faith; and (4) over death itself.[17]

These were indeed mighty acts. However we interpret them, they are an integral—and, for the Evangelist's aim and purpose, a necessary—part of the Gospel record. Their explanation puzzles us, relying, as we often do, on a "natural" understanding of them. But, as we have already learned,[18] they were miracles, and as such fulfilled a twofold aim: they witnessed to the fact that the kingdom of heaven was at hand; and they were the signs of God's endorsement of Jesus as the Son of man who was being revealed to the world as the chosen Messiah. Were not the Incarnation and the Resurrection the greatest of all miracles to the early Christians among whom the Gospels were

---

[16] Luke 10:22. See also John 5:17-31 and John 17.

[17] An interesting note on demonology appears in Brooks Atkinson's review of Elizabeth Sprigge's book, *The Strange Life of August Strindberg,* in *The New York Times,* August 7, 1949, in which the reviewer says: "He [Strindberg] was anything but a sadistic monster, although he frequently behaved as though he were one. But the sufferings he visited upon his wives [he was three times married] and children must have been shattering; for they were the victims of demons that possessed him. . . . *The Confession of a Fool* . . . is pure malevolence—a scream of rage and vilification; and Strindberg was horrified by it as soon as he had written it." The Gadarene demoniac, mentioned in Mark 5, has here a convincing modern counterpart.

[18] See pp. 182ff.

edited and composed? Obviously, such a point of view must even then have been Christological. And such, in fact, it was; and it was held no less by Mark than by Matthew and Luke. Christology—by which is meant an interpretation of the meaning of the divine person and work of Christ on earth—is the very sum and substance of the culminating Gospel of John.

It is admittedly, we must observe, difficult for us to comprehend such a descent into nature as that which Christ made in the Incarnation and such an ascent as that accomplished by him in the Resurrection. These divine historic truths are apt to be vague theological concepts to us and little more. But to help us to an insight into them, our daily experience offers us this suggestive parallel: the human mind, too, descends into nature and rises out of it again. When this is accomplished, the result is human civilization and world history. Now, by analogy, when God accomplishes this, we call it divine history; and the incarnation and the resurrection of Christ are the beginning and the conclusion of this divine act.

We moderns, if it will better content us, may call these miracle stories by the name of legends; only we must remember that there was a reason why there should be such legends at all told about Jesus. Mark the Evangelist reports that the mighty deeds of Christ were possible because of the people's faith in him; and this faith was shared by those who communicated them as an integral part of the oral Christian tradition, and later also by those who put them into writing. But the miracles were not works of the disciples' deluded fancy. They were accepted facts. Moreover, we read that the Pharisees, who did not look with favor on the work of Jesus, did not deny them; they merely offered their own explanation of what they saw by saying, for example, of one such typical occurrence, that Jesus exercised authority over demons through the power of Beelzebub the prince of devils.[19] The plain truth underlying the stories is that Jesus was believed by everyone to be a very extraordinary person. The disciples close to him, like the surrounding multitudes, increasingly marveled, and now "feared exceedingly," as they

[19] Mark 3:22.

began to say to one another : "What manner of man is this, that even the wind and the sea obey him?" [20]

Clearly, the time was ripening toward the season of a greater manifestation of Jesus' person to these men who were now more and more close to him. This divine "secret" of who he was—that he was indeed none other than the Messiah—was to come to light at Caesarea Philippi. When that time came, hostility toward Jesus, as well as loyalty to him, was to become a twofold major issue. People on the outer orbit of the circle of his followers were to drift away from him; those at the center were to be held faithful to him by a strange new attachment. It was no longer to be his preaching, but his person, that was to claim their allegiance. A time of great dividing was at hand—like that of the time of Moses in the desert, and of Elijah on Mount Carmel.[21] Jesus, himself pointing to that impending crisis, may be heard saying, [22]

> I am come to cast fire upon the earth;
> And how much I wish it were already kindled!
> Think not that my coming will bring you peace:
> Verily, it will not bring you peace, but a sword.

The drama of redemption was reaching its second act; and the Evangelists who in a later day looked back upon it all were—by writing the story of the earthly life of Jesus—but filling in the necessary details of this Christological and eschatological history.

Meanwhile, according to the story, the disciples had gone forth on their evangelistic mission and had returned. And having reported their extraordinary success, they awaited the future. The immediate days before them were shrouded in mystery. Did they dream of the time beyond that, when they would become the first apostles? We do not know. The Evangelists, of course, looking backward from the apostolic age in which they lived, saw and knew it all. Did they, too, dream of the ages of Christendom yet to come? We, now, who look into

[20] Mark 4:41.
[21] See Exodus 19, and I Kings 18.
[22] Luke 12:49-51, and Matthew 10:34-36.

world history through the intervening centuries, should be able to find the answer to the first disciples' question: "What manner of man is this, that even the wind and the sea obey him?" The evidence is plainly before us. Have not the wind and the sea been obedient to the gospel: first, on the lake of Galilee; then, on the Mediterranean; after that, on the Atlantic; and, at last also, on the Pacific? Let the modern Christian disciple stand in wonder and take heart.

Chapter 21

DISCOURSES ON THE KINGDOM OF GOD

I

THEIR GOSPEL SETTING AND BACKGROUND

Before undertaking to discover what Jesus taught—and before assuming that he was a teacher at all—we must bring his entire earthly life into a closer focus and ask ourselves who, in reality, he was and what he came into the world to do. For the "sayings" of Jesus, like those of any great historic teacher, must be studied by a threefold approach: (1) in their "ideological" context, that is, in the light of the principal ideas illuminating the age; (2) from the point of view of the specific intent and aim of the teacher; and (3) in a manner that will make them intelligible to us who live in our own time. We must therefore ask ourselves three pertinent questions. First, from what background—not chiefly of race or place but of thought—did Jesus speak? Second, what, against this background, looking at his own time and into the future, did he mean to say and do? Finally, how are we, who are both helped and hindered by the intervening centuries, to understand and apply these teachings to our modern life?

In our age, and for some time past, two prevailing views have been held concerning the person of Christ. They are aptly designated by the terms "pietism" and "liberalism." Pietism has been strongly individualistic and anti-intellectual. It has stressed personal salvation, been active in building moral character, but passive toward world problems. Its strength has been its unalterable faith in Christ the God-man whose kingdom is not of this world but through whose coming into the world individual men are offered redemption from sin and a spiritual new birth into an everlasting life in the kingdom of heaven.

Liberalism, born of modern times and rising in the nineteenth century out of a background of humanitarianism, has been predominantly sociological. It has directed its attention toward the perfection of man and toward the building of an ideal Christian society. According to it, Jesus is the ideal man, the example of true manhood, the representative of man's "higher self" toward which, by an evolutionary process, he is destined more and more to grow. Salvation, by this liberalistic view, is the humanizing process through which the kingdom of God is to be progressively realized. The kingdom of God itself is defined as an ideal brotherhood, free from sin, whose seat is the lower or sensual part of man. Evil is a deficiency which the gradual and inevitable enlightenment of man will overcome.

Where pietism is pessimistic, liberalism is optimistic. It believes in Man—underestimating his own helplessness against sin, overestimating his natural goodness. The liberalist has called himself a modern Christian. He believes he has outgrown the primitive views of the pietist; he regards historic orthodoxy as out of date; he has abandoned the church's past interest in doctrine for "practical" Christianity; and he welcomes a more secular idea of religion, a more simple and applicable one—so he thinks—in which the kingdom of God is pictured as an ethical-cultural ideal, and Jesus is regarded as the gentle and unsophisticated teacher.

It must be said that neither of these views offers us an adequate interpretation of the gospel and of Jesus' teaching concerning it. A more profound historic significance underlies our Lord's discourses on the kingdom of God. Theologians and historical critics have lately become very much aware of this fact. Consequently a third viewpoint, under the name of Neo-Orthodoxy, has come to the timely forefront among Biblical scholars. It seeks to stress anew both the divinity and the humanity of Christ, and to look upon the teaching of Jesus as having its implied setting in what is called the history, or drama, of divine revelation.

The sayings and parables which constitute this teaching are, by their context and character, an integral part of this history. To be understood they must be examined, first, in the light of

Jesus' coming to bring the Good News of the kingdom of God, and, after that, in consideration of his announced assumption of the role of Messiah by which the Kingdom is to be further defined, interpreted, and at last consummated. In other words, the teachings of Jesus are discourses on the *meaning* of the gospel. They are not simply the wise sayings of a social and ethical philosopher. It is taken for granted that these teachings are moral; but they have to do with a morality that is not merely natural, or humanitarian, but Christian. They have to do with the "good life" as defined and lived within the gospel pattern. That pattern—as it has yet to be examined in greater detail—is (1) Christological, and (2) eschatological.

Tested by what the gospel says of it, the good life is not simply idealized or commended. It is clearly outlined, divinely judged, and blessedly rewarded. The virtue called "goodness" takes on a new meaning. In its absolute sense it belongs to God only; yet it is distinctly enjoined on everyone who would follow Christ.[1] In short, the good life becomes a law, the law of the Kingdom. According to it, our Christian duty is not only to have a sensitive conscience but to obey the gospel. In a more direct and urgent sense than that implied by the poet Wordsworth, the voice of duty to the Christian is the "stern daughter of the voice of God."[2] The compulsion that we must feel as we read the Sermon on the Mount, or the Kingdom parables, is no less than that which was upon Christ himself when, proceeding to his own trial in Jerusalem, he said to a wealthy young man who would be one of his disciples:

> If thou wilt *enter into* life,
> Keep the commandments: ...
> Thou shalt do no murder,
> Thou shalt not commit adultery,
>
> Thou shalt not steal,
> Thou shalt not bear false witness;
> Honor thy father and thy mother;
> And, Thou shalt love thy neighbor as thyself....

[1] Matthew 19:16-21.
[2] Wordsworth, "Ode to Duty" (1805).

If thou wilt *be perfect,*
Go and sell that thou hast, and give to the poor;
And thou shalt have treasure in heaven;
And come and follow me.[3]

Clearly, here the Old Testament law is now annulled by the law of the Gospel. The old commandments are still in force. But they are described as only opening the door to a new life. On the door's panel, we may say, are written these words: "They who enter here must love their neighbors as themselves." And they who, having entered into the Kingdom, would find its hidden treasure, must leave behind them their worldly goods and their love for them and follow Christ. For as we near the climax of the Sermon on the Mount, we are told:[4]

Enter ye in at the strait gate:
For wide is the gate, and broad is the way,
That leadeth to destruction,
And many there be which go in thereat;
Because strait is the gate, and narrow is the way,
Which leadeth unto life;
And few there be that find it.

We can see how all moral values are here being transvaluated as the gospel passes through them. For instance, in one of Jesus' typical sayings, recorded in Matthew 5:16, we are bidden to let our "light so shine before men" that they may see our "good works" and glorify our "Father which is in heaven." But in the background of this commandment is the reminder, as Francis Quarles several centuries ago so well expressed it: "Thy flame is not thine own: it is a debt thou ow'st thy Master." Again, at the beginning of the Sermon, the virtue of meekness is enjoined on all Christians. Its reward is the inheritance of the earth. The outward paradox of such a statement is obvious. It must mean that the meek are the strong whose strength is in the gospel. This truth is well interpreted by the words and life of Saint Paul: "I can do all things through Christ who strength-

[3] Matthew 19:17-21.
[4] Matthew 7:13-14.

eneth me." It is by the power of the gospel, the Apostle says, that the world will one day be overcome and ruled.

II

Their General Character and Content

These examples serve to illustrate how the teachings of Jesus, like his life, have their setting within the framework of the Christian gospels. On closer view it will be observed to be the gospel (1) preached as the good tidings of the impending kingdom of God, (2) interpreted to the world through the Messiahship of Jesus and symbolized in the doctrine of the Cross, and (3) represented as coming to its full consummation in history through the church and, beyond history, in a final world judgment and an everlasting glory of the saints. All the sayings and parables fit into this framework like the monologues and dialogues of a great drama. The drama of divine redemption may indeed, without compulsion, be viewed successively in three acts —mighty Acts of God—in which Jesus is the heroic figure, the strong Son of God, the protagonist of mankind for the redemption of the world. In the first act he appears as the mighty prophet and healer; in the second, as the "transfigured Jesus," assuming the role of the Suffering Servant of God; in the third, as the dying savior and risen Lord of men.

Some of the teachings of Jesus—if we may so classify them —belong only to one of these "acts," or aspects, of the Kingdom's unfolding history. Wherever, in the Gospels, certain of the sayings and parables refer to questions having to do with the disciples' immediate guidance and conduct, and by that fact are given a setting that is eschatological—pointing to the hourly awaited goal and triumph of the heavenly kingdom—they may be listed in the category of "interim-ethics." These teachings make their appearance in the drama's first act, recede to the background in the second, and reappear in the third. Their intent is to heighten the anticipation of the climax of the divine drama and so to keep in clear sight the end toward which God in His wise providence is directing the course of gospel history.

Among such sayings or teachings, for example, are the following:

> Take ... no thought for the morrow.
>
> Resist not evil.
>
> Give to him that asketh thee, and from him that would borrow of thee turn thou not away.
>
> The kingdom of heaven is at hand: Go, preach, heal the sick, cleanse the lepers, raise the dead, cast out devils.
>
> Provide neither gold, nor silver, nor brass ... nor scrip for your journey.
>
> Render to Caesar the things that are Caesar's.
>
> Leave the dead to bury the dead: come and follow me.
>
> Be ... ready.
>
> He that endureth to the end shall be saved.

These sayings, and others like them, are so obviously tied together with the context of an apocalyptic outlook as to be inseparable from it. They are not simply moral teachings dispensed to us through maxims or precepts. They are gospel prophecy. For, by comparison, moral teachings as such are broadly philosophical. They have their roots in an observation of human behavior; they spring up and grow in a certain climate of opinion; their expression takes the form of a cultural pattern; and their justification is grounded in man's reasoning faculty. Morality, in this broad sense, is the application of wisdom—reduced to "common sense"—to the necessary task of living. Certainly, we may not say that Jesus possessed no such wisdom and that he did not act on it. He is represented in Luke 16:1-8, for example, as comparing the wisdom of the sons of light with that of the children of the world, and as saying that the sons of light ought, in matters pertaining to their kingdom, to be as wise as the children of the world are in theirs. But the point of distinction is that the kingdom of God is its own realm, and that it has therefore its own moral law. The consideration of this law is the study of gospel ethics.

The general background of Jesus' teaching, as the Synoptic Gospels present it to us, is clearly eschatological. Many of the sayings and parables are cast in the mold of apocalypses: they are revelations of the breaking through of God's kingdom into

the world, together with directions to those who eagerly await its coming. Other teachings—traceable, some scholars think, to the elaborating influence of the early church—have a more general application to Christians of all time. Among them are those found, for example, in the Beatitudes, the discourses on the Mosaic law and on prayer,[5] and in certain parables on the growth of the Kingdom[6]—the parables of the Sower, the Mustard Seed, the Leaven, the Hidden Treasure, and the Pearl. In them we can foresee the establishment of the Christian church and its historic growth throughout the world. Nevertheless, even in these parables, the stress on the Kingdom's immediacy and urgency is unmistakably present.

To look on the sayings of Jesus as though they were idealized "social teachings" to be applied to a later established historic church is to distort the picture. That Jesus founded the church no one can deny. He built it by his own life, and more particularly by his death and resurrection. It is, in a historic as well as symbolical sense, his risen body of which believing Christians of all time are the several living members. As his bodily life on earth was real, so the church, too, is a historic fact and a reality. Its founding was the last of the "mighty acts" of God accomplished through the earthly life of Christ.

The church on earth is not the entire kingdom of God. The Kingdom is a heavenly one; it is absolute; in it the will of God is done perfectly; and to it belong also the saints who have departed this earthly life and are in a state of everlasting blessedness. The church on earth, we should rather say, is the Kingdom's full and complete *historic* revelation. All that God can tell us through history is revealed in the person and life of Christ; and all that Christ has meant to the world is summed up in the historic Christian church. But, ultimately, the kingdom of God is above history. That, we must conclude, was its essential meaning to Jesus; and the early Christian tradition, on its way toward becoming the written Gospels, does not alter or distort it. It is we who distort this meaning when, yielding to the pragmatic secular temper of our time, we try to make of

[5] Matthew 5-7.
[6] Matthew 13.

the kingdom of God a social Utopia, a land of Eldorado, to be reached by humanitarian efforts and inhabited by an assorted population of men of natural good will.

When, however, the Gospels speak of the heavenly kingdom, they do not mean a purely transcendental one. The kingdom of God does not transcend the earth; rather, the earth is encompassed by it, as the temporal is encompassed by the eternal. The gospel, as history, is this eternal kingdom breaking into time, continually disturbing it by the mighty acts of God, disturbing it with the sense of guilt and sin and the promise of salvation from sin, and never leaving it until time ends and eternal peace reigns in heaven. That, we must remind ourselves, is what is meant by saying that the kingdom of God is an eschatological concept. And it is within the pattern of this concept that the sayings and parables of Jesus are to be understood.

The words no less than the works of Jesus have their setting in this eschatological pattern. Both, in this sense, are acts of God. The parables and the miracles have the same origin, move toward the same outlook, are characterized by the same urgency. They are "signs"—proofs, in history (1) that the kingdom of heaven is at hand, (2) that it is forcibly active in grace and judgment as both a permeating leaven and a kindled fire, and (3) that, after a time of turbulence and testing on earth, it will be brought to its glorious conclusion in the marriage feast of Christ and the saints. History will have ended: and, as we read in the parable of the Ten Virgins, they that are "ready" will go in with the Bridegroom to the feast of the marriage; and the door to the temporal order will be shut.[7]

The symbolism here put to use in an interpretation of history may appear to us today as ancient and Oriental. Yet no language could better express what all men deeply know about the meaning implicit in it: the joy of hope fulfilled; the tragedy of wasted desire; the warning against "the ungirt loin and the unlit lamp"; and the finality of all temporal things. Here, we will admit, is a philosophy of history with a goal. If, in contemplating the parable, that goal may yet seem far off, we do unwisely to fall asleep. The signs of the Kingdom's coming

[7] Matthew 25:13.

are most surely seen at midnight. Therefore, from the parable's context, we are to take this warning:

> Be ready:
> Trim the lamp of your faith;
> Replenish your lamp with the oil of grace;
> Wait for the hour of the Lord's coming.
> For, behold, the kingdom of heaven is at hand.

Chapter 22

THE SAYINGS AND PARABLES OF JESUS

I

Jesus the Word of Life

We have already said that we must begin our study of what Jesus said by asking ourselves who he was. The verdict of the early church, as the Gospel of John records it, was that Jesus himself was the Word of God.[1] This was said to mean that God was Himself speaking through the entire earthly life of Christ. The inference is that Jesus' acts and words alike are a divine revelation. What Jesus teaches, according to this Gospel, is therefore centered in his own divine nature as the living Word of which every saying and parable spoken by him is but an unfolding exposition. Again, the Fourth Evangelist tells us that when—at a crucial moment in what we now call gospel history—Jesus addresses the disciples with the question, "Will ye also go away?" Simon Peter answers for them, saying, "To whom shall we go? Thou hast the words of eternal life." [2]

It is in this context that the sayings and parables of Jesus are to be approached and examined. Such an examination does not at this time concern itself with the question of whether or not these sayings have been literally recorded by the Evangelists. A greater and more important fact is established by them. For just as the kingdom of God is itself the symbol of divine history breaking through world history, so in Jesus' discourses on the Kingdom the word of God is continually breaking through the barriers of communication into language whose peculiar symbolism, like that of the parable, is intended to convey the "secret," or hidden mystery, of the Kingdom. Both the word of God and the Kingdom of God, in this sense, are mysteries—

[1] John 1:1-14.
[2] John 6:67-68.

that is, truths supernaturally revealed; and human language and human history are—and must be—used to interpret them. For though we may know inwardly these divine truths of which the Gospels speak—as, for instance, we may be fully aware of space and time without at all comprehending them—there is for us, except through the vocabulary of symbolism, no other way in which they can be rationally understood. In all this our attempted study we should keep ourselves reminded of the words of Saint Paul, that "we have this treasure in earthly vessels."

Let us try, now, to state the facts more simply. The outer framework for our understanding of the sayings and parables of Jesus is given us in the form of a situation or a story. But within this story or situation there lies the concealed truth ready to be revealed to the person who is looking for it. The Kingdom of God is such a revelation. Only he who awaits it eagerly, and with insight into its nature, can comprehend its coming. An example taken from the Gospels, found in Luke 14, will illustrate how this truth is made plain. The setting in the narrative is an incident that occurs in the house of a prominent Pharisee. It is the Sabbath day, and Jesus has been invited to a meal. Other guests are present, and everyone is extremely curious to see what will happen. Luke says that "they watched him." But Jesus, too, is observant. He notices how the guests look about as they arrive and "choose out the chief rooms." Then Jesus begins to give the guests some good advice on choosing a modest place at a wedding and waiting for the host to assign to the most worthy their places of distinction. The advice is homely; it seems merely to suggest prudence and good sense. But Luke calls these remarks of Jesus a parable.[3] Evidently the saying has a deeper symbolical meaning not discerned by the guests generally—who here represent the multitudes of the world. But one of them—symbolizing those that "have eyes to see, and ears to hear"—understands and sums up the meaning in these Messianic words:

> Blessed
> Is he that shall eat bread
> In the kingdom of God.

[3] Luke 14:7.

There is good reason for believing that we have in many of the sayings and parables of the Gospels a record of the very words—*ipsissima verba*—spoken by Jesus on various occasions during his earthly ministry. The sayings are strikingly original in form, too obviously original to have been invented or distorted by the ensuing time. It is a sign of originality in any spoken or written paragraph to recognize in it a certain quality of structure that remains firm—like the texture of wool or the fiber of oak—no matter how hard and frequently it may be put to later use. It is this very quality in the language of things said or written that makes hearers or readers like them, want to learn, to quote, and to preserve them. That, in the accepted sense, is what is meant by the living word. Jesus' word, we have said, was Life to his hearers; and the poetry in which it found expression often made a twofold appeal to them: to the outer sense and to the soul. It had the quality of the Hebrew vernacular, the Aramaic tongue. His utterances were rich in the use of epigram and familiar Palestinian imagery; and they were generally characterized by the three distinguishing traits of Hebrew poetry: repetition, rhythm, and antithesis.[4] Illustrations of these traits are to be found throughout the Sermon on the Mount which has come down to us through the source Q in the form of a memorable collection of our Lord's sayings. Here is an example in which repetition is forcibly used with a pleasing, rhythmic, and indelible effect:[5]

> Ask, and it shall be given you;
> Seek, and ye shall find;
> Knock, and it shall be opened unto you.
> For everyone that asketh receiveth;
> And he that seeketh, findeth;
> And to him that knocketh it shall be opened.

Another example in which repetition and antithesis are rhythmically joined together to reach a balanced and satisfying

---

[4] See M. Goguel, *The Life of Jesus* (New York: The Macmillan Co., 1933), pp. 296 ff.; C. F. Burney, *The Poetry of Our Lord* (New York: Oxford University Press, 1922).

[5] Matthew 7:7-8.

conclusion is presented to us in this passage taken from Matthew 6:19-21:

> Lay not up for yourselves treasures upon earth,
> Where moth and rust doth corrupt,
> And where thieves break through and steal.
> But lay up for yourselves treasures in heaven,
> Where neither moth nor rust doth corrupt,
> And where thieves do not break through nor steal.
>> For where your treasure is,
>> There will your heart be also.

We must admit that these signs of originality and poetry in the words of Jesus are sometimes obscured in the narrative the Evangelists have preserved for us. It is noticeable, however, that Matthew has retained their primitive form more literally —and in a closer adherence to their Old Testament background —than has Luke, who in his own lively style of composition has added much that is interesting and new but has allowed the original pattern of Jesus' sayings to be slightly changed—not detrimentally but nevertheless actually—as the following comparison will show. In Matthew 5:44-45, for example, we read:

> I say unto you:
> Love your enemies,
> Bless them that curse you,
> Do good to them that hate you,
> And pray for them which despitefully use you, and persecute you:
> That ye may be the children of your Father which is in heaven.

In Luke 6:27-29 we note the altered rhythm, the continuation of the theme, and the omission of the summarizing conclusion:

> I say unto you which hear:
> Love your enemies,
> Do good to them which hate you,
> Bless them that curse you,
> And pray for them which despitefully use you.
> And unto him that smiteth thee on the one cheek,
>> Offer also the other.

Of the sayings of Jesus, those contained in the Sermon on the Mount are, as we have said, of first importance. Among them the Beatitudes and the Lord's Prayer are especially noteworthy. In the Beatitudes the good life is given its definitive gospel setting. It is the good life designed for those who seek to enter the kingdom of heaven. Nothing, except by implication, is said of valor, of courtesy, of honor, or of liberty, equality, and fraternity—such shibboleths and codes as those based on a philosophy of natural morality—though there is room, and to spare, for the exercise of all the human virtues as the event of the kingdom touches them in its course of breaking through history and into secular society and charging them with its supernatural presence and power. For nothing in nature or history escapes this penetrating and transvaluating power since the event of its release into the world. The kingdom of heaven, we must note again, is but a name for the event in history by which, since its occurrence, all things are changed: all kingdoms, all powers, all acts of men, including their deeper motives, are affected by it, stirred to activity: all evil, to open hostility; all good, to a friendly acceptance; and to it, at last, all authority on earth is to be subjected. The kingdom—by this Hebrew-Jewish-Christian concept of divine revelation—is itself supernatural and absolute. Its coming is an event in history. The earthly life of Christ is the historical medium through which this act of God is accomplished; and the Christian community, remembering Jesus and treasuring this divine history, is its perennial witness on earth. Such is the gospel message of which the Gospels tell us; and it is from this point of view that all that Jesus said and did is to be interpreted.

The Beatitudes, therefore, are so many expressions of the blessedness of belonging to this kingdom. And since the kingdom is itself an eschatological concept, the Beatitudes are also, or at least mainly, eschatological. We note, by the Gospel record, that two of the blessings imply that the Kingdom is a present possession, while six refer to it as a future promise. The poor in spirit, and those who suffer persecution for the kingdom's sake, already possess it; those that mourn, that hunger

for righteousness, the meek, the merciful, the peacemakers, and the pure in heart have the promise of its future possession. Meanwhile, until the Kingdom is fully come, these "blessed ones" are the salt of the earth and the light of the world.[6]

The Ten Commandments—if the sayings here grouped together may, for the moment, be regarded as being of one piece —still stand. Men, living together here on earth, must obey them. But the Gospels, at this point, let us see their Christian transvaluation. They not only undergo a turning inward "from code to conscience" but are placed in another category of values. Jesus is demanding of his followers what is clearly beyond the strength of unaided human nature when he says, "Love your enemies," adding to the commandment this supernatural reward: "That ye may be the children of your Father which is in heaven." The Lord's Prayer which Jesus teaches the disciples follows the same pattern. It is kingdom-centered from the beginning to the end: from its communal "Our Father which art in heaven," through the invocation "Thy Kingdom come," to the great petition "Deliver us from evil," ending in its climax of affirmation, "For thine is the kingdom, and the power, and the glory, for ever. Amen." So also do the rest of the sayings of Matthew 5-7 which may here be briefly summed up in these words:

Lay up no treasures on earth. Be not anxious for tomorrow. Do not your alms publicly. Pray in secret: your Father knows what you need. Do not appoint yourself as judge of men. Do not desecrate that which is holy: cast not your pearls before swine. Ask, and it shall be given to you. Beware of false prophets. Bring forth good fruit. Do unto others as you would have them do unto you. Enter in at the strait gate that leads to eternal life. Hear what I, your Master, say: build your house on the rock, against the day when the rains will descend, the floods come, and the winds blow to beat upon that house. Hear, and do—while the kingdom is to you a day of grace, and the day of judgment is not far off.

[6] Matthew 5:13-14.

II

Parables of Grace and Judgment

What has thus far been said is also true of the parables of
Jesus. They are not merely stories told for our entertainment
or our general edification. Nor are they neatly composed alle-
gories serving us as examples of good literature—though in the
Evangelist's hands, especially in those of Luke, their literary
character is abundantly demonstrated. They are figurative expressions, similitudes, pictures in story form and analogies from
nature, implying indeed a close "inward affinity between the natural order and the spiritual order," [7] but setting forth a specific
single truth applicable to the kingdom of God which is their
general theme. Thus, for example, when Jesus says, in Matthew 6:26-30, "Behold the fowls of the air:... Your heavenly
Father feedeth them"—a saying which contains the germ of a
parable—we are obviously not simply to learn a lesson on the
care of birds or of wild life. Nor are we only to be reminded
again of the frequent declaration of the ancient Psalmist that
there is a divine providence in the order of nature. The context itself is the key to the meaning of the little parable: God
cares for the birds of the air, the lilies of the field, for the very
grass which is green today and "tomorrow is cast into the
oven." He will care for you; but "seek ye first the kingdom of
God." How else also, except in this setting of the urgency
with which Jesus preached the meteoric advent of the kingdom,
can we understand the parabolic saying of Jesus: "I am come to
set fire to the earth, and what will I, if it be already kindled"? [8]

When now we look at such a collection of parables as that
found in Matthew 13, we do not try to find their context in the
chapter's opening words referring to the day that Jesus went
"out of the house, and sat by the seaside." If we did, we
should ask: "Whose house?" and we would not find the answer.

[7] C. H. Dodd: *The Parables of the Kingdom* (London: James Nisbet &
Co., Ltd., 1935), p. 21.
[8] Luke 12:49.

Rather, we read through the parable of the sower who went forth to sow; we hear about the seeds falling by the wayside, upon stony places, among thorns, and into good ground; and we come upon the declaration which is the key to the parable's meaning: "Blessed are your eyes, for they see; and your ears, for they hear." If we should ask: "What is it that we should hear?" the answer would follow: "When one heareth the *word* of the *kingdom,* and understandeth it." The other parables, from there, follow a straight course, only with the added introductory phrase, "The kingdom of heaven is like" these things: good wheat growing among the tares; a grain of mustard seed; a baker's leaven; a hidden treasure; a priceless pearl; and a net cast into the sea. And the series of parables closes with the suggestion that a good disciple—Jesus says, a good "scribe"; we might say, a Christian, or perhaps simply, a good man—is one who is well "instructed unto the kingdom of heaven."

To illustrate the truth further, we may go to another collection of parables, found in Luke 15. As the introductory context informs us, they are designed to show that publicans and sinners may enter the kingdom of heaven. The Pharisees and scribes were outraged at the thought that Jesus should choose to eat bread with sinners. It will help us to understand our Lord's necessary use of parables when we note that these murmuring legalists altogether missed the point. He was by his act inviting sinners to feast with him. Now, in the parable of the Prodigal Son, he is foreshadowing that Messianic feast with the redeemed in the Father's everlasting kingdom of heaven. The three parables in the chapter are of one piece. In the first we have a picture of the Great Shepherd of Souls seeking to bring even the last lost sheep into the fold. So great is His divine compassion, so instant His pursuit, so self-propelled, that He will not rest from His mighty action in the world until His work in human history is accomplished. That is also the meaning of the parable of the lost coin: the divine solicitude knows no bounds; it reaches to the darkest corners of the earth in pursuit of one lost soul; when it is found, "there is joy in the presence of the angels of God." One thinks here of the lines of the Saint Luke-like poet and physician, Henry Vaughan:

> How kind is Heaven to man! If here
> One sinner doth amend,
> Straight there is joy, and every sphere
> In music doth contend.

These parables, it will be observed, show the strong allegorical and humanitarian tendency so characteristic of Luke. But there is no reason to doubt either their germinal Messianic content or the trustworthiness of their setting in the earthly life of Christ. They are kingdom parables through and through. And no better situation in the Gospel narrative could be found for the parable of the Prodigal Son than that provided by the elder brother, the type of the Pharisees who themselves would not enter the Kingdom and forbade entrance to those who would come.

There remains now only the need of mentioning the judgment parables which find their best adapted setting in the Jerusalem period of Jesus' earthly ministry. That they are parables of crisis, and are therefore eschatological, is at once evident. That the church saw its life reflected in them is also clear.[9] Their theme, throughout, is the kingdom of God. In them the Kingdom offers itself once more, and finally, in grace to Israel and—through the later interpretation that the Evangelists give to it—to mankind. But the main accent is on the Kingdom's judgment. It descends upon those who (1) refuse its invitation, (2) are disloyal to their trusteeship of its "talents" or its "vineyard," and (3) remain asleep and unready, like the five foolish virgins, when the marriage feast is prepared and Christ the Bridegroom comes to join his bride, the community of the redeemed —symbolized in Christian history as the church—in everlasting joy and peace. The language used in the parable is symbolical, just as such language would be used elsewhere in thinking of great and ultimate values. But the symbolism is not unreal, no more so than are the sculptured figures of liberty and justice, or of the arts and sciences, exhibited in our national galleries. The meaning is disclosed in terms already familiar to people living in Bible times. It is that God in His wise providence has sent Christ

9 Matthew 21-25 and Luke 16-20.

into the world to set up His kingdom, and that this kingdom will have no end. Other kingdoms rise and fall; God's kingdom endures. It involves history, enters into history, acts on all things temporal, but is itself supernatural and eternal. It denies nothing that is natural in man: his gifts, his aspirations, and his limitations. Instead it affirms all these; but it regards man not as an animal, rather as a being having a soul. Man, according to the gospel of this kingdom, is a pilgrim of eternity. The earth is not his abiding place. His citizenship is in heaven.

But that is not all that is implied in this concept of the kingdom of God. The Kingdom is above all a community. It is a society of the redeemed, of saints—that is, of men delivered from evil. The community is on earth for those who live on earth; in heaven for those who have completed their earthly task. For Christians living today it is the community of the Faith symbolized in the risen body of Christ, the "unique fellowship of Christian believers throughout the world—Orthodox, Roman, Anglican, Protestant, and all others who name the name of Christ." [10] This fellowship is a historic reality, the continuation of God's mighty act in human history, begun in ancient times and brought to a climax in the earthly life of Christ. In other words, it is the church spoken of by the first apostles and by Matthew the Evangelist who records Jesus as saying to Peter after his confession of our Lord's Messiahship:

> Thou art Peter:
> And upon this rock I will build my church
> And the gates of hell shall not prevail against it. [11]

Finally, we must remind ourselves again that this central concept of the kingdom of God is an eschatological one. The Kingdom will one day have an end on earth, but never an End. Time, itself but a concept by which earthly things are measured —and we know how strangely inadequate is its measure of life —is for this community, as the Gospels tell us, an opportunity

[10] Charles Clayton Morrison, *What is Christianity?* (Chicago: Willett, Clark & Co., 1940).
[11] Matthew 10:18.

for sowing and reaping.   The kingdom of God, here and now, is sown in grace and harvested in judgment.   It is a vineyard for the ingathering of souls.   The good wine is everlasting life. As a "philosophy of life," therefore, this Hebrew-Jewish-Christian interpretation of history has for us today a strong appeal. It is both realistic and free from a corroding pessimism.   Breaking through the naturalistic order of things, nature's cycle of eternal recurrence, of birth and death, it offers the world a challenge and a hope.   Though ancient in its origin, this concept of the kingdom of God, as the Gospels present it to us, is also the most "modern."   The world today, with its spirit broken on the wheel of purposelessly revolving events, needs a sense of direction.   It needs an assurance of its ultimate destination.   The kingdom of God conceived as divine history furnishes the pattern for the achievement of this goal.   In summing up our present study, it is of interest to note that Matthew, in recording the parables of Jesus, concludes his account of them [12] with this practical test for all men to read and to ponder—lest, talking urgently, and perhaps too loudly, of *ends,* they overlook the active *means* to attain them:

> Then shall the King say unto them: ...
> I was an hungred, and ye gave me meat;
> I was thirsty, and ye gave me drink;
> I was a stranger, and ye took me in;
>   Naked, and ye clothed me;
> I was sick, and ye visited me;
> I was in prison, and ye came unto me.
>   Come, ye blessed of my Father,
>   Inherit the kingdom prepared for you
>   From the foundation of the world.[13]

[12] Matthew 25:31-46.
[13] Matthew 25: 34-36.

Chapter 23

THE GALILEAN CRISIS

I

THE HOSTILITY OF HEROD

The Gospel accounts agree that the opposition to Jesus in Galilee developed gradually. It began as a series of minor repulses, irritations felt by the Pharisees, whose first major effect was an inaugurated cold war against him. It was inevitable, from the start, that they should question him. The scribes were continually preoccupied with disputation. It was, one may say, their daily bread; and the diverse teachings of the schools of Hillel and Shammai, for example, offered them an instant opportunity to whet their appetite. Jesus must have expected such positive aggression and been prepared for it. The question of divorce, mentioned in Mark 10:1-12, was a good case in point, since the Shammaites held severely puritanical views about it and the Hillelites regarded themselves as the modern liberals.

But the situation took on gravity as it involved questions of supernatural import. Accordingly, when the Pharisees accused Jesus of breaking the Sabbath which God had ordained, or of forgiving sins which God alone could forgive,[1] their attitude was definitely inquisitorial; and when, finally, they saw him casting out demons, he was summarily condemned by them as being allied with the prince of devils.[2] Thus did the tares of opposition to the gospel grow on Galilean soil. Yet that opposition, until it was outwardly implemented, was ineffectual, since it remained in the free realm of religious conviction and theological opinion. What was required to make it an open danger was its re-enforcement by the state. This political power pre-

[1] Mark 2:1-12, 3:1-5.
[2] Mark 3:22.

sented itself for action through the suspicions and fears of King Herod.

The Evangelists now tell the story of Herod and John the Baptist in order to indicate how this open enmity took threatening form. The accounts are not agreed in full detail, but this much is obvious: Herod sensed trouble; and he had his own reasons for action. Chiefly because of John's pronounced influence through the missionary work of his disciples, and partly, we are told, to please Herodias, his wife, Herod had ordered the prophet executed; and now the rumor was spreading that he had returned from the dead and was continuing his work in Galilee in the person of Jesus. It is doubtful that Herod believed this rumor; but he would have been guileful enough to give the impression that he did. Behind this craftiness lay a fear for the security of his position. The current of Messianism was running strong through Palestine, and the party of the Zealots, its supporters, was opportunely active in the underground. Herod, therefore, would give the impression that he sincerely wished to inquire for himself who Jesus was and what he taught.[3] Through the Herodians, his emissaries —more probably, his spies—he inquired what Jesus might think about the payment of the tribute money. Answering them by the use of one of those pithy aphorisms by which we recognize the primitivity of the tradition containing the story, Jesus said: "Render unto Caesar the things that are Caesar's, and to God the things that are God's."[4] Luke adds that Jesus perceived their craftiness and that his answer left both the Herodians and the Pharisees without a word to say. One fact ought to have been evident to them from this typical encounter: the fact that Jesus was no political rebel. Perhaps they sensed it well enough, but found themselves confronted only with differences between themselves, and agreed only in their dire determination to destroy Jesus. Thus a powerful two-headed engine was at work, driving blindly toward a goal. But the Evangelists, in all this fateful devising of blinded men, see the fulfilment of a divine

[3] Hence Mark's report, in 6:14, quoting Herod as saying that John was risen from the dead.

[4] The incident, found in Mark 12:17, Matthew 22:21, and Luke 20:25, and placed in Jesus' ministry in Jerusalem, is here out of its natural context.

plan whose meaning could be made clear only when the whole story had finally been told.

This fact is evident in Jesus' reply to Herod's emissaries in an incident of tradition, preserved in Luke 13:31-33, that has since become a classic. "Go ye and tell that fox," he said,

> Behold I cast out devils,
> And I do cures to day and to morrow,
> And the third day I shall be perfected.
> Nevertheless I must walk to day
> And to morrow, and the day following:
> For it cannot be that a prophet
> Perish out of Jerusalem.

It is apparent from the record that a series of repulses had borne heavily against Jesus and that his ministry was now becoming less public and "itinerating" and more private and "wandering." The reasons for this change, stated summarily, were two: (1) The unmitigating hostility of the Pharisees and the Herodians; (2) the rising popular tide of Messianism culminating, as the Fourth Gospel tells us, in a forthright determination to make Jesus king. The effect of these circumstances on the thought of Jesus can only be conjectured by us from what actually occurred. For some time, now, the preaching of the Good News of the Kingdom had been eagerly received. There had been a buoyancy, a hopefulness, felt by all who heard the message, that might naturally have been likened, by those who witnessed it, to the bright sunshine falling on the Galilean lake. But lately storms had risen which, though they left Jesus calm in spirit,[5] had influenced his action and thinking. The Pharisees had cried "Beelzebub" at his mighty works; the people in his own home town of Nazareth had driven him out of their community; and even the swineherds of Gadara had asked him to leave their secluded region. At one time he had said, hopefully: "He that is not against me is for me." Now he was compelled to say regretfully: "He that is not for me is against me." So changed had become the attitude of persons who may have thought of becoming his followers that he said to a certain

[5] See Mark 4:36-41.

scribe who wished to join him, and whose sincerity he must
have appreciated: "The foxes have holes, and the birds of the
air have nests; but the Son of man hath not where to lay his
head." [6]   It was in this mood, and confronted by a wholly
changed picture of the Galilean towns in which he had once been
so warmly welcomed, that Jesus uttered these climactic words
of sorrow and of judgment:

> Woe unto thee, Chorazin!
> Woe unto thee, Bethsaida!...
> It shall be more tolerable for Tyre and Sidon
> At the day of judgment, than for you.
> And thou, Capernaum,
> Which art exalted unto heaven,
> Shalt be brought down to hell....
> It shall be more tolerable for the land of Sodom
> In the day of judgment, than for thee. [7]

There could be no question of Jesus' sustained popularity.
The people crowded about him in even greater numbers and
with an unmistakable intensity of purpose.   For a time he seems
to have decided to take up quarters in Peter's boat on the lake
in order to escape the feverish desire of the multitudes to see
him.   We must assume a reason for this insistence of Jesus on
being alone, either with his disciples, or in prayer, as the Evangelist indicates in Mark 6:46. [8] Matthew, supplementing Mark's
narrative, suggests a sufficient cause. [9]   The people, he says, had
become discontented, irresponsive, even perverse; they looked
for a prophet, only to reject him.   That had been their treatment of John the Baptist; and it was even so with their attitude
toward Jesus.   It was indeed a generation of children to which
both John and he had come—"children sitting in the markets,
and calling to their fellows":

---

[6] Matthew 8:20.
[7] Matthew 11:21-24.
[8] According to Mark, Jesus withdraws from the multitudes for prayer and
communion with God on three occasions: (1) at the beginning of his preaching in Capernaum (Mark 1:35-38); (2) after the feeding of the five thousand (Mark 6:45-46); (3) in Gethsemane (Mark 14:32-42).   All three
point to crises in Jesus' ministry.
[9] Matthew 11:1-19.

> We have piped unto you,
> And ye have not danced;
> We have mourned unto you,
> And ye have not lamented.[10]

They acted like the children, not of wisdom, but of absurd and pitiful ignorance: for "Wisdom," Jesus concluded, "is justified of her children." What they required was a kingdom that would take them into it by force. Yet Jesus had not wished it so, had the people but heeded; for it had hitherto been his work on earth to offer to them the news of the good time to come, to preach forgiveness to sinners, and to bring deliverance to men under the yoke of sin. And that—as the early church, a generation later, came clearly to comprehend it—was, even in the face of the impending crisis, Christ's great desire as, reviewing again the work given him to do of the Father,[11] he said:

> Come unto me,
> All ye that labor
> And are heavy laden,
> And I will give you rest.
> Take my yoke upon you, and learn of me;
> For I am meek and lowly in heart:
> And ye shall find rest unto your souls.

It ought here to be granted that we cannot be sure of the exact context of the various groups of sayings as we now find them in the Gospels. For the arrangement of them is topical rather than chronological; and such a *pericope,* or preaching unit, as this that we have just quoted would in apostolic times have found many an appropriate setting. But we may rightly assume that it was with such thoughts as these—thoughts of judgment and of grace—that Jesus reviewed the scene before him. Accordingly, by now, three facts are reasonably clear: (1) that Jesus' plan of future action was not dictated simply by a fear of Herod; (2) that he very well understood the multitudes as being wandering sheep without a shepherd; (3) that, as the Son of the heavenly Father, he was now fully conscious

---

10 Matthew 11:19.
11 Matthew 11:28, 29.

of the meaning of the earthly work assigned to him.   It was
therefore with thoughts of John the Baptist's death and of
Herod's evil designs that Mark the Evangelist again takes up
the narrative and has Jesus say to the disciples:[12] "Come ye
yourselves apart unto a desert place, and rest a while"; and then
he adds, emphatically, that "they departed . . . by ship privately."

II

THE MIRACLE OF THE LOAVES

It is at this stage, approaching the climax of Jesus' Galilean
ministry, that the Gospels record the miracle of the Feeding of
the Five Thousand.   Noteworthily, it is the only miracle recorded by all four of the Evangelists.[13] Mark gives us, besides,
another account of a miracle of Loaves and Fishes, indicating
by the fact that some particular significance was attached to the
event at the time the Gospel narratives were written.[14] The
versions of Matthew and Luke show few variants of the story
as told by Mark; and the Fourth Gospel's later report verifies
the miracle's larger meaning in full detail.

The story is simple. Its setting is the natural amphitheater
of Jesus' larger Galilean ministry. The "desert place," probably
near Bethsaida, is actually an isolated grassy hillside. Mark emphasizes the fact that when Jesus looked on the scene he "saw
much people and was moved with compassion toward them,
because they were as sheep and not having a shepherd."[15]   In
the next chapter the Evangelist adds that "in those days the
multitude was very great, and having nothing to eat."   The
account continues by saying that "the day was now far spent,"
and lets the disciples reiterate: "This is a desert place, and now
the time is far passed."   The disciples, with no apprehension of
the divine drama implicit in the forthcoming event, say to Jesus:
"Send them away."   But Jesus answers: "Give ye them to eat."
They ask: "Shall we go and buy . . . bread?" Jesus inquires:
"How many loaves have ye?" The company is seated, in order,

---

[12] Mark 6:31-32.
[13] Mark 6:30-44; Matthew 14:13-21; Luke 9:10-17; John 6:1-13.
[14] Mark 8:1-9.
[15] Mark 6:34.

on the green grass, "by hundreds, and by fifties." Now the miracle takes place. Jesus takes the five loaves and the two fishes: he looks up to heaven, blesses and breaks the loaves: he gives them to the disciples; and they, in turn, distribute them among the people. And the narrator says, pointedly: "And they all did eat and were filled." But that was not the whole effect of Christ's mighty doing; for, when all was done, "twelve baskets full of the fragments" remained unused.

It is obvious that the Evangelists were here not only, or mainly, interested in their story. They saw in it a deeper twofold significance: it summed up all that, until then, Jesus had been doing and teaching his disciples to do; and beyond that, it pointed to the complete fulfilment of Christ's work in the world. In Jesus' earthly life the feeding of the multitude represented the climax of his public Galilean ministry. All that he had wished to accomplish by signs of his mighty work was here dramatized in one act, and emblematized, besides, in one great historic symbol—that of the good shepherd who led his sheep in green pastures and by still waters, even as King David had expressed it in the well-known Twenty-third Psalm.

But there was, we must infer, for Jesus a deeper meaning in the event—one which the church, a generation later, was quick to grasp and establish as a basic fact of the Christian faith. It had its historic foundation, first of all, in what was happening in Galilee at the time, and in the changing attitude Jesus himself experienced in the face of the developing circumstances. In his consciousness of his own vocation, from having regarded himself as the divinely appointed messenger of the impending advent of the kingdom of God, he had, through the evidence presented to him—and—more particularly because of his contact with sinful humanity and the consciousness of his own sinlessness—come to see in himself the chosen Son who was to carry out on earth the will of the heavenly Father. Instead of simply announcing Messiah, he was himself to undertake the work of Messiah already announced. This was the "Messianic secret" now fully revealed to him; and it signalized the crisis of his ministry in Galilee. Of the earliest dawn of this revelation to Jesus we have no knowledge. It will content

us to know that it was given to the Son at a time chosen by his Father. But we are not here altogether left without historical information. For in the progressive references to the Son of man, made by the Evangelists, we can see something of the manner in which the earlier Danielic concept of his sudden coming in the clouds is now being associated with the older Davidic concept of Messiah-king as a deliverer of his people. The apocalyptic emphasis, already familiar to us, is not displaced; it is assimilated, by stages, to the Messianism of First and Second Isaiah; and it reappears in the later Jerusalem ministry of Jesus with an even greater urgency—the urgency of an impending final world judgment.

But now, for Jesus, the thought of Messiah as the Suffering Servant of God was taking an ever greater possession of his mind. The repulses he had experienced, his rejection in Nazareth, the opposition of the Pharisees, and the hostility of Herod could not but remind him of the familiar words of Isaiah 53:3, where the prophet had said:

> He was despised
> And rejected of men;
> A man of sorrows,
> And acquainted with grief.

Was this the direction his own life, too, was taking? We shall see, and the Evangelists knew, that it was. Therefore, in its subsequent interpretation, the miracles of the feeding of the multitudes could come to be comprehended in the revelatory light of its full meaning. In the language of the ancient prophets, that meaning was Messianic; to the early church, it expressed itself in the symbolism of the Holy Eucharist, commonly identified by Christians today with the Lord's Supper. The doctrinal basis for it is found in the Fourth Gospel where Jesus, after the miracles, is heard to speak of himself as the Bread of Life—or, more traditionally, as the bread of God come down from heaven.[16] John, in introducing his account of the miracle, says, moreover, that it occurred at the time of the Jewish Passover. Plainly, the inference is that the miracle was to be asso-

[16] John 6:26-59.

ciated with Christ's passion. Luke, in his story of the risen Christ, has already by then written down the transcendent truth that "he was known of them in the breaking of the bread" (Luke 24:35. See also Acts 2:42, 20:7, and 27:35). And St. Paul, whose work as an apostle has long since been completed, has given to the death of Christ its definitely redemptive meaning in these words:

> The Lord Jesus, the ... night ... he was betrayed took bread:
> And when he had given thanks, he brake it, and said,
>> Take, eat: this is my body, which is broken for you;
>> This do in remembrance of me.
> After the same manner also he took the cup, ... saying,
>> This cup is the new testament in my blood:
>> This do ye, as oft as ye drink it,
>> In remembrance of me.[17]

The subsequent effects of this miracle are plainly seen in the events that follow. Jesus' very first act after that, Mark tells us, is to send away the disciples in a boat on the lake in order that he may be free to withdraw into the hills to pray. When, later, they see him by the shore, all radiant to their sight, they are filled with fear and wonder until Jesus says to them: "Be of good cheer, it is I; be not afraid"; and the Evangelist adds: "They were sore amazed ... and wondered; for they considered not the miracle of the loaves." [18] A new power seems to them to have entered his person. The people, we read, "ran through the whole region round about," eager to reach him; [19] and as many as touched even "the border of his garment" were healed.

One cannot but observe, here, how persistently the theme of the narrative moves forward. In the very next incident the Pharisees arrive on the scene just as the disciples are eating bread; but the bread, so the scribes maintain, is eaten with "defiled hands." Jesus is represented as moved to indignation toward these ceremonious and hypocritical dispensers of the Mosaic law—and later, arriving in Caesarea Philippi, he warns

[17] Corinthians 11:23-26.
[18] Mark 6:50-52.
[19] Mark 6:55.

the Twelve, charging them to "beware of the leaven of the Pharisees, and of Herod." [20]

The miracle of the loaves and fishes, mentioned in the Markan passage, had a wider intent and a deeper meaning than the simple story indicates. In its setting and action it gave dramatic expression to what the apostolic church believed Christ had come to signify to the world. And, with the passing years, it was the Fourth Evangelist who comprehended most clearly its highly symbolic implication. By his range of vision extending through history from Sinai to Calvary, and his extraordinary gift of summing up a great truth in a single metaphor, he saw Christ the living Bread coming down from heaven, taking the place of the manna that Moses had given; and he heard Jesus say: [21]

> I am the living bread....
> If any man eat of this bread
> He shall live for ever:
> And the bread that I will give is my flesh,
> Which I will give for the life of the world.

Finally, it should not escape our attention that these continuous allusions, having their origin in the story of the feeding of the multitudes, point in retrospect to Jesus' last supper with his disciples, and in prospect to the Messianic feast which Christ is one day to celebrate with his faithful followers in the blessed kingdom of heaven. [22] Later, in the history of the church, they attain their full meaning in the miracle of the divine presence as it is symbolized in the Holy Sacrament commemorating the vicarious death of Christ and his achievement of man's redemption. The perennial mystery of this divine presence underlies our universal Christian faith. It is, in the language of Peter's confession, the rock on which the church is built. The cross on every altar or church spire today attests it.

This divine mystery is perhaps nowhere in our literature more familiarly portrayed than in Tennyson's poem *The Holy Grail*. In it Sir Galahad is pictured as the blameless knight of

[20] Mark 8:15.
[21] John 6:51.
[22] Matthew 26:17-31.

the Round Table, in search of the Holy Grail, the legendary chalice of the Lord's Supper. He comes to a forest chapel, lays his lance against the open door, and kneels at the altar in prayer. The elements of the Holy Sacrament lie there before him under the altar cloth. The young knight later recalls the scene:

> I, Galahad, saw the Grail,
> The Holy Grail, descend upon the shrine.
> I saw the fiery face as of a child
> That smote itself into the bread, and went.

But that is not the whole story. For what follows may be regarded as the poet's way of summing up the history of the divine Sacrament through the ages, symbolizing the fact that Christ's death upon the cross has followed men through the world since that day, a haunting, waylaying presence not to be put off. Here, in Sir Galahad's words, is the record of that presence, pursuing mankind across the centuries, a sheltering cloud of grace in days of peace, a pillar of fiery judgment in nights of blackening war:

> And hither am I come; and never yet
> Hath what thy sister taught me first to see,
> This Holy Thing, fail'd from my side, nor come
> Cover'd, but moving with me night and day,
> Fainter by day, but always in the night
> Blood-red, and sliding down the blacken'd marsh
> Blood-red, and in the sleeping mere below
> Blood-red.

Chapter 24

THE GALILEAN CRISIS (CONTINUED)

I

THE GREAT CONFESSION

The leaven of the Pharisees and of Herod was indeed at work in Galilee, fermenting and preparing for Jesus the eating of the bitter bread of suffering. The Evangelists are agreed in recording that a crisis was at hand, the first of two crises around which the Gospels were written—the second being that which centered in Jerusalem and led directly to Jesus' death.

Galilee, once so hospitable to our Lord, is now pictured as increasingly hostile ground. It was not that the multitudes had become disinterested. On the contrary, they pressed upon him as never before; but with a different motive. They were led less, now, by a desire to hear the good news of the impending advent of the kingdom than by a mass movement to establish Jesus at once as their temporal leader and king. It was obvious that the summarized result of his Galilean ministry had been to arouse the ever-ready Maccabean hope of setting up a Davidic ruler over Palestine, and so effecting a situation as displeasing to Jesus as it must have been pleasing to the patriotic Zealots. Accordingly, the greater end, or aim, of the Messianic kingdom, which was to establish, by a direct but gracious intervention, the role of God in the lives of men and so to effect the immediate accomplishment of His will on earth, was being obscured. It was this fact, and not simply a fear of Herod, that (1) accounted for Jesus' decision to leave the borders of Galilee, and (2) offered the outward occasion for his open acknowledgement of his Messiahship.

We rightly assume that Jesus' consciousness of his vocation had been clear to him from the beginning of his earthly minis-

try. Now, too, the direction in which it was leading him was equally manifest. The beginning and the end of his mission were alike before him. His earthly life, begun in lowliness, must end in humble abnegation, and so be of one piece—a royal robe without a rent or seam. It must, indeed, be so manifestly of one human-divine nature, from first to last, as to be able to be compressed into one single great truth, and to be expressed in one climactic moment or event. The Gospel narrators wisely perceived the truth and recorded it in one sentence: "The Son of man must suffer"; and, with one accord, they pointed to the passion story as the climactic expression of the consummate truth about him. Mark does so briefly and intensely; Matthew and Luke treat the theme more elaborately, offering a full explanation, using their source material freely to accomplish that single end, which is to repeat after Mark, "The Son of man must suffer, . . . be rejected . . . be killed, and after three days rise again"; and they preface their more elaborate accounts of Jesus' earthly life with appropriate birth stories in order to round out the full revelatory and Christological picture. It goes almost without saying here that the Gospel writers were under the kind of compulsion that kept them continually aware of their entire story, and of its meaning to them, while they were engaged in writing each integral part of it.

Perhaps, at this juncture in our study, we ought to remind ourselves again that, to the Evangelists, the life of Christ they were writing was not a biography but a revelation. And by this revelation they did not simply mean that their minds were being enlightened to behold divine truth, but that history was unfolding itself before them as divine drama. Through the gospel tradition of which they were the chosen heirs, they were confronted in the person and work of Jesus with a demonstration of the mighty action of God's love and judgment against a world of sin and evil. We who read the narrative are, therefore, not to look for any gradual progress represented by the periods of Jesus' earthly life. For the picture which the Gospels present to us is not an evolutionary but an eschatological one—that is, it is one in which the final issue of Christ against the evil of the world is brought to light in a series, or succession,

of dramatic scenes, all of which are directed toward a single end. This end or meaning is best explained to us—as it is in all true drama—by such a typical declaration as this one, for example, found in Luke 11 :20, in which Jesus says: "But if I with the finger of God cast out devils, no doubt the kingdom of God is come upon you."

This fact need not disturb us in our attempt to understand the events that transpired in Jesus' life on earth. They were real events. Things happened to Jesus, as they do to all men who live eventfully. But it is not the events themselves, their natural causes or sequences, or the order in which they appear on the pages of the narrative, but their religious and theological interpretation that is finally important. For, tested by theological standards, all Christian history is divine drama. The events belong to human history; their ultimate issue, or end, is something beyond the events themselves. It is in God's hands.

But let us now return to our story. Looking again at the Evangelistic record, we note that there now began for Jesus and his disciples a period of wandering more continuous and extensive than at any previous time. The waves of Messianism, like those on the stormy lake, were running high. Herod was craftily alert. He could not have failed to hear the report that, after the miracle of the loaves, the people had tried by force to make him king.[1] Jesus was well aware of these culminating circumstances. But his course of action was not determined by them. They were, as the Gospel writers imply, the signs by which he discerned the way by which God's will was leading him. As, in the beginning of his ministry, he had been "led up of the Spirit into the wilderness," so now he "arose and went into the borders of Tyre and Sidon."[2] We are arrested by the terse and pertinent statement of Mark that Jesus "would have no man know it," followed by an opposite effect: "but he could not be hid." Then, reading further, we come upon Mark's story demonstrating the faith of the Syrophoenician woman. That the story is typical and deliberately chosen is clear from the manner in which the narrator feels himself still captivated by the recent

[1] John 6 :15.
[2] Matthew 4 :1, Mark 7 :24.

miracle of the loaves and fishes. One cannot fail to hear its
overtones in the words he reports Jesus as saying to the woman:
"Let the children first be filled: for it is not meet to take the
children's bread and cast it unto the dogs," together with her
answer: "Yet the dogs under the table eat of the children's
crumbs." [3]

The journey from Tyre and Sidon to Caesarea Philippi has
been variously outlined. If Mark's account is accepted, it was
a long and circuitous one, taking the travelers northwestward
over rugged hills to Tyre on the Mediterranean and along the
coast to Sidon, then eastward across the Lebanon Mountains
to the springs of the upper Jordan and from there southward
within close view of Mount Hermon, through Caesarea Philippi, down to the region of the Decapolis. The journey would
give to Jesus just the kind of opportunity he desired for detachment from the Galilean scene. Historic, scenic, out of
reach of popular followers, and conducive to intimate association with the Twelve, it offered days of solitary reflection and
lofty perspective. Mount Hermon, rising 9,000 feet above sea
level, was within clear and compelling sight, suggesting to Jesus,
as we shall see, Mount Sinai of Mosaic history and Mount
Carmel associated with Elijah's fame. From what springs of
thought Jesus' mind was fed, in that rich region between Lebanon and Hermon, where the rivers Leontes and Jordan have
their source, we are left to conjecture. Did he have sight of
a hill outside Jerusalem, more historic and meaningful than
Sinai or Carmel? We do not know. But it is impossible to
escape the inference that the Gospel writers saw in this lofty
setting a sign of the divine grandeur of the events soon to
follow.

An incident occurred in the region of the Decapolis that
may serve to illustrate to us the topical character of much of the
Gospel material. A poor deaf-mute is brought to Jesus who
heals him. (Mark 7:31-37.) The story has all the traits of an
ideal theme for evangelistic preaching. It has human interest,
is dramatic, and comes to a fitting climax as the evangelist,
preaching perhaps in Jerusalem or Caesarea or Antioch, acts

[3] Mark 7:27, 28.

out the details of the healing as he tells how Jesus took the man aside from the crowd, put his finger into the unhearing ears, touched the mute tongue, and looking up to heaven and sighing, said: "Ephphathá . . . Be opened." Mark preserves, in the tradition, the exact Aramaic word which Jesus himself used and with which the sermon could come to the moving conclusion that Christ "hath done all things well: he maketh both the deaf to hear and the dumb to speak." [4] The inescapable inference would be that the miracle, according to prophetic predictions,[5] was a sign that the Messianic age had come—the time of Zion's redemption, when

> The eyes of the blind shall be opened,
> And the ears of the deaf shall be unstopped.
> Then shall the lame man leap as an hart,
> And the tongue of the dumb sing:
> For in the wilderness shall waters break out,
> And life-giving streams in the desert.[6]

At Dalmanutha—possibly Magdala, the home of Mary whom Jesus had healed and befriended [7]—the Pharisees appear, demanding that Jesus present them with a sign from heaven. Mark's account, dismissing the demand by an abrupt refusal, is supplemented, in Matthew 16:1-4, by a vivid and detailed picture of a typical situation. The Pharisees want miracles that can be naturally explained. So Jesus talks to them of *nature,* where they think they are at home. They say, "It will be fair weather: for the sky is red"; but they cannot read the signs of the true heaven of whose kingdom Jesus speaks. They do not know that his coming is itself such a sign; and no sign will be given to their generation, Jesus adds, but the sign of the prophet Jonah. Symbolically interpreted, as it was by the early Christian church, the story referred to the death and resurrection of Christ. Jesus' death and resurrection were henceforth to be the sign that he was sent of God. The incident of this encounter with the Pharisees requires, for our understanding of it, no

4 Mark 7:37.
5 Isaiah 32:3-4, 35:5-6.
6 Isaiah 35:5, 6.
7 Matthew 15:39.

special chronological setting. It sets forth, and once more sums up, the meaning of Christ's earthly ministry as having its final climax and interpretation in the events of his passion. And we are led to conclude that the Evangelist Mark considered the incident appropriately placed in its present context, to illustrate the timely pronouncement sentence of Jesus: "Beware of the leaven of the Pharisees." But Matthew, as we have seen, gives to it a larger Messianic significance.

The Synoptic Gospels depict Jesus' Galilean ministry as coming to a climax with the incident at Caesarea Philippi: situated on the southern slopes of Mount Hermon, in a region of isolated grandeur, the spot itself symbolized the meaning of what was to take place there. The thought had by now taken full possession of the mind of Jesus that he must assume outright the Messianic office to which since his baptism—according to the earliest gospel tradition—he had been conscious of being drawn. Now, and for some time past, it had been revealed to him that the office of the Son of man was to be one of sorrow, and that the holy nature and activity of that office, as defined by the Unknown Prophet of Isaiah 53, was moving toward a consummate fulfilment in his earthly life.

This inner consciousness, we have already learned, was corroborated by the outward historic facts. The outward events had not produced but evoked the consciousness, deeply latent from the first. The time, therefore, had come to convey this truth to the disciples. It was imperative that these men, hitherto so close to Jesus, be informed of the goal and meaning of the suffering toward which all that had until then transpired before their eyes was being directed by the will of God. They must know the Messianic truth less for his own sake than for theirs and the world's. For the events that were to follow were not simply the rough road to his own martyrdom, but the fulfilment of the divine plan for the redemption of the world. By the road that he must travel, thereafter in history to be known by the name of *Via Dolorosa,* the prolonged ancient hope of Messianism, and the Good News of the kingdom of God which had been so joyously preached to them, were both to be fulfilled.

The plan and will of God in bringing this to pass had not been changed; nor had Jesus misunderstood them. The message that had begun in joy would end in joy. The apocalyptic outlook, as we shall see, was not to be abandoned; rather, it was to manifest itself the more radiantly, like sunshine above the stormy mountain peaks, as Jesus entered the valley of sorrows. The Ancient of days was still in the heavens and the Son of man would one day be seen coming in the clouds to judge and rule the world. But, before that day came, the work of Messiah must be accomplished through suffering; and it was Jesus who had himself been chosen for this sacred office.

This was the great mystery that had been revealed to him. It was indeed a "mystery" hidden from his followers—and has ever since remained one; but to Saint Paul of the early church it became known as the "exceeding great" mystery of our redemption; and we have already noted that to the Evangelist Matthew, the early church's most distinguished Gospel narrator, these words of Jesus himself summed up the conclusion to which he had fully come: [8]

> I thank thee, O Father, ...
> Because thou hast hid these things
> From the wise and prudent,
> And hast revealed them unto babes.
> Even so, Father: for so
> It seemed good in thy sight.[9]

The episode in Caesarea Philippi centers in Peter's great confession. All the four Gospels contain varying versions of it. Those of Matthew and Luke are clearly based on Mark; that of the Fourth Gospel points to an original background and source but is otherwise in accord with the Synoptic account.[10] The essence of the conversation, as stated by Mark, is contained in these words:

[8] Matthew 11:25-26.
[9] Pondering this mystery, we may do well to remember the saying of Saint Augustine concerning Holy Scripture: "Whilst it contains pools at which lambs may drink, it also contains depths in which elephants must swim."
[10] Mark 8, Matthew 16, Luke 9, John 6.

> And Jesus ... asked his disciples, saying unto them: Whom do men say that I am? And they answered: John the Baptist; but some say, Elias, and others, One of the prophets. And he saith unto them: But whom say ye that I am? And Peter answereth and saith unto him: Thou art the Christ.

Matthew's account reads: "Thou art the Christ, the son of the living God," and adds these words of Jesus to Peter: "Blessed art thou, Simon Bar-jona; for flesh and blood hath not revealed it unto thee, but my Father which is in heaven; and I say also unto thee, that thou art Peter, and upon this rock I will build my church; and the gates of hell shall not prevail against it." Luke's record differs only in certain individual details, the most important being that instead of saying, "Thou art the Christ," Peter answers, "Thou art the Christ of God." The version of the Fourth Gospel presents us with its own context and should here be quoted:

> From that time many of his disciples went back, and walked no more with him. Then said Jesus unto the Twelve: Will ye also go away? Then Simon Peter answered him:
>> Lord, to whom shall we go?
>> Thou hast the words of eternal life.
>> And we believe and are sure
>> That thou art the Christ
>> The Son of the living God.[11]

II

HUMILIATION AND GLORY

Such was the record preserved and clarified by the Evangelists for the early church to cherish and remember. It indicated that the truth that lay at the heart of the gospel message had at last been laid bare. The gospel was the gospel of Christ the Son of God. This exposition, and its clarification by the Gospel writers, had not been something arbitrarily added to the simple human history of Jesus, but had been a part of the gospel tradition from the beginning. It had, in fact, been the very essence of that tradition: "flesh and blood" had not revealed it; nor did

[11] John 6:66-69.

Courtesy of The Art Institute of Chicago.

5. THE TEMPTATION OF CHRIST. The Master L C Z.

Courtesy of The Art Institute of Chicago.

6. The Crucifixion. Hans Baldung (Grün).

a knowledge of it come as an afterthought to the church a generation later. The truth was that Old Testament prophecy was being fulfilled; the meaning of Jesus' coming into the world was being made clear. Messiah was indeed come. The suffering that still awaited him was clearly a part of God's plan: divine history was being written on pages of world history. The humiliation that the Son of God was to undergo was but the climax of his entire earthly life which was itself the humiliation foretold for him in the prophetic vision of Isaiah 53, after the pattern of which Jesus had seen his life to be taking shape; and all this that had occurred was seen by him as the express will and act of God of which the whole of prophetic history was an expression. The glory that awaited the Son of man still lay in the future. But the humiliation and the glory were of one piece, even as prophecy was of one piece—the garment of the word of God, having a variety of colors but a single design. As Jesus had come in humiliation to accomplish his work on earth, so he would come again in glory to consummate the advent of the kingdom of heaven. All this was implied in Peter's confession that Jesus was the Christ the Son of God. Of course the disciples, at the time, only dimly perceived this truth. In the borrowed words of Saint Paul, they but saw it "through a glass darkly." The full vision of it was to come after the morning of the resurrection. But the truth of Jesus' Messiahship had been declared, as it had been revealed to the disciples, by the Spirit of truth.

We are offered a compelling picture of how this divine drama of redemption—thus far begun and continued in the earthly ministry of Jesus—was to be concluded, in the story of the Transfiguration. The story had already been enshrined in the oral gospel tradition when the Evangelist Mark came upon it. Luke, elucidating Mark's account, discerned the incident's meaning for Jesus by referring to the "decease which he was about to accomplish in Jerusalem." [12] The very language used by the Evangelists in telling the story suggests an entrance into a profound mystery; not a puzzle, but a revelation hidden in the symbolism of the appearance of the historic personages of

[12] Luke 9:31.

Moses and Elijah, and so uniting the law, the prophets, and the gospel into a single pattern setting forth the divine plan of mankind's redemption. It was necessary for the early church —as it is for us today—to lift its vision to this lofty viewpoint. The high mountain, the dazzling light, the holy conversation of Jesus with Moses and Elias, and the voice of heaven in the overshadowing cloud were figures of Holy Scripture tinged with associations familiar to the first Christians. These figures, taken together, signified to them that Jesus was the Christ, or Messiah, and the Son of God; that in him all the hope of Israel was, as it were, summed up in one effulgent burst of light filling this dark world with a divine radiance. It meant that a new Israel had come into being in which the law and the prophets were overshadowed by the gospel of Christ. Henceforth, in this world yet shrouded in darkness, men might lift up their eyes unafraid, seeing "no man, save Jesus only."

But the Evangelists tell us that the disciples did not comprehend all this at the time. Clearly, the Gospel narrators, when they wrote, lived in a time already made light by the gospel truth. They understood what the disciples did not; and the story they tell reflects the contrast; thus showing that the Gospels as literature have their setting in the apostolic age but that they reflect primitive history. The disciples could not know beforehand the nature of the changed person they perceived Jesus to be. They could only be dazzled into amazement, and thereafter stand in wonder and awe recalling their vision of the transfigured Jesus. Behind the story, for the church to remember, was the fact that the person of Christ took on a new meaning when he assumed the role of the suffering Messiah. At the time the incident occurred, this fact was known to Jesus only. It was not until after Jesus' resurrection that it was recognized as divine history. Moses and Elias then faded from the picture. The old dispensation gave place to the new. The followers of Jesus were no longer Messianists. They had become Christians.

In a word, the transfiguration of Jesus stood, in the minds of the early Christians, for that moment in divine history when the redemption of man became an anticipated fact. The seed

of Israel's ancient faith, like a grain of wheat planted in rich soil, was at that moment ready to spring up for growth and harvest in the Christian church. Jesus, according to John's Gospel, had himself pointed to it when he said: "Except a corn of wheat fall into the ground and die, it abideth alone; but if it die, it bringeth forth much fruit." And, in the same discourse, following the raising of Lazarus, he had added: "And I, if I be lifted up from the earth, will draw all men unto me." [13] Clearly, this was the beginning of what, in the language of Saint Paul, was to be called the gospel of the Cross. And the Gospel writers confirm this fact by indicating that, as Jesus came down from the mountain of the Transfiguration, he began to teach the disciples, and to say to them repeatedly thereafter, that

> The Son of man
> Is delivered into the hands of men,
> And they shall kill him;
> And after that he is killed,
> He shall rise the third day.[14]

New vistas open before the eyes of the Evangelists as they reflect on the tradition they are here putting into writing. They note that Jesus began again to "teach his disciples," and that they "understood not" what he said, but "were afraid" to ask him what he meant. Matthew, looking back upon the scene, discerns the full meaning, as it is one day to apply to them, when he quotes Jesus as saying:

> If any man will come after me,
> Let him deny himself, take up his cross, and follow me.
> For whosoever will save his life shall lose it;
> And whosoever will lose his life, for my sake,
> Shall find it.[15]

Discipleship, then, was to mean suffering. Membership in the kingdom of God was to be obtained through a new type of humility. For the greatest in this kingdom were to be those

---

[13] John 12:24, 32.
[14] Mark 9:31.
[15] Matthew 16:24-25.

whose spirit was that of a little child.[16]   It must have seemed, for the moment, that all the grandeur of the Messianic concept that the disciples had entertained was to come to nothing.   But it was not to be so.   For Jesus assured them with a vision of the fruit of their self-sacrifice, with the words: "Verily I say unto you, there be some standing here, which shall not taste of death, till they see the Son of man coming in his kingdom." [17]

Thus, as we review all that has hitherto been said, we see that the Gospel writers offer us a narrative that is at once Christological and eschatological—a study, first, of the divine person, and, second, of the entire redemptive work of Christ. They do so by letting us see the person and work of Christ, by stages, in its threefold character: (1) in his birth, or divine incarnation, as Messiah-king; (2) in his earthly ministry, or divine humiliation, as the Suffering Servant who offers his life as "a ransom for many" through his death on the Cross; (3) in his exaltation, or divine lordship, as the Son of man who, by his resurrection, ascension, and coming again is the acknowledged giver of life, the judge of men, and the ruler of the world.

It was, accordingly, with the climactic thought of his death on the Cross that the Synoptic Gospels looked on Jesus' Galilean ministry as now coming to its close.   It is no surprise to us to see them stand in wonder and awe at the prospect before Jesus.   For before them, outside Jerusalem, to where he was to go, loomed the hill of skulls, called Golgotha, where he must finish the work given him to do by his Father.   There, in the story of Christ's passion, they saw it all exhibited and accomplished: the humiliation and the glory, the mystery enshrouded and revealed, in the historic fact and the divine symbolism of the Cross.   It was this story, told again and again by the early apostles, that had taken ultimate form as the Christian gospel, and to the true telling of which the Evangelists had dedicated themselves and their special gifts.   In doing this, as has been elsewhere noted, they were but recording the primitive tradition from its source and following the example of Saint Paul, whose work antedated theirs, in giving to the story its original Chris-

16 Matthew 18:1-6.
17 Matthew 16:28.

tological pattern and in placing the Cross at the center of this Christology. It is, therefore, from this center—expressed in the doctrine that Christ died for man's sin—that we must think our way through the Gospel narrative to an understanding of the meaning of Christ's earthly life. This is what is implied by the theological method that must accompany our historical as well as our devotional study of the Gospel literature with which we are confronted. By it we shall endeavor now to be guided as we proceed to outline the course of Jesus' activity during the remaining periods of his Perean and Jerusalem ministry.

But, perhaps, one word of guidance may here be welcomed. The study of these Gospels is not a factual examination only. It is also a revelatory experience. And we shall lose our way on this journey to Jerusalem which Jesus is now to take if we fail to travel with him under the overshadowing cloud by which he himself was led.[18] The life of Christ, we must again be told, is not secular but divine history; and only he can read it aright who, in the words of Shakespeare, has traversed

> Those holy fields
> Over whose acres walk'd those blessed feet
> Which fourteen hundred years ago were nail'd
> For our advantage on the bitter cross.[19]

[18] Compare, in this connection, Mark 1:10-11, 9:7, 15:39.
[19] *King Henry IV.*

Chapter 25

IN THE BORDERLAND OF PEREA AND JUDEA

I

THE STORY'S SOURCE AND SETTING

The incident of Caesarea Philippi was past. It was now also gospel history. And with it a new setting was furnished for what was to follow. Up to that time it had only been the Kingdom of God that had seemed a mystery to the disciples. Now, above the Kingdom, it was the person of Christ that was becoming more and more mysterious to them. We read in the Gospels that they were held in amazement and fear as he moved among them. What he said mystified them. They had come to call him Messiah, but the deeper meaning of that title had escaped them. The reason for this fact lay in the consciousness of Jesus—where it still lies for us today to give rise to the age-old question: What, actually, is meant by the claim that Jesus is the Christ or Messiah? The author of the Fourth Gospel found his own answer to it by calling him the eternal Son of God. But the mystery remains to waylay the Christian and to confound the unbeliever, as also do the more concrete facts of the Jesus of history and the undeniable existence of the historical society of Christian believers known in gospel language as the living body of Christ.

Yet the Synoptic Gospels carefully point out that the mysterious transfigured Christ and the human Jesus are one and the same person. The disciples now, in this later stage of his earthly life, see in him a human being of almost more natural traits than at any previous time. He is weary, often fatigued, in body and mind; he is capable of impatience, and even of anger, at the blindness of the opposing Pharisees; he is gentle with little children and tender toward the loving ministry of

women. He experiences moods of cheerfulness and depression;
he is continually moved by great pity toward Palestine's poor
and unfortunate people.

But there is in all this behavior of Jesus a strange mysterious
quality that makes it, real as it is, seem almost symbolical. This
is more particularly true of his pity and compassion. It is a
divine compassion, not merely, or only, noble and admirable but
also redemptive. It is the compassionate pity of Christ who
sees in his giving of himself not simply a salutary evidence of a
trait of natural goodness in man but the sign of a divine plan
whereby he is offering his own life as a "ransom for many."
This particular underlying purpose overrules all human desire
in him; it rules him and directs him toward an end beyond all
human desire for happiness and achievement.

It is this divine plan, or end, that makes Jesus so different
from even while he is so near the disciples as, in the words of
the Gospel narrative, he sets his face to go to Jerusalem. In
reading Mark's account one notices again the urgency so typical
of his narrative. The theme—three times mentioned—of this
section is "Behold we go up to Jerusalem." [1] Matthew, as usual,
elaborates the story and fills in the details from his own individual source. Luke likewise follows Mark, stressing no less than
five times the thought expressed in these words: "And it came to
pass, when the time was come that he should be received up, he
set his face to go to Jerusalem." [2] But instead of only elaborating the story of Mark, the Third Evangelist here introduces
material from a Proto-Lukan source and expands the narrative
by inserting into it the major section of his Gospel, found in
Luke 9:51-19:28. By the addition of this rich and important
weight of material, the fast-moving narrative of Mark is slowed
down in its rapid progress toward its goal. But time is gained
thereby to indicate to us that this later ministry of Jesus was not
simply a hastened journey to Jerusalem but was a rather prolonged period of activity associated with the historic border-
lands of Samaria, Perea, and Judea.

That there was, in fact, such a period is sufficiently clear.

[1] Mark 10:17, 32, 33.
[2] Luke 9:51, 57; 10:38; 13:22; 17:2.

The "journey" was therefore not a mile-by-mile movement toward the Holy City, as it is sometimes pictured. Rather, it represented an epoch in Jesus' earthly life to which, by close agreement, the Evangelists give the setting of the region surrounding the Jordan River Valley. The events in it included a farewell visit to, and a lament over, Capernaum, a brief mission in Samaria, a considerably lengthened sojourn in Perea—despite the risk involved in being in a territory of Herod Antipas—and a short period of activity in the lower Jordan, not far from Jericho. Luke interestingly records, early in his interpolated section, that Jesus during this period was entertained at the home of Martha and Mary who—as we know from the account of the Fourth Gospel—lived in Bethany.[3] Did he at that time also visit Jerusalem, as the Gospel of John tells us he did on several occasions before making his final entry there? Quite probably. For recent New Testament scholars—more than those of a generation ago—tend to substantiate the general historicity of the Johannine account.[4]

Another question of interest here presents itself. Did Jesus, in his journey toward Jerusalem, pass through Samaria? Or did he simply reach its borders only to be rebuffed and so turn his footsteps to cross the Jordan into the Decapolis and go southward into Perea? We do not know. Nor does it matter to us, except that in either case he was traveling in territory that, from all appearances, did not welcome him.[5] Luke says that Jesus was warned against going into Perea, which was in the territory governed by Herod Antipas, and that the Samaritans did not receive him "because his face was as though he would go to Jerusalem." But the record implies that Jesus, having a foreordained purpose, was determined to travel there at his own risk. For he was no longer simply *itinerating,* as in the early days in Galilee, nor *wandering,* as he had done through the region of Tyre and Sidon during the climactic weeks, or months, culminating in the crisis in Caesarea Philippi. He was now a determined traveler to the Holy City, a resolute pilgrim

[3] Luke 10:38, John 11:1.
[4] Nevertheless, in its broad outline the Synoptic narrative with its lesser emphasis on chronology is here as elsewhere given a place of precedence.
[5] Luke 9:51-56, 13:31.

who followed the course laid out before him, not knowing the precise circumstances of the way but conscious of the outcome awaiting him at his open declaration of himself as the Messiah and the Son of man.

Luke in his universalism cannot, as he writes, let Jesus feel himself repulsed by the Samaritans for whom there is very definitely a place in the kingdom of God. The parable of the Good Samaritan is proof of his desire to show that, on the highway toward this kingdom, the Samaritan is a good neighbor to the Jew—that in the kingdom itself there is neither Samaritan nor Jew. As for Herod Antipas—if the passage in Luke 13:31-32 belongs to this period in Jesus' ministry—he was but the evil adversary permitted to oppose but not to impede the kingdom's coming and the accomplishment of God's will. Against this opposition of Herod and rebuff in Samaria—their evil design and injured pride—Jesus pursues the course outlined for him. There can be no doubt now that, like Isaac of old,[6] the son walking by the side of the father on the road leading to the place of sacrifice on the hill at Moriah, Jesus as the son of the Father went on his way, questioning but trusting, perhaps pondering the old story:

> And Isaac spake unto Abraham: ... My father.
> And he said: Here am I, my son.
> And he said: Behold the fire and the wood;
> But where is the lamb for a burnt offering?
> And Abraham said: My son,
> God will provide himself a lamb for a burnt offering.

For the story of the journey to Jerusalem we are referred mainly to the record found in Mark 10 and Luke 9:51-19:28. An account parallel to that of Mark is found in Matthew 19:1-20:34. All three accounts, though differing in some detail, are in major agreement. Mark's is direct and brief. It stresses these facts: that Jesus begins again to teach; that he seeks privacy from the multitudes that gather about him; that the Pharisees pursue him with tempting questions, particularly on marriage and divorce; that he stops by the roadside to bless the

[6] Genesis 22:1-13.

little children; that he discourses on how hard it is for those whose hearts are set on riches to enter the kingdom of God. His hearers are "astonished out of measure" when Jesus says: "It is easier for a camel to go through the eye of a needle, than for a rich man to enter into the kingdom of god." [7] But the disciples are even more astonished at what Jesus says about the events to come and at what they perceive in his own person. He seems to them to be invested with an inconceivable solemnity as he goes before them, "striding on ahead," while they follow him, talking to one another. He has twice before spoken to them of the suffering that awaits him in Jerusalem, and they now listen with amazement and fear as he says to them:

> Behold, we go up to Jerusalem; and the Son of man shall be delivered ... unto the scribes, and they shall condemn him to death; ... and shall mock him, and shall scourge him, and shall spit upon him, and shall kill him; and the third day he shall rise again.[8]

But Mark's record—though composed in obvious retrospect—indicates that the disciples do not then understand what Jesus means. And so the narrative moves forward to a more concrete climax. The Evangelist introduces a very human story centering in James and John, who ask for places of honor in the kingdom they think Jesus is soon to set up as he goes to the Holy City. They do not realize that he is going there to drink the cup of suffering. If they are to follow him, it will have to be into the glory of self-sacrifice. Thrones in the kingdom of God are not gained by ambition, they are told; and crowns there are composed of thorns. Jesus is thinking of the Suffering Servant, mentioned in Isaiah 53, as he says:

> Even as the Son of man
> Came not to be ministered unto, but to minister,
> And to give his life a ransom for many.[9]

Luke's account of the Perean ministry extends into ten chapters. The section containing it [10] comprises about one third of

7 Matthew 19:24.
8 Mark 10:33-34.
9 Matthew 20:28.
10 Luke 9:51-19:28.

the entire Gospel.   This Travel Document is famous for its
striking sayings and rich parables.   Scholars see in it some parts
derived from the source Q; but its main source is an independent
Palestinian document accessible to the Evangelist.   Its order of
events is topical rather than chronological.   Held together by
a series of reiterations that Jesus is going up to Jerusalem, the
story deals with these topics: (1) the inhospitable Samaritans;
(2) the three would-be followers of Jesus; (3) the mission of
the Seventy; (4) Mary and Martha; (5) Pilate's slaying of
the Galileans; (6) the healing of the crippled woman; (7) the
threat of Herod, the "Fox"; (8) the healing of the dropsical
man; (9) the ten lepers; (10) Zacchaeus, the publican.

Into this outline of events Luke has incorporated certain
relevant sayings of Jesus, supposedly from the document Q.
These sayings, in the main, may be listed under three headings:
first, those having to do with the question of Christian discipleship; second, those dealing with a designed opposition to Jesus'
message; third, those centering in the imminent future: the time
of crisis, the consummation of the Kingdom, and the advent of
the Son of man.

Finally, there is that remarkable body of material found
nowhere in the New Testament but in the Gospel of Luke.   It
is composed, first, of sayings of Jesus on such important topics
as prayer, the moral life, and the keeping of the holy Sabbath,
and, second, of such famous parables as those of the Good
Samaritan, the Rich Fool, the Lost Sheep, the Prodigal Son,
Dives and Lazarus, the Importunate Widow, and the Pharisee
and the Publican.   In them the ethical teaching is distinct and
final, centering in the concept of the kingdom of God, and presented to us in an unmistakable eschatological setting.

This placing of universal moral teaching in a framework of
eschatology is clearly noticeable throughout the entire Travel
Document.   Luke no sooner seems to settle down to the exposition of an all-time social ethic when he stops in his narrative to
assure us that there is an urgency about what Jesus says that
admits of no delay.   The time for teaching and preaching is
short: the Seventy, on their mission, must not delay the passing
hour; they must not go "from house to house," but simply pass

through the villages, entering here and there, and saying, "Peace be in this house." Similarly, after talking with a certain lawyer about the good life, Jesus begins to speak about prayer. These are universal subjects; all great men discourse on them. But here, note what happens. To his emphasis on the petition "Give us this day our daily bread"—surely a very earthly need—Jesus adds a parable to show that even though the time is late the door to the Kingdom is not yet shut. The thought that seems to be conveyed is that, while there is yet time, God will give us bread enough for the coming day.[11]

It is the same story when Jesus talks of the peril of riches. The topic is "Beware of Covetousness"—surely also a good and timely topic for any age. But the moral advice Jesus gives has its setting in the parable of the Rich Fool. The accent is on "This night is thy soul required of thee"; and the discourse moves toward a climax on the theme of the kingdom of God, by slow degrees, from "Consider the ravens . . . consider the lilies," through "Fear not, little flock: for it is your Father's good pleasure to give you the Kingdom," to the urgent eschatological ending:

> Let your loins be girded about,
> And your lights burning; . . .
> Be ye therefore ready also:
> For the Son of man cometh at an hour
> When ye think not.[12]

Again, Jesus seems to be talking in an almost rabbinical vein of discourse on doing good deeds on the Sabbath day, and on the table manners at a wedding feast, when the theme of the Kingdom begins to unfold itself as the story gets under way. We note the accelerating tempo of Luke's style as the eschatological vision enlarges before him in the parable of the Great Supper.[13] The guests are bidden: "Come, for all things are now ready." Then follow the excuses: "I have bought a piece of ground" . . . "I have bought a yoke of oxen" . . . "I have married a wife" . . . "I pray, have me excused." The master of the

11 Luke 11:1-8.
12 Luke 12:35-40.
13 Luke 14:16.

house, "being angry," invites the poor, the maimed, the halt, and the blind to the feast. The lesson is, at last, clear: they that would enter the Kingdom must act at once, and not count the cost:

If any man come to me, and hate not his father, and mother, and wife, and children, and brethren, and sisters, yea, and his own life also, he cannot be my disciple.[14]

The parables that follow are delivered in the same strain: from the parable of the Prodigal Son to the parable of the Talents. And the interspersed sayings—some of which are found in Matthew's collection under the title of the Sermon on the Mount—breathe the same spirit. They are, as it now appears, plain enough—eschatologically presented. Were they also so conceived and spoken by Jesus himself? Probably so. For if the eschatological pattern was Luke's own, or that of the early church, what of the sayings themselves? Are the ethical teachings more *original* than their eschatological setting? Scholars of New Testament criticism are divided on this question. But what Luke quotes Jesus as saying is clearly before us; and it is through this concept of the Kingdom that we ourselves may enter most fully into the deep consciousness of Jesus.

II

THE OVERSHADOWING CROSS

It is now evident that we are here, as in our study of the Galilean period of Jesus' earthly ministry, face to face with one of the major questions of New Testament interpretation. Did our Lord look on the kingdom of God as eschatological and as therefore lying wholly in the future? Did he view it as an apocalyptic or sudden revelation to be accompanied by signs of demonic violence in nature and the final overthrow of Satan's rule in the world, according to the picture presented to us in the Book of Daniel?[15] Or is this apocalyptic-eschatological element in the Gospels but the outer shell or husk of the Kingdom's

14 Luke 14:26.
15 Daniel 7:13-22.

essential and ethical teaching? Stated more simply, did Jesus teach that the kingdom of God was already come or was yet to come? Combining these questions, may we answer them categorically by saying that the Kingdom was, in fact, present in the person of Christ, and that it was yet to come in its full and consummate glory (1) after Jesus' resurrection, (2) during the courses of future world history, and (3) at the end of time? Finally, against such considerations, what of the significance of Jesus' ethical and social teaching for our time?

Here, surely, we find material enough for the exercise of our thought; for these questions, we can see, involve both the integrity of the New Testament and the meaning and message of Christ to the modern world. To find their answers requires careful critical study. But, answer them as we may, the ultimate solution, as in all Bible study, lies in our response to the gospel record as the word of God. That it is indeed such, we know; and that Christ is himself the Kingdom's pivoting fact we know also. When, therefore, Jesus says "The kingdom of God is within you," we may believe him. But when, speaking eschatologically, he uses language already familiar to all faithful adherents to Judaism, we need not say that such language was but the—to us now dried up and wasted—shell of the kernel of truth he taught. Least of all, will it be ours to say that all that is eschatological in the Gospels was later put into them by the practical necessity of the early church. Finally, the problem is not solved by supposing that Jesus' own views, as time passed, underwent a marked change. All that we can say is that, despite all disparate views, the eschatological note in the Gospels remains. Without this clear note they would contain less than the Christian gospel; for they would be like a violin, one of whose strings had lost its tension.

We have by now noted that, side by side with Jesus' outgoing compassion toward the multitudes, the Evangelists present us with a picture of his forward-going passion as he proceeds on his journey to Jerusalem. In the one we seem to see the human, in the other the divine motive driving him into activity. In reality they are but one mighty activity to him, representing the social and the eschatological dimensions of the

kingdom of God. Jesus' social passion was intense and out-reaching; but it was his forward-going passion by which he drew all those whom he touched with him in the Kingdom's onward progress toward its goal. The whole creaturely world is thus drawn to him and carried toward its redemption. In plain words, the social motive in him is controlled by the higher all-governing motive of the Kingdom. To Jesus, as the Evangelists picture him to us, the Kingdom was everything. It was the great divine event in which he was God's chosen agent. To state the fact differently, in a hierarchy of values it was the transposition of a lower into a higher good—like the transposition, as C. S. Lewis says,[16] by which, for example, "the sensation that accompanies joy becomes itself joy." This highest good was represented in Jesus' sacrifice of himself to bring in the Kingdom. In the language of Saint John's Gospel, it was to be the Cross by which he was at last to draw all men unto him.[17] And while he went alone, he bade his disciples to follow after him into the fellowship of that kingdom, that is, into the divine glory of a self-surrendered life. In it the gospel as history was to stand fully revealed. And there the Cross stands today, the symbol of redemptive reality, calling us to a Life beyond life:

> Up to Mount Calvary
> If thou desir'st to go,
> Then take thy cross, and follow Christ,
> Thou canst not miss it so.[18]

It was this urgency by which Jesus was now moved. This, we say again, did not mean for him any absence of an interest in contemporary life or in the world around about him. He found in it room enough for the exercise of mundane virtues and for enjoining them on his disciples and through them on mankind. It was not solely an "interim ethic" that he taught. We know well enough that he had a message for men of all time. And when at last, after Christ's death, the curtain to the apocalyptic hope was lifted and Christian history began, the

---

[16] C. S. Lewis, *The Weight of Glory* (New York: The Macmillan Co., 1948), p. 27.
[17] John 3:14, 12:32.
[18] Samuel Rowlands, "The Highway to Calvary" (*Circa* 1600).

church—and the prolonged era of Christendom thereafter—was to have given to it a faith to sustain it until, in the end, God's will could be declared as being done and the eschatological fulfilment of the gospel could be realized. But now, in that segment of historic time in which Jesus did his work, the world was a field ready for harvest and the kingdom of God, though having begun, was still mainly yet to come. It was both present and future—perhaps best conceived by us in modern philosophical terms as the absolute in time, but pressing upon time, working, so to speak, against time toward time's fulfilment, the existential in the midst of the circumstantial, the seed germinating in the soil, the net cast for the gathering of souls. Never had there been more need of goodness than now, of meekness and righteousness and mercy and of the self-sacrifice implicit in the Kingdom's Good News. Jesus indeed now demanded of his disciples that self-sacrifice to which the Evangelists, later recording the narrative, gave the name of cross-bearing. The shadow of the Cross, the gospel tradition tells us, was upon him. To those who followed him—noticeably to Peter, who later recalled the events—it made Jesus seem like a changed person. The early sunlit days of the Kingdom's announcement were over. The Messianic crisis was close at hand. In the words, here pertinent, of the theologian Julius Wellhausen:

> The Gospel, as the Apostles taught it, now really begins. . . . A transfigured Jesus stands before us. . . . He is now no longer preoccupied with public instruction but with prophesies about himself. It is no longer the people to whom he speaks; it is now the intimate little company of disciples. . . . He accepts Peter's confession that he is the Messiah. . . . He goes up to Jerusalem, not to set up the Kingdom, but to be crucified. . . . The demand to follow him . . . is addressed particularly to the few; for it is a demand to follow Jesus to death.[19]

Such, in essence, is Mark's story. The figure he presents to us in the person of Jesus is severely noble yet serene. It is the figure of the strong Son of God about to take on himself the office of Messiah so recently attributed to him by the disciples

[19] *The Gospel of Mark,* Section 43.

through the spokesmanship of Peter.   In the twilight into which his earthly life is passing, he seems to hear the voice of the great Unknown Prophet of the Exile—who himself lived in a time of twilight between two ages—directing him to assume the role of the Suffering Servant of God by his offering of himself as a "ransom for many."   There, in the darkness of the Cross that awaits him—as the disciples are later to understand it and the Evangelists to record it—the will of God is to be fully done. As in his life thus far, in his words and acts, he has discerned the signs of the Act of God, so by his death this mightiest of God's Acts is to be accomplished.

The risk of it all must have passed before the mind of Christ as he contemplated its meaning to him and to the world.   And the Synoptic Evangelists, though they knew the outcome as they later told the story, did not minimize the risk.   Jesus was to be "despised and rejected of men, a man of sorrows, and acquainted with grief"; even the disciples were to "hide their faces from him"; and Peter—how true is here the story!—was to "esteem him not." [20]   Mark tells that Jesus knew the cost at which the Kingdom was to be brought in.   It was to be born of agony, through being mocked and scourged and spit upon; it was to involve drinking the cup of suffering and being baptized with the baptism of death.[21]   Could anything be more concrete and real than that?   Those who then looked upon the kingdom of God as a nationalistic dream—like those who look upon it now as a sociological utopia—could well pause to take note of how, in such a crucible of suffering, the mundane virtues and social teachings of the Kingdom were to be alchemized and transformed into an ethic of heavenly pattern.   Such a program required action, immediate and wholehearted.   There was no room now for any expanding and interrogating argument. Everything within the Kingdom was to be compressed into one act and toward one end: one precious pearl to be bought; one hidden treasure to be sought, at great risk and cost.   We are not surprised, therefore, that Jesus, as he enters Jericho and sees Zacchæus, curious and observant of the procession passing by,

[20] Isaiah 53:3, Mark 14:66-72.
[21] Mark 10:34-40.

says to him: "Zacchæus, make haste and come down, for today I must abide at thy house." [22] Luke tells us that the rich little publican made haste and came down from his place of vantage in the sycamore tree and received Jesus joyfully. The incident and the gospel truth it conveys are enshrined by Francis Quarles in these apt words:

> Methinks I see with what a busy haste
> Zaccheus climed the tree. But, O, how fast,
> How full of speed, canst thou imagine—when
> Our Saviour called—he powdered down again!
> He ne'er made trial if the boughs were sound,
> Or rotten; nor how far 'twas to the ground.
> There was no danger feared. At such a call,
> He'll venture nothing, that dare fear a fall,
> Needs must he down, by such a spirit driven;
> Nor could he fall, unless he fell to Heaven.
> Down came Zaccheus, ravished from the tree;
> Bird that was shot, ne'er dropped so quick as he.

[22] Luke 19:1-10.

Chapter 26

HOSTILITY IN JERUSALEM

I

COLLISION WITH THE PRIESTS AND SCRIBES

Before undertaking our study of the closing days of Jesus' earthly ministry, we ought again to remind ourselves of the point of view from which the Evangelists composed their narrative. They were but wishing to preserve the tradition as it assumed shape immediately after the death and resurrection of Jesus. That Jesus was indeed the Christ had by then been demonstrated by the resolute serenity with which he had accepted his trial at the hands of his enemies and by his death on the Cross. The disciples had come to realize that this final offer of himself in his death had not only been by the will of God but an act of God—the mightiest act and the most meaningful event in gospel history. Through this event the divine plan for the redemption of mankind lay openly revealed to them. Now Christ was risen and was the Lord of life, and there was a gospel to be preached, as Luke the Evangelist could record it, first, "in Jerusalem and in all Judea and Samaria," and thereafter "unto the uttermost part of the earth." [1]

But before all this information had been written down and preserved, it had become the subject of a generation of apostolic preaching. It will be recalled that, in reality, "Jesus did not come to preach the gospel: he came that there might be a gospel to be preached." He did not come only to proclaim the word of life. He was himself that Word. And as it was preached it took form, centering in the passion story to which, in a following chapter, we are to give our attention. Almost immediately, around this great central story other stories began to

[1] Acts 1:8.

267

gather, based on the acts and sayings of Jesus as these were
related to his Messianic mission: stories of miracles, parables,
and other teachings on the dominant theme of the Kingdom of
God, which was the event in divine history of which Christ,
through his coming, was the providentially appointed agent. As
the chosen Messiah he was both the Son of God and the Son
of man. Accordingly he was called of God, first, to a life of
humiliation—his entire earthly life was that humiliation—culminating in his acceptance of the office or role of the Suffering
Servant, and, second, to a transcendent place of glory as the
prospective judge and ruler of mankind. Now, as the gospel—so evidently both Christological and eschatological—was
preached, there began to take form, from this nucleus of the
living truth, the first body of Christian doctrine as it is now
preserved for us, for example, in Acts 2:22-24 and in I Corinthians 15:3-11, in which both Saints Peter and Paul bear early
witness to the fact

> that Christ died for our sins, according to the scriptures; and that
> he was buried; and that he rose again the third day according to
> the scriptures; and that he was seen of Cephas [Peter]; then of
> the twelve;...and, last of all, that he appeared to me [Paul] also.

It is against this background that we must now view Jesus'
triumphal entry into Jerusalem. All four of the Evangelists
record the event. Mark's brevity, here as elsewhere, is our
surest guide; though Matthew, Luke, and John add certain important details to the story. The time is five days before the
last Passover of Jesus' earthly life. The Fourth Gospel tells us
that Jesus was staying in the house of Mary and Martha, awaiting the time when he should inaugurate the divine history of
his passion. In a setting in which Lazarus, lately raised from
the dead, is present, Mary is depicted as anointing the feet of
Jesus and wiping them with her hair. The Synoptists place the
anointment later in the narrative, but the symbolism of the act
remains the same: Jesus is Messiah; he is king; he is to rule
not through self-exaltation but through self-humiliation; he is
anointed unto death to rise again as the Lord of life. The oint-

ment pleasing to God is not poured out for social charity but to bring in the kingdom of God. The care for the poor is not allowed to serve as a substitute for the Kingdom. The gospel is not humanitarianism; it is self-sacrifice for the absolute ideal of the Kingdom. And the Gospels quote Jesus as saying that the reason that the gospel is hereafter to be preached to the poor is the impending fact of his own passion. It is for this reason also that even today in the church's celebration of the holy sacrament of the Lord's Supper an appeal is made to give alms to the poor. All true Christian charity has this Eucharistic background. It is the sweet odor of Christ's sacrifice on the Cross.

The symbolism of Jesus' Messiahship is carried further in the story of the triumphant entry. In reading it we notice, first of all, its prophetic context; and, after that, its specific application to this signal act of Jesus. The picture of the kingly Christ riding into Jerusalem on the lowly ass is of one piece with that of the humble birth of the child of the house of David in the stable at Bethlehem. It is a picture of divine humiliation. Luke uses something of the same language in describing both: the palm-waving multitudes echo the voice of the angels in the birth story, as they say, "Peace in heaven, and glory in the highest!" [2] There is rejoicing in heaven and on earth at this demonstration of the manner in which God is bringing in the Kingdom. Even the lowliest creation is thereby glorified. The poet G. K. Chesterton gives us a moment of insight into this homely truth as he speaks in behalf of "a colt, the foal of an ass":

> The tattered outlaw of the earth,
>   Of ancient crooked will;
> Starve, scourge, deride me: I am dumb,
>   I keep my secret still.
>
> Fools! For I also had my hour;
>   One far fierce hour and sweet:
> There was a shout about my ears,
>   And palms before my feet! [3]

[2] Cf. Luke 2:14 and 19:38.
[3] "The Donkey," from *The Wild Knight and Other Poems*, 1927. Used by permission of the publishers, E. P. Dutton & Co., Inc., New York.

We note, besides, in Luke another vivid contrast: while the multitude rejoices, Jesus looks on the Holy City and weeps. The Messiah is the prince of peace; but Jerusalem does not know "the things which belong unto peace." [4] The King comes; but he is to be rejected; and for this rejection the Holy City is under the judgment of destruction. The keynote of the incident is Hosanna, meaning "God save us now!" The voice of the ancient prophet announces: "Rejoice greatly, O daughter of Zion . . . behold, thy King cometh unto thee." [5] And the people answer their glad acceptance of him—Matthew saying that they "spread their garments in the way," and John adding that they met him waving palm branches in their hands—in these words:

> Hosanna!
> Blessed is he that cometh . . .
> Blessed be the kingdom . . .
> That cometh in the name of the Lord.
> Hosanna in the highest! [6]

Mark tells us that it was evening when Jesus reached Jerusalem and entered the temple, and that "when he had looked round about upon all things . . . he went out unto Bethany with the twelve." [7] Is this statement intended to tell us that the day ended in an anticlimax? If so, it was prophetic of what was to follow. On the next day he returned to the city and, entering the temple, found it crowded with people. But what he saw outraged his spirit; for he found it filled with money-changers, buyers and sellers of animals for the temple sacrifice. The spirit of commercialism had taken possession of the religious leaders of Judaism. Seized with prophetic indignation, Jesus overturned the tables of the money-changers and closed the outer door to the Court of the Gentiles and cried out against this desecration and said: "My house shall be called a house of prayer—but ye have made it a den of thieves." [8] Truly, Juda-

[4] Luke 19:42.
[5] Zechariah 9:9.
[6] Mark 11:9-10.
[7] Mark 11:11.
[8] Mark 11:17.

ism needed a divine cleansing. It was the carrier of a great faith. No one knew this better than Jesus; he had himself been brought up under the shadow of the synagogue, had visited Jerusalem, and had been taught the Torah, the Jewish law, in accordance with the commandment in Deuteronomy 6:6-9:

> These words ... shall be in thine heart; and thou shalt teach them diligently unto thy children, and shalt talk of them when thou sittest in thine house, and when thou walkest by the way, and when thou liest down, and when thou risest up.

But Judaism, with all its great history, was spiritually decadent. It was like a barren fig tree which, as Luke says, had been digged about and dunged but bore no fruit. Mark says—if the story may be given this symbolical meaning—that Jesus was hungry to see fruit on this tree. But it bore only leaves. How typical of men's spiritual lives, then and now! Jesus' indignation was justified; it was the sign of God's judgment on those whose religious life was outwardly flourishing but withered at the root.

Mark seems to regard these events as preliminary to Jesus' brief Jerusalem ministry. The coming of Messiah and the cleansing of Israel to receive him prepare the way for the scene of divine judgment whose theme is introduced by the cursing of the fig tree and is carried to its climax in the "Little Apocalypse" recorded in Mark 13. The period is viewed by the Evangelist as a single historic act in the divine drama of redemption. The incidents reported form a unit of gospel tradition, a kind of gospel in miniature, an aggregation of preaching elements held together by the Christological-eschatological concept of the Kingdom's coming: first, in grace; and finally, in judgment. Mark sees Jesus' Jerusalem ministry beginning with the salutation, "Blessed is the Kingdom that cometh," and ending with the final foreboding words: "Seest thou these great buildings? There shall not be left here one stone upon another which shall not be thrown down." [9] The apocalypse, or epiphany, that follows is directed to the disciples. It may be regarded as an epilogue to the Act on the topic of the Kingdom's final consum-

[9] Mark 11:10, 13:2.

mation, ending in the Last Judgment and the sudden coming of
the Son of man "in the clouds with great power and glory." [10]

Matthew's and Luke's narratives generally follow the Markan
plan, expanding it here and there and giving to it the direction
of the aim and intent of their respective Gospels. No passage,
perhaps, so well sums up the Jerusalem ministry of Jesus, its
characterizing notes of divine compassion and judgment, as that
which Matthew and Luke have preserved for us from the source
Q. The passage seems to be misplaced in Luke 13:34; but it
is given its appropriate setting in Matthew 23:37, where it combines Hebrew prophecy, Jewish history, and Christian eschatology in an utterance of unparalleled poignance and beauty:

> O Jerusalem, Jerusalem,
> Thou that killest the prophets,
> And stonest them which are sent unto thee
> How often would I have gathered thy children together,
> Even as a hen gathereth her chickens under her wings,
> And ye would not!
> Behold, your house is left unto you desolate.
> For I say unto you,
> Ye shall not see me henceforth, till ye shall say,
> Blessed is he that cometh in the name of the Lord.

The passage in Mark 11:27-12:37 is controversial. It is at
once obvious that Jesus is here on hostile ground. He is not
invited, or allowed, to teach and to preach as he did in Galilee.
There is almost no one who hears him gladly. The disciples,
as yet loyal, are filled with strange misgivings, while the scribes
and priests and Sadducees push to the forefront of the scene.
The atmosphere in the temple where, Mark says, Jesus is walking is tense with feeling as the representatives of the Sanhedrin
press on him with their questions. The passion week is turned
into one of inquisition, crowding out the memory of Israel's
wondrous deliverance from the bondage of Egypt. The lamb
of sacrifice is being prepared, but in a sense far greater than
the officiating priests at the time realize. As we read on through
the story, we are aware of the providential plan—the divine

[10] Mark 13:26.

history, as we have called it—in all that takes place; and it is not difficult for us to trace the movement of the Evangelist's editorial hand as he shapes the material of the gospel tradition toward this great end. That end, or aim, is the open declaration (1) of Jesus as Christ the Messiah, and (2) of the coming of his kingdom in suffering and glory. Everything pushes toward this final conclusion. The argument proceeds. The controversy moves to and fro. But as the tension heightens, Jesus' inquisitors are left behind to wrangle among themselves in their intense hatred, while he goes onward, forward toward the fulfilment of his divine task, leaving us to follow him with wonder, pondering on the meaning of it all. The poet Swinburne, groping as we do for the ultimate meaning, expressed it, though vaguely, in these words:

> Ye shall seek me and shall not reach me
> Till the wine press be trod;
> In that hour ye shall turn and beseech me,
> Saith the Lord God.[11]

Five controversial issues present themselves in the Markan passage to which we have referred. They center in these timely themes: (1) the divine authority of Jesus as Lord and Christ; (2) the question of loyalty to God and to Caesar—we would say today, of church and state; (3) the doctrine of the resurrection of the dead; (4) the first and great commandment of God; (5) the definition of Messiah. The controversy is followed by Jesus' word of warning to the disciples to take heed of those Pharisees who "sit in Moses' seat," imposing the jot and tittle of the law on others, but who themselves "devour widows' houses and for a pretense make long prayers." Over against them Jesus gives us the picture of the poor widow who brought her hard-earned farthing to the temple treasury and thereby judged the rich who gave ostentatiously what they could easily spare.

> Two mites, two drops, yet all her house and land,
> Falls from a steady heart, though trembling hand:

---

[11] "What shall be the Sign?" from the poem *The End of the World.*

The other's wanton wealth foams high, and brave,
The other cast away, she only gave.[12]

Observing closely the Evangelistic record before us, we note that while the people greeted the Messiah with Hosannas and waving palms, the Sanhedrin confronted him with armed disputation. Shielding themselves behind the Law, they threw their baiting darts at him. But Jesus was no martyr to Messianism. He was its bringer. He would concede to no compromise with the enemy of the Kingdom. Divine wisdom and strategy, he knew, were necessary to combat the casuistry and evil design of those who had appointed themselves the protectors of an established Ezra-Mosaic cult. We can easily imagine them entrenched in their power and pride, these solemn and cunning sages of the Sanhedrin shaking their heads, having their will, awaiting the day of their victory which—according to the Gospel narrative—was but the prelude to their defeat and Jerusalem's fall.

This pride and legalized opposition was the more regrettable since Judaism, as we have said, was the carrier of a great tradition, both Mosaic and Messianic, in which Moses and the prophets—the law and the hope of Israel—were jointly stressed. Jesus had no desire but to maintain this great tradition. The concept of the kingdom of God was definitely set within its framework, its one aspect being ethical and social, its other, prophetic and historical. The doctrines of righteousness, of holiness, and of love, preached, for example, by the prophets Amos, Isaiah, and Hosea, were both ethical and supernatural. They were in reality synonymous with the righteousness, the holiness, and the redemptive love of God as these were presupposed in the teaching of Jesus. The law as taught alike by Israel's prophets and priests was clearly preparatory. It was an integral part of the gospel tradition. Old Testament prophecy, in particular, had made a great contribution to this tradition through its emphasis on the twofold order of the world: the temporal and the supratemporal. The one was easily recognizable in the political history—the rise and fall, for example, of

[12] Richard Crashaw, "The Widow's Mite." (Seventeenth century.)

the Hebrew nation; the other was just as recognizable in the prophetic word of God which was "from everlasting to ever-lasting," and in the frequent allusion to the Kingdom that would "have no end." It was obvious enough to those who read the Old Testament with a discerning insight that the supernatural order was in a continuous state of suspense above the natural order: it was like the overshadowing pillar of a cloud by day and the pillar of fire by night during the journey of the children of Israel in the wilderness.[13] That symbolism was a picture of the manner in which the Lord watched over Israel's history: the nation's day of glory and its night of humiliating exile. But it was a matter of certainty to her prophets and seers that God was Himself making history, divine history, by means of these events. He had indeed chosen Israel—so the prophets said repeatedly—toward this divine historic end.

Jesus' controversy with the Jewish leaders is to be interpreted against this historic background. Its essential content is well summed up in the Markan account of the parable of the vine-yard.[14] The parable was more than an answer to a question about Jesus' divine authority. It was an indictment of his hostile inquisitors. Had not the Kingdom been both offered to them and entrusted to their care? They were, by their own proud claim, the keepers of their Lord's vineyard. But they had failed in the task entrusted to them. Judaism was indeed good tillage, but it was kept from being fruitful by its faith-less husbandmen. Now their time of grace was ended. Their day of judgment had come. And this was the sign that the day was at hand: the wicked keepers of the vineyard were about to kill the Owner's son; they would slay the rightful heir that they themselves might lay claim to the inheritance. The plain truth was that Jesus was talking to his own self-revealed mur-derers. Were they, self-betrayed and inflamed with anger, now ready to stone him for what he had said? If so, Jesus did not fear or spare them. After telling them that the stone which they the builders of God's temple had rejected was destined to

13 Numbers 9:15-23.
14 Mark 12:1-12.

become the "head of the corner," he is quoted by Matthew as surprising them with words like these:

> Does this saying offend you? You will be shocked to hear that it is you who will be rejected. The stone of the building will stand, except as God Himself will lift and move it to rebuild His Temple. But hear this final warning:
>> He that falleth on this stone
>> Shall be broken to pieces;
>> But he on whom it shall fall,
>> It will scatter him as dust.[15]

II

DISCOURSES ON THE FINAL JUDGMENT

This initial encounter of Jesus with the Sanhedrin which now so bitterly opposed him was typical of those that followed. We can see in them the larger evangelistic pattern of the discourses on the final judgment with which his Jerusalem ministry is to come to its close. The controversy on the tribute to Caesar [16] further increases the tension between Jesus and the Pharisees who are now joined by the Herodians. The particular area of tension is that between the kingdom of God and the kingdom of this world. We note at once the allusion to the satanic wickedness that calls forth the statement: "Why tempt ye me, ye hypocrites?" And we marvel at the manner in which Jesus captures the initiative in the dispute as he says, "Show me the tribute money." And they brought unto him a penny.... "Whose is this image and superscription?" His opponents are startled at his answer that men owe an allegiance to a temporal as well as to a supratemporal authority. The two orders or dominions are not confused; each is given its own and rightful existence. But there can be no question of which transcends and so ultimately embraces the other. For all Creation is God's; and the state whose right to exist is here acknowledged is within the category of divinely ordered things, and so subject to Him.

[15] Matthew 21:42-44. (Variant translation.)
[16] Mark 12:13-17.

All is God's; yet 'tis true
All we have is Caesar's too.
All is Caesar's; and what odds,
So long as Caesar's self is God's.[17]

It is with a pleasing sense of relief—or is this but the stillness before the storm?—that we come upon the story of the
good scribe [18] who asked to know the first great commandment
of God and who, according to the report of Mark, was in full
agreement with Jesus' answer.[19]   The sympathetic scribe was
no doubt acquainted with the quotations from Deuteronomy 6
and Leviticus 19.   It seems to have delighted him to hear how
Jesus joined together the two commandments by implying that
to love God wholly, that is, with all one's heart, and soul, and
mind, and strength, meant, in its full and final application, to
love one's neighbor as one's self.   For, to apply the truth also
to ourselves, no one can wholly love God and not love mankind
which is His creation.   But there can be no question of where,
by Christian standards, the emphasis is to be placed.   All social
and humanitarian virtue—whatever modern political or economic pattern it may assume—is conditioned on man's vital
and moral and intellectual love of God.   What makes this commandment Christian is the doctrine that God Himself is love.
To know God is to know this love by which all things in heaven
and on earth are moved.

But this pleasant interlude of conciliation between Jesus and
the temple authorities is all too soon interrupted.   The climactic
moment is impending.   The iron curtain of Jewish hatred,
reinforced by Roman authority, is slowly descending on the
scene.   Once more the Pharisees occupy the central stage, and
we listen to Jesus' description of them as men who like to be
seen walking in long robes, to be envied as they sit in the chief
places at the feasts, while to demonstrate their hypocrisy they
"devour widows' houses and for a pretense make long prayers."

[17] Richard Crashaw, "Render to Caesar ... and to God."
[18] Mark 12:28-34.
[19] Cf. the parallel accounts in Matthew 22:34-40 and Luke 10:25-28, in
which the "tempting" scribe, or lawyer, reflects the later attitude of the
Jews toward the Christians.   But note, for further comparison, Luke 20:
39-40.

We see Jesus linger a little while near the temple treasury where he observes how the rich are casting in of what they do not need, while the poor widow is giving of her want and therefore her very living.   And, continuing with Mark's account, we follow Jesus as he leaves the temple—the little company of the disciples going with him—and passes through the gate of the city on his way to the Mount of Olives.   We look back with one of the disciples and hear him say: "What an imposing pile of stones!   And what magnificent buildings!"   Jesus' answer comes to us direct and ominous: "There shall not be left here one stone upon another, which shall not be thrown down." And so, quite abruptly, we come to the end of our Lord's public ministry.

Much discussion has centered on the Little Apocalypse recorded in Mark 13.   Some scholars see in it only the reflected view of the later Christian church as, in a time of persecution, it looks backward upon the destruction of Jerusalem and forward to its deliverance at the victorious coming of the Son of man.   This view seems indeed to be justified by the facts of the story as one notes them in the scenes depicted in the chapter and in the versions of Matthew and Luke based on the Markan account.   But it is not to be supposed that this apocalypse is the Evangelists' invention.   The backward look is there, more particularly in Luke's narrative,[20] with its accurate reference to the manner in which, in A.D. 70, Jerusalem was encompassed by the Roman army under Vespasian and Titus; and it is noticeable in the account of Matthew in which the apocalyptic vision is heightened by an emphasis on the *signs* [21] that are to accompany the Parousia—that is, the advent of the Son of man and the consequent end of time.   But at the center of this cosmic drama, at the core of the apocalypse, we may clearly see the figure of Jesus and hear the words which actually and most naturally came from his own lips as he sat with the disciples on the Mount of Olives overlooking Jerusalem.   The reference, in Mark 13:14, to "the abomination of desolation" is clearly based on Daniel 9:27 in which the prophet is alluding to the

[20] Luke 21:20-24.
[21] Matthew 24:3.

desecration of the temple by Antiochus Epiphanes in 168 B.C. The description that follows has the vividness of an act of historic drama:

> Let them that be in Judea flee unto the mountains:...
> Let him that is in the field not turn back for to take his
>   garment....
> Woe unto them that are with child...in those days!

But there remains the Danielic discourse on the coming of the Son of man. The time, the signs, the warning against false prophets, the eschatological picture of the last judgment, and the climactic "Watch, therefore, for ye know not when the lord of the house cometh," are in keeping with what we may read elsewhere in the Gospels in which the apocalyptic note is clearly present and which formed a part of the primitive tradition. Most impressive in the story as we read it is "the difference in tone between Mark 13 and the Galilean Gospel which began and ended with 'the Kingdom of God is at hand.'" In contrast, the burden of Mark 13 is as follows:

> Wait: Do not always be imagining that the End is coming. It
> will seem a long time to you and you will have a hard time of it;
> but be firm and patient, and above all things be ready, and you
> will not lose your reward. The great Day will come: this gen-
> eration will not pass before you see Daniel's Heavenly Man
> descend and gather together the Elect. You cannot tell when it
> will be, but watch, watch, let Him not find you unprepared! [22]

There remain the eschatological parables to be found in Matthew 25. This is their urgent text: "Be prepared; be faithful; be occupied in the work of the Kingdom." The chapter is a part of Matthew's version of the Little Apocalypse. It reflects conditions within the church as they existed near to the year A.D. 75. Jerusalem had fallen; yet the Parousia, the second coming of the Lord, had not taken place. Was it not now daily imminent? [23] What were the signs to which the faithful were to look, and the duties to which they were to apply

---

[22] F. C. Burkitt, *Jesus Christ: An Historical Outline* (London: Blackie & Son, Ltd., 1932), p. 49.
[23] See in this connection Saint Paul's letters to the Thessalonians.

themselves while they waited? The answers are given in the three parables of the Ten Virgins, the Talents, and the Last Judgment. They exactly fit the later apostolic time—and ours. What they say is that some Christians are wise; others are foolish. Some use their Godgiven talents; others do not. Some do genuine deeds of Christian charity; others neglect them.

But one cannot read the parables merely as ethical exhortation. They are not "sacred" inventions—story-teachings penned by someone wishing to commemorate the good life of Jesus. They have their roots in the actual sayings of our Lord and are an integral part of the primitive Christian tradition. For these parables are Kingdom-centered, with the stress on the Kingdom's delay but its certainty of coming, in precise keeping with the pattern of Jesus' later eschatological discourses. If we accept the change in Jesus' outlook from an earlier "Rejoice, for the kingdom of heaven is at hand" to a later "The coming of the Kingdom is delayed—but watch, pray, be ready: it will come suddenly, in glory and in judgment, at an hour you know not," [24] we shall understand these parables to mean what they obviously intend to say. They will no longer seem to be only "a curiously involved mixture of ideas drawn from various sources," [25] or to have a merely antiquarian or "interim" place in the gospel record. They will become real to us, unlimited in their interpretation by the category of any given time. That, we must conclude, is what the early church believed them to be; and it is for this reason that they have become Holy Scripture.

The parable of the Last Judgment is a dramatic summing up of all things at the world's end. [26] Here the world is indeed the stage. God, the King, is Himself on the throne. Christ and his brethren, represented in the Son of man, are beside Him. Before them are the world's nations and peoples: those on the right are the sheep; those on the left are the goats. It is the great judgment day. The question now is not: "How good and humane and honest have you been?" It is: "Have you been loyal to the Kingdom—to Christ whose cause is now one

[24] See Mark 13; Matthew 24; Luke 12.
[25] T. W. Manson, H. D. A. Major, and C. J. Wright, *The Mission and Message of Jesus* (New York: The Macmillan Co., 1941), p. 534.
[26] Matthew 25:34-46.

with his brethren? The Kingdom has been brought in at a cost, at the price of hunger and thirst, homelessness and nakedness and imprisonment. What share have you had in these sacrifices?" Those on the King's right hand have not been conscious of the cost: their minds have been wholly on the great enterprise of the Kingdom. Those on the left have been unaware that the Kingdom has been brought in at such great cost. They have done nothing. There is no need now for any arbitrary decree. The nondoers have separated themselves from God everlastingly. That is their terrifying punishment. The faithful doers of the Kingdom enter into everlasting life.

Chapter 27

JESUS ALONE WITH HIS DISCIPLES

I

THE LAST SUPPER

There is a wise saying of Martin Luther that "the Scriptures are the crib wherein Christ is laid." This truth becomes increasingly evident as we look closely at the manner in which the Biblical record presents us with the life of Christ. It is not a magic story, or a golden biography, that we have here before us, but a plain substantial history overshadowed by a divine Providence, as the manger of Bethlehem where the Christ child lay was watched over by the star and overshadowed by the angels. Within the pages of this record, Luther means to say, lies the cradled living Word "wrapped in swaddling clothes"; but above and around it is "the multitude of the heavenly hosts." It is not the crib but the Christ that we need to know and, like the ancient Wise Men, would worship.

This truth has a special bearing on the Gospel narrative of the Last Supper. Much more is contained in it than the report of a final meeting of Jesus with his disciples. The event itself is clearly the outer shell enclosing an inner living fact. As we remove the reported incidents one by one—as we might remove the leaves of an ear of corn—we find the vital kernel kept intact for us in a group of great and related historic symbols: the Upper Room; the Paschal Lamb; the Bread and Wine—the Christian symbols of the sacrament of the Lord's Supper, or Holy Eucharist. In them, rather than in the story itself, the church found, and still finds, nourishment for its faith.

These symbols are, so to speak, the germinal core of the gospel: that is, in them the revealed truth of divine history, of what God has done for mankind, is put into the language and

form of a meaningful liturgy for our easier understanding. The incidents themselves are of course authentic. They belong to history. The truths they contain and the symbols enshrining them are above history. What we mean to say is that everything spoken of as historical takes place in time: it has a today, a yesterday, and is no more. But the truth it conveys lasts. It endures. In the Gospel narrative it is the gospel's imperishable part; it is the Word of God that will not pass away. The distinction will become clear to us when we put it this way: the Last Supper is history; the Lord's Supper is a sacrament celebrating the perennial presence of Christ in the world. Yet the history and the sacrament are inseparably joined together, as we may see in these simple lines of an unknown sixteenth-century poet who wrote of Jesus' words, "This is my body":

> He was the Word that spake it,
> He took the bread and brake it;
> And what that Word did make it,
> I do believe and take it.

Mark the Evangelist presents us with the story of the Last Supper in its true and larger framework. It is one of antithesis, setting forth the scene of world conflict in which Jesus is the center. On one side of the stage are the chief priests who discuss their plot to kill Jesus; on the other stands Judas Iscariot, ready to betray him. At the foreground of the preliminary scene we see the woman anointing Jesus for his burial. The atmosphere, on the shadowy border, is one of aggressive hatred and an uneasy show of discipleship; but before us, in the clear light, we witness the divine drama in the outpouring of the priceless ointment of love on the head of Christ. Finally, as the narrative proceeds,[1] from the central figure of this preconceived drama of redemption about to be enacted on the Cross, we hear these words:

> Verily, I say unto you,
> Wheresoever the gospel shall be preached...
> That also which this woman hath done
> Shall be spoken of for a memorial of her.

[1] Mark 14:1-21.

The Evangelists, together, tell us that the time was now the beginning of the Passover. There can be no doubt that their record is correct. But it is obvious that this setting especially suited the story they were about to tell. It was in this form that the tradition had come down to them, not only to the Synoptic writers but to the author of the Fourth Gospel. We must conclude, in the light of his foreknowledge of the events to come, that Jesus himself had so planned it. If so, it was his purpose by his own act to unite in one supreme concept the memorial of Israel's deliverance from bondage to Egypt[2] and the current hope of the coming of Messiah[3] with the Unknown Prophet's greater vision of a world redemption through the office of the self-sacrificing Servant of God.[4] Thus the entire history of the Old Testament might serve as a framework for the later interpretation of his anticipated passion and death. That the Evangelists so interpreted the story of Christ's passion is easily seen. Saint John, in particular, was quick to see in Jesus the paschal "Lamb of God which taketh away the sin of the world."[5]

We note again how definitely Christological the early gospel tradition was, especially as it converged on the story of the passion. Everything in that tradition centered in the person and Messianic mission of Christ. It was not that Jesus' teaching was considered unimportant; and his self-sacrificial life was certainly a holy example to the early church. But Jesus was to the first Christians predominantly neither a philosopher nor a saint. He was the bearer of God's will and word to the world. His coming was a special revelation of God. The meaning of his life was made plain to them by his death on the Cross, and authenticated by the fact of his resurrection from the dead. Thereafter he lived among them both in his broken and in his risen body; and the Last Supper, which was to them a historic memory, became the Lord's Supper which was a sign and sacrament of his perpetual presence among them.

It will be seen, as we examine the records, that the Synoptists

---

[2] Exodus 12, 13.
[3] Isaiah 9:1-9.
[4] Isaiah 53.
[5] John 1:29.

and the Fourth Gospel differ in their account of the Last Supper.[6] But the differences are not important except as they serve to verify the trustworthiness of the story. The Synoptic Gospels, for example, indicate that Jesus kept the Passover with his disciples on the evening—after sunset—before the day of his crucifixion, and that the institution of the Lord's Supper took place at that time. The author of the Fourth Gospel records the Last Supper as having occurred twenty-four hours earlier; and his reason for doing so is to indicate that Jesus' death on the Cross took place at the very time when the Paschal lambs were being slain and made ready for the Passover meal. To the later church of John's time, such an appropriate setting in Hebrew history for the mystical symbolism of the use of bread and wine in the celebration of the Lord's Supper would serve an important purpose: it would help to keep the Christian sacrament free from the taint of paganism represented in the Greek Mysteries then everywhere current in Asia Minor where the Fourth Evangelist lived when he wrote his Gospel.

But here a noteworthy fact presents itself to us. The Fourth Evangelist omits from his account the inaugural ceremony of the Eucharist at the Last Supper. He is acquainted with the story of its inauguration; and it is certain that he can himself have no objection to the sacrament's observance, since of all the Evangelists he is the most eucharistic in his interpretation of the entire gospel message. The reason for the omission is not far to find. Saint John has already presented Jesus to his readers as the Bread of Life.[7] It remains for him now to incorporate in his narrative, from a source accessible to him, the account of Jesus' washing of the disciples' feet. In this act, too, there is something sacramental. It represents Christ as laying aside his sovereignty to unite his followers with him in an act of cleansing. It is interesting to note that Peter demurs at having a part in his lord's humiliation. But Judas Iscariot does not. And when the sop is given him—the token of particular affection—his resolve hardens in him to betray his

---

[6] Mark 14:22-26; Matthew 26:26-30; Luke 22:15-21; John 13:21-30. See also I Corinthians 11:23-25, 10:14-22; John 6:35; Acts 2:46, 20:7-11.

[7] John 6.

Master.   John says that "Satan entered into him."   Jesus, in
pity and sorrow, tells him privately, "What thou doest, do
quickly." Judas rises and goes; and the Evangelist adds: "And
it was night." But on that night, within the circle of the little
company of faithful disciples, there is a visible radiance as—
using the word five times in two verses of John's Gospel—Jesus
says:

> Now is the Son of man *glorified,*
> And God is *glorified* in him.[8]

On reading Luke's account of the Last Supper, we note that
he gives to the cup of the sacrament a twofold meaning.   The
first is that of a tryst and pledge between Jesus and his disciples
to meet again at the Messianic feast in the kingdom of heaven;
the second, that of a new covenant between Christ and his followers, made possible by his death on the Cross.[9]   Here mention should also be made of Saint Paul's well-known account,
in I Corinthians 11:23-26, of the manner in which the sacrament of the Lord's Supper was actually observed by the primitive church.   The apostle's record is the earliest in existence
—though, according to some scholars, Mark's account is traceable to an antecedent oral tradition.[10]   The formula followed
by the Corinthian church, together with Saint Paul's authority
for it, is hallowed by its use through the centuries and is worthy
of a treasured place in every Christian's memory.

Looking once more at the Gospel story of the Last Supper,
we observe its *backward,* its *outward,* and its *forward,* look,
in these successive words: (1) "This do in remembrance of
me"; (2) "This is my body broken for you": (3) "This do
ye, as oft as ye drink it."   The sacrament is thereby made
commemorative, communal, and continuous.   That it is also
vicarious, reflecting the office, or mission, of the Suffering
Servant of God, mentioned in Isaiah 53, is clearly stated in the
words of Mark: "This is my blood of the new covenant, which
is shed for many"—to which Matthew adds, "for the remission

---

[8] John 13:31.
[9] Luke 22:14-20.
[10] See M. Goguel, *The Life of Jesus* (New York: The Macmillan Co.,
1933), pp. 443 ff.

of sins." [11]   Last of all, it is significant that Matthew and Luke alike give to the sacrament a final eschatological meaning when they say, with Mark: "Verily I say unto you, I will drink no more of the fruit of the vine, until that day that I drink it new in the kingdom of God." [12]

Altogether, therefore, it is not difficult to understand why the Last Supper, symbolized and variously celebrated as the Lord's Supper, Holy Communion, the Eucharist, and the Mass, has come to occupy an ever increasing place of importance in the life of the church. Its significance does not merely revolve about an interest in ritual or liturgy, or speculative theology, or the "love to lose one's self in a mystery." The sacrament is rooted in the very center of the gospel tradition—that is, in the story of Christ's incarnation, his passion and his resurrection. It was from this threefold root, or source, in gospel history that the Christian faith itself originated; and it is from a contemplation of this fact that our faith derives its active and perpetually energizing substance.

II

JESUS' FAREWELL DISCOURSES

But now, by the side of what the Synoptic Gospels tell us of the Last Supper, we must place the Fourth Evangelist's record of the event.   He does not controvert or ignore anything that Mark and Matthew and Luke have said.   He has read and knows their accounts of our Lord's institution of the Eucharist: he is acquainted also with Saint Paul's observance of the holy sacrament in the churches he has founded.   But years have passed since the apostle's death, a whole generation of them; the time is now A.D. 95; the Parousia, or earthly return of Jesus, has not occurred; and, as is natural, a certain solidification within the ordered life of the church has taken place, pointing to its permanency as an historic institution in the world.

[11] Mark 14:24; Matthew 26:28.
[12] Mark 14:25; Matthew 26:29; Luke 22:18.

Wherever, therefore, the Lord's Supper was being observed, it indicated Christ's living presence among the communicants who broke the bread together and drank the cup of covenant. It now remained for John to sum up the entire meaning in a symbol associated with the last meeting of Jesus with his disciples in the upper room. That symbol, as we have already noted, was the washing of the disciples' feet. Nothing else so human could have been done to demonstrate a truth so divine —the representation of divine love in human form. It was to exhibit this love that the body of Christ had been broken on the Cross and that he had drunk the cup of suffering. The bread of sacrifice and the cup of suffering: these were the demonstrable sign, as the Evangelist had from the first declared, that

> God so loved the world,
> That He gave His only begotten Son,
> That whosoever believeth in him
> Should not perish,
> But have everlasting life.[13]

But in this dramatized parable of the foot-washing we have already noted an additional meaning. Besides being an act of divine humiliation, it is also one of purification. By the death of Christ the world is to be cleansed of its sin.[14] It is to be observed that the Fourth Evangelist is not merely thinking of some fit symbolism, or mystic rite, by which to represent Jesus to the Greek-speaking world. The writer is himself a Jew. His thought is on Israel's great and ancient law of purification; and the thought will not leave him that Christ is he through whom a new and purified Israel is to arise. As, according to John, Jesus begins his earthly ministry with the cleansing of the temple, so now with his own hands—before his purifying blood is shed—he washes the disciples' feet. How certainly also the Evangelist remembers the Eucharistic words in Mark and Matthew, "This is my blood of the new testament which is shed for many for the remission of sins," [15] is inferred from

---

13 John 3:16.
14 I John 1:7. Cf. also Mark 14:24 and Matthew 26:28.
15 See Matthew 26:28; Mark 14:24.

what he later writes in his First Epistle, when he says: "If we walk in the light, as he is in the light, we have fellowship one with another, and the blood of Jesus Christ his Son cleanseth us from all sin." [16] Was there not sufficient proof of the fact of sin in the perfidious design of Judas to betray his Master?

With the Last Supper—the Agape, the feast of love—now nearing the end, and Judas gone out into the night, Jesus turned to the eleven remaining disciples and addressed them, saying: "Little children . . . I am with you." Yet it was to be so only for a little while; for, as we read later in the Gospel, the *Hour* had come.[17] It was the hour at which the Son of man was to be glorified—glorified through his death. That death was not to be a tragedy: the tragedy, already enacted, was that he had come into the world—to be its Living Bread—but that the world had not received him. But God's will and plan were not thereby frustrated. For the death of Christ was not to be an *ending,* but a *going,* to be followed by a *coming again.* There was indeed to be an interruption—as evil interrupts all good, as darkness interrupts the day—but the delay was to be expected. Time would bring changes: that was the way with all things subject to time; but time and place were themselves subject to eternity. The earth was not the faithful one's only abode, or God's only concern; for, as Jesus assured those near to him:

> In my Father's house are many mansions: . . .
> I go to prepare a place for you. . . .
> I will come again and receive you unto myself;
> That where I am, there ye may be also.[18]

One cannot sustain the impression, as one reads these farewell discourses,[19] that they are the Evangelist's own invention. They clearly represent the tradition—also represented in the writings of Saint Paul—that Jesus is the Christ the Son of God, and that men are saved by faith in him. The open-minded reader of the chapters will readily agree with the verdict of

[16] John 1:7.
[17] John 17:1.
[18] John 14:2-3.
[19] John 14-17.

Luther that here as elsewhere "the Scriptures are the crib wherein Christ is laid." There is no need of a sacrosanct defense of the Gospel text. To the original quizzical doubter, Thomas the disciple, Jesus speaks the reproving yet assuring word: "I am the way, the truth, and the life: no man cometh unto the Father, but by me." [20] And to Philip—typical of those who ask to see but do not place the necessity of *being* before the possibility of *seeing*—who insists with, "Shew us the Father, and it sufficeth us," Jesus replies in words like these:

> You are looking for some sign of God's physical appearances. Look at me. I am the Word of God made flesh. The work of healing, teaching, and preaching that you have seen me do has in reality been the work of God done through me. You may therefore begin by remembering what was openly done by me before your very eyes. Then look about you, upon this scene, and draw your own conclusion. But now, presently, it will be necessary for me to leave you, and the world will see me no more. I am returning to God the Father who sent me. But the Father's work, given me to do, of which all you here have been the witnesses, will remain. It will not end. I who say this am here before you now. I ask only that you believe in what you see. Believe in me.

But, in speaking of the earthly work of Christ, were the disciples now only to be consoled by their memory of it? What of the future years and generations in the life of the church? Jesus assured them by saying that they would not be left alone. For the Holy Spirit, the Comforter, the Teacher, and the great Doer, was to come, and He would continue the work Christ had begun. Meanwhile their calling as disciples was to live in daily consciousness of his divine presence. The sign, or proof, of this consciousness was to be their knowledge of his love—the love that was presently to lead Jesus to the Cross. It was to help them toward an understanding of this love that Jesus was calling them together at this Last Supper. It was the *Agape*, the Love Feast, in which their oneness with him was to become a realized fact. Love, Christlike love, was henceforth to be their lord and to rule their lives. Now, at

[20] John 14:6.

this feast, they were Love's guests: they were no longer to
be fearful, but to share with him Love's trust and power and
peace. One recalls here how well George Herbert expressed the
response to which the disciples must have been awakened:

> Love bade me welcome....
> "You must sit down," says Love,
> "And taste My meat."
> So I did sit and eat.

The Fourth Evangelist closes Jesus' discourse, in Chapter
14, with the saying, "Arise, let us go hence." But the discourse
is resumed in Chapters 15-17—perhaps suggesting an interval
in the author's plan and progress of composition—with the
parable of the Vine and the Branches. In it the reader is returned once more to the theme of the Last Supper. The central
thought in it is that the disciples are to be bound to their Lord
through all time in an intimate and living bond of fellowship.
Its symbolism is both apt and historical. Israel, from the beginning, has been God's vineyard; the prophets have been its
faithful husbandmen; and now Christ himself is the Vine from
which the new Israel, the Christian church, is to derive its
perennial sustenance. His life on earth is this new vineyard's
first fruit. In a little while his life is to be taken to the wine
press of suffering, and his blood is to be the wine of life to
all who believe in him, forever.

But the disciples, while partaking of this fruit of the vine,
are themselves to be fruit-bearing. The condition of their fruit-
bearing is to be their inseparable union with Christ. His life
has been of the Father's own planting. Now, through them,
by the inflowing vitality of the Holy Spirit, this life is to pro-
duce a harvest of love in the souls of men unto eternity. To
John the Evangelist, living late in the first century, this allegorical setting forth of a great truth had a special meaning. It
was intended to make plain the fact that the faith of the church,
severed from this close union with Christ, was destined to
wither and die, and that to engraft this faith on some other
vine of doctrine would result in its bearing wild fruit. This
was the twofold danger that confronted the church. Jesus

foresaw this danger; and John, after two generations had passed, observed its effect upon the then established Christian communities of Asia Minor. The only way to prevent this heresy, and the church's consequent decline, was to keep its Christ-given life flowing from the wine press in a continuous and loving self-sacrifice. The whole truth for John, as he reviewed the church's history and looked into its future, was summed up in the words of Jesus: "Greater love hath no man than this, that a man lay down his life for his friends." [21] It was there that the great truth lay. As in the beginning of his Gospel, so now as it moved toward its end, the saintly Evangelist was impelled by the thought of Jesus' divine historic sacrifice. From the Incarnation to the Cross, the story was the same: it was one of the transcendent self-humiliation of the Son of God who took on our human flesh to have his life so pressed into ours that we might live in him.

> Most blessed Vine!...
> How wert thou pressed
> To be my feast!
> In what deep anguish
> Didst thou languish,
> What springs of sweat and blood did drown thee,...
> Doubling thy griefs, when none would own thee! [22]

The Johannine discourses of Jesus come to a close with his great high-priestly prayer. Its keynote is the consummating utterance: "Father, the Hour is come: glorify thy Son, that thy Son also may glorify thee." [23] In it the Evangelist reviews the entire mission or work of Christ, from the Incarnation through the story of the Passion to the Resurrection. The will of God has been accomplished. There remains now only Jesus' self-commitment to the Father's care. But in this commitment, holy in its completion and trust, he is not alone. His prayer, especially, is for those beside him and who believe in him. Jesus' mind is directed wholly toward this twofold end: "I am

21 John 15:13.
22 Henry Vaughan, "I am the true Vine."
23 John 17:1.

no more in the world . . . I come to thee," and "Holy Father,
keep those whom thou hast given me." The prayer's essence
is contained in these words: "I in them, and thou in me." In
their divine synthesis, human expression melts into a vision
of the Eternal. Words can go no farther. The earthly work
of Jesus is finished. He is ready for the betrayer and the Cross.

Chapter 28

THE ACCOUNT OF JESUS' PASSION

I

The Arrest and Trial

Mark tells us that when the Last Supper was ended and Jesus and the disciples "had sung a hymn, they went out unto the Mount of Olives." It was—we are to imply from the Evangelist's outlook—a song of victory, sung against the impending agony of Christ for the world's sin. For there in Gethsemane, the garden of the olive press, Jesus knelt and prayed. Matthew, following Mark, records that he was "exceeding sorrowful, even unto death," and that, going forward a little distance, he fell upon the ground, "on his face," and cried out: "O my Father, if it be possible, let this cup pass away from me; nevertheless, not as I will, but as thou wilt!" Luke, recording the scene of agony, adds (1) that "his sweat became as it were great drops of blood falling upon the ground," and (2) that "there appeared unto him an angel from heaven, strengthening him." [1] The Fourth Evangelist, omitting the story of the agonizing struggle, does not discount the great cost when he records Jesus as saying: "The cup which the Father hath given me, shall I not drink it?"

The picture here presented to us through the combined Gospel narrative is not intended simply to show how utterly human Jesus was but how fully, in assuming his divine mission, he took upon himself our humanity. The inference is that, except for this divine mission, the human suffering he endured might have been averted. The Gospels are unanimous in declaring that Jesus chose this way of suffering for a cause, or end, which he clearly conceived to be the will of God. Having chosen the

---

[1] Mark 14:32-42; Matthew 26:36-46; Luke 22:39-46; John 18:1-11. Cf. here Hebrews 5:7-8.

office of the Suffering Servant, he was fully resigned to it.
Sidney Lanier strikes the appropriate note of the prelude to
Christ's passion in the familiar strain:

> Into the woods my Master went,
> Clean forspent, forspent. . . .
> Out of the woods my Master came,
> Content with death and shame.

The story of Jesus' arrest follows that of Judas' act of
betrayal. For thirty pieces of silver the betrayer has sold the
secret either of Jesus' place of seclusion or of his Messianic
mission.[2] He has done so with a traitor's kiss—that perfidious
act in which repulsive treason has since been summed up, as
here by Shakespeare:

> So Judas kissed his Master,
> And cried, "All hail!" whenas he meant all harm.

Then the multitudes—as the Evangelists say together—
break in upon the scene out of the night, led by the chief priests
and scribes and elders, with Judas himself heading a band of
soldiers and officers, carrying, among them, such implements as
swords and staves and lanterns and torches. Against all this,
the account of Peter's sword and Malchus' ear is a piece of
well-recorded and grim irony.[3] But the whole scene represents
a gross misconception of Jesus' person and mission. His is not
a kingdom of daggers, like that sought to be established by the
Sicarii and the Zealots. So he must here rebuke even Peter,
well-meaning but not yet a Rock, eager to wield a sword in his
Lord's behalf but, in another moment, weak against the accusation of the woman who said: "Thou also wast with the
Nazarene, even Jesus."

Jesus is now led away for a quickly improvised trial. Witnesses are gotten together to substantiate the accusations of the
chief priests and their demand that Jesus be put to death. The
witnesses appear to have been hired. For there is no agreement
among them even when several of them, approximating the

2 Matthew 17:3-9.
3 John 18:10.

truth but perverting it, report having themselves heard Jesus say that he will destroy the temple at Jerusalem and will build another temple "made without hands." [4]   From Mark's account it is apparent that the trial will fail unless some strong man who can see to things steps in to take hold.   Caiaphas, the high priest, who knows how to force the issue, now questions Jesus. The high priest's dignity, and that of his distinguished family and office—he was the son-in-law of Annas and the Sanhedrin's presiding ruler—command instant attention.   Jesus stands before him in silence, but without fear.   As Mark and Matthew say, Jesus "held his peace."   He stands with hands crossed and bound, not in the ecstasy or with the will of a martyr, but as the appointed and compassionate Son of God.   According to the gospel tradition, two ages meet here in open conflict, representing two authorities: (1) that of ancient Israel's priestly law, and (2) that of the newly covenanted kingdom of Christ the Messiah.   It is Caiaphas against Jesus, there on the high priest's porch, while the scribes and elders look on at the scene, and the disagreeing witnesses stand by, and Peter, having followed Jesus "afar off," has entered the courtyard and sits with the officers, warming himself by the fire before dawn.

Then Caiaphas addresses Jesus.   Matthew, augmenting Mark's account, says that the high priest adjures him "by the living God," saying: "Tell us whether thou be the Christ, the Son of God."   Jesus answers: "Thou hast said ... I am."   Then, in a setting in which he is now clearly the Suffering Servant, "despised and forsaken and rejected of men, a man of sorrows and acquainted with grief," [5] Jesus utters the apocalyptic prophecy: "And ye shall see the Son of man sitting at the right hand of power, and coming on the clouds of heaven." [6]   At such "spoken blasphemy," the high priest rends his garments—when, at the gospel's summons, men should rend their hearts as they see Jesus the Son of man and Son of God smitten and spat upon and mocked for declaring himself to be the Christ.   And so the scene of the first trial ends.

[4] Mark 14:59.
[5] Isaiah 53:3.
[6] Mark 14:62; Matthew 26:64; Luke 22:69.

Meanwhile, the disciples, terror-stricken, have fled to safety —all but Peter who is beneath in the courtyard warming his hands. The scene that follows, according to Mark, is an interlude between the two trials: (1) that before Caiaphas, and (2) that before Pilate.[7] It affords the Evangelist an opportunity to separate them in a manner that has suggested to some scholars the existence of two independent traditions in Mark's Gospel: the one Palestinian and the other Roman. To bring them into harmony—or, by their study as separate documents, to place the final responsibility for the death sentence imposed on Jesus—has long engaged the attention of historical critics.

But our thoughts, with those of the four Evangelists, turn irresistibly to Peter. Mark's Gospel, and Matthew's after it, here almost certainly contain Peter's memoirs. If so, we can see with what unsparing vividness Peter has turned the searchlight on the incident in which he was the central figure. That fact is further shown by the exactness with which the four Evangelists report what happened. The little details in which the narratives differ add to the story's general trustworthiness. Some of them have a touch of particular interest, as for example (1) Mark's statement that Peter "began to curse and to swear," (2) Matthew's reference to Peter's rustic Galilean dialect, and (3) more especially, Luke's poignant remark that, at the moment of the third denial, Jesus "turned and looked upon Peter." The concluding words, "And Peter remembered . . . and . . . went out and wept bitterly," are among the most touching and treasured in our Gospel literature. Poets have vied with one another to catch a glimpse of the scene. Among them, Thomas Hardy thus depicts the disciple with characteristic directness and restraint:

> His face convulses as the morning cock that moment crows,
> And he droops, and turns, and goes.[8]

[7] In addition to these two trials, the Fourth Gospel records a trial before Annas, in John 18:12-24, and Luke records one before Herod Antipas, in Luke 23:6-12. Their contribution to the main story is incidental.

[8] From the poem, "In the Servants' Quarters." Used by the permission of The Macmillan Co., New York, publishers.

In the next scene Mark presents Jesus before Pilate. It is necessary, here, to remember that Palestine was under Roman rule and that, in matters concerning Jewish life and customs, there were two separate courts of justice to which defendants could be brought for trial. The one was ecclesiastical, and was represented by the Sanhedrin; the other was civil, and was invested with power delegated in this instance to Pilate, by the emperor at Rome. Hence the double trial to which Jesus was being subjected. In the one he was accused of declaring himself to be the Christ, or Messiah—as, in fact, he was; in the other, he was falsely charged with insurrection against the state by allowing himself to be regarded as the king of the Jews. Both trials were instigated by the powerful party of the chief priests, supported by their subordinates who saw to it that the necessary popular clamor for Jesus' conviction was not wanting.

Perhaps, on first thought, it may seem to us that the whole story resolves itself into the fact that the Jews killed Jesus. We must guard against an oversimplified and easily misleading conclusion. If to instigate murder was to commit murder, the leaders and others of the Jewry of that time could not well be absolved of its guilt. But we must here assume a historical attitude—remembering how heavily the sins of the human race bear on us all, and how long we ourselves in our modern age have kept "Christ writhing on the cross." [9] But the point of historic significance has to do with the Evangelists' *interpretation* of what actually happened. They did not look only on the event but on its meaning. And the death of Christ was the most meaningful of all the events in his earthly life. Everything involved in it—Peter's denial, Judas' betrayal, Caiaphas' accusation, and Pilate's judgment—had taken place by the expressed plan and will of God. It all happened in order that Holy Scripture might be fulfilled and that the kingdom of God might come. That, it was believed, was the manner in which divine history was being written on the pages of human history. The gospel writers had no thought of producing documents of complaint or accusation against Judaism. There was in their minds, and in the minds of those who first told the story that became the

[9] From Edwin Arlington Robinson's sonnet, "Calvary."

Gospel tradition, no cause for complaint. For all was as it should be, since the gospel was being preached to the world.

The trial of Jesus before the civil court of Pilate was now begun. But it appears to have been wholly perfunctory. That Pilate perceived no reason for condemning Jesus to death is openly indicated. Mark says that the Roman governor marveled at the accusation brought against him. Surely this man standing bound and serene before him was not guilty of political insurrection. How unlike Herod was this self-declared king of the Jews! Matthew emphasizes Jesus' kingly dignity, the chief priests' anger, and Pilate's astonishment. The Fourth Evangelist interprets Jesus' kingship by having him say: "My kingdom is not of this world." And John follows up this answer with a dialogue [10] typical of his literary style and Christological outlook:

PILATE.   "Art thou a king then?"
JESUS.   "Thou sayest that I am a king. To this end was I born; and
           for this cause came I into the world, that I should bear witness
           unto the truth."
PILATE.   "What is truth?"

The trial before Pilate seems, at first sight, to be an exhibition of Roman justice against Jewish fanaticism. Pilate is considerate, inquiring, merciful, and just; the chief priests and elders are wary, opinionated, insistent, and revengeful. Pilate says: "I find no fault in him"; he makes a concession by offering to have Jesus scourged and released; he listens to his wife's warning in a dream to have no part in persecuting "that righteous man"; he washes his hands before the multitude as a symbol of his innocence of the "blood of this righteous man." The chief priests, on the contrary, resort to subterfuge, drag in the case of Barabbas the notorious robber, prefer to have him released rather than Jesus, and stir up the multitude to cry out against Jesus: "Crucify, crucify him!"

But to get a true picture we must look deeper into the situation. Pilate was a detached onlooker and preferred to be such. He did not wish to be involved in a disturbance that would

[10] John 18:37.

require careful attention and might seriously affect his status with the government at Rome. He could well afford to be cool-tempered and equably minded, contenting himself with an evasive inquiry into the philosophical nature of truth, while safeguarding his position—with the help of his legions, of course—by a show of Roman justice. On the contrary, the little colony of Jewish leaders in Jerusalem was literally and desperately fighting for its life: its racial identity, its capital city, and its religious heritage as represented in its temple worship and its sacred scriptural law. In such a parallel situation natural philosophy might be expected to support anyone sufficiently to bear the ills of others. But what of that which touches men vitally and more than all else grips their very souls? In the name of justice, therefore, we shall need to reappraise Pilate who, having the power to act on his virtuous knowledge, did not use it. This, then, may be our inviting word to him:

> Thy hands are washed, but O, the water's spilt,
> That labored to have washed thy guilt:
> The flood, if any be that can suffice,
> Must have its fountain in thine eyes.[11]

II

THE CRUCIFIXION AND BURIAL

With the trial now ended, the Evangelists introduce us to a scene of painful tragedy. Mark records that Pilate, conceding to the clamor of the crowd, released Barabbas the robber, and delivered Jesus to the Roman soldiers to be scourged, mocked, and crucified. The scourging was inhuman. Even strong men, when submitted to it, often died during the ordeal. But it was when subjected to bitter mockery that Christ stood for the first time before the world as the despised and rejected Son of God —the figure and representation of a divine and infinite pity, calling forth pity and penitence in the human heart. We note the restraint and realism of the record—the scarlet robe, the plaited crown of thorns—and perceive at once that we are in

[11] Richard Crashaw, "To Pontius Washing His Hands," from *Divine Epigrams*.

possession of authentic gospel history. The event and its meaning to the Christian church are of one piece. The poet Spenser,
moved by this close identity of what occurred and what was
believed, wrote:

> And looke at last how, of most wretched wights,
> He taken was, betrayd, and false accused;
> How with most scornefull taunts, and fell despights
> He was revyld, disgrast, and foule abused,
> How scourged, how crownd, how buffeted, how brused.

Here, in the story of the Crucifixion, gospel history meets
face to face with Christian doctrine—the doctrine of the Cross.
Now, at last, the entire Gospel narrative is interpreted to us;
the reason why there should be any Gospels at all is made plain.
What impresses us is the fact that the first apostles and the
Evangelists did not see in the death of Christ simply a historic
tragedy. On the contrary, it was a part, a most important part,
of the gospel story that began with the first Christmas and came
to its climax with the first Easter. The story of the Cross stood
at the center of the Good News concerning Christ. It was the
Good News that through the death of Christ men had found a
way to get rid of their sins. The coming of Christ into the
world was God's own act. That act was the Incarnation. The
death of Christ, accordingly, was God's own sacrifice of His
Son in the person of the Suffering Servant; it was an expression of His love, an act of divine and forgiving grace, whereby
men could free themselves from despair, from bargaining with
God, from the delusion and false pride of moralism, and come
empty-handed and trusting into the divine presence and so find
peace for their souls.

It was in this doctrinal-historical manner—difficult, perhaps,
for the modern naturalistically minded man to understand—
that the Christian gospel was originally interpreted. We have
already said that, to the first Christians, the death of Christ was
more than an event in Jewish or Roman history. The Cross
was to them the symbol of divine history. It was the gospel.
Therefore, in following through the story of the Crucifixion,
we must keep in mind this point of view from which the gospel

message was first preached and later committed to writing.   It
was preached and written as the Word of God, not merely to
inform men but to transform their lives.   Only when so read
and interpreted does the gospel story, especially that of the
Cross, yield up its meaning to us today.   All else is literary history, something good to know and to remember, but insufficient
to account for the birth, the spiritual strength, and the subsequent influence of the Christian church.

All four of the Gospels give us a careful account of the
Crucifixion.   Though differing in certain details, their reports
are in remarkable agreement.   Matthew follows Mark's narrative almost literally, indicating again his reliance on it as his
primary source.   Now and then he omits a fine point of reference, as when, for example, he only mentions Simon of Cyrene
whom Mark further identifies as the father of Alexander and
Rufus.[12]   But here and there Matthew adds a note of sharp observation, as he does early in the crucifixion scene when he says:
"And they sat and watched him there."   Only in recording the
moment of Jesus' death when "the veil of the temple was rent
in twain, from the top to the bottom," does Matthew add to
Mark's account the portentous statement—perhaps to symbolize
the effect of Christ's death on all creation:

> And the earth did quake,
> And the rocks were rent;
> And the graves were opened:
> And many bodies of the saints which slept arose,
> And came out of the graves after his resurrection,
> And went into the holy city, and appeared unto many.[13]

Luke's account, in general, follows the order of events in the
Markan tradition: the initial reference to Simon of Cyrene;
the arrival at Golgotha, "the hill of the Skull"; the Crucifixion;
the parting of the garments; the reviling mockery; Jesus' sudden
outcry and death; and the comment of the Roman centurion.
But textual differences indicate that Luke is not primarily dependent on Mark for his narrative.   His access to another and
independent source—it is certainly Palestinian, and gives signs

[12] Mark 15:21; Matthew 27:32. See here also Romans 16:13.
[13] Matthew 27:51-53.

of being feminine—is shown most particularly in the note of divine outgoing compassion that runs through the narrative: (1) toward the women who follow Jesus to Calvary and remain with him to the end; (2) toward the Roman soldiers for whose cruel deed he asks the Heavenly Father's forgiveness; and (3) toward the penitent malefactor whom he invites with him through death's gateway into Paradise.

John's account of the Passion is the most brief, definitive, and dramatic. As we should expect, it is written with a knowledge of both Mark and Luke, whose narrative it condenses, adding and omitting details, in keeping with the Evangelist's aim of presenting Jesus as the Son of God. John's omission of the reference to Simon of Cyrene and his statement that Jesus went to Calvary "bearing the cross for himself," indicate the author's stress on Christ's sovereignty—expressly demonstrated —in the hour of his humiliation and death. The familiar allusion to the robe of Christ, worn next to his person, and being without seam, aptly illustrates John's universalism, already pointed out to us in these earlier words of Jesus: "And I, if I be lifted up from the earth, will draw all men unto me." [14]

The Christian church, looking back upon the scene of the Crucifixion, was not long in gathering together the Seven Words spoken by Jesus on the Cross. Arranged according to the manner in which they appear in the four Gospels, they are the following:

In Mark and Matthew

1. "Eloi, Eloi, lama sabachthani: My God, My God, why hast thou forsaken me?"

In Luke

2. "Father, forgive them, for they know not what they do."
3. To day shalt thou be with me in paradise."
4. "Father, into thy hands I commend my spirit."

In John

5. To his mother: "Woman, behold thy son!"
   To the disciple: "Behold thy mother!"
6. "I thirst."
7. "It is finished."

[14] John 12:32.

Jesus' work on earth was indeed finished. In the language of John, the Word of God had now been spoken. It had been spoken, first, by Christ's coming into the world in the form of a man, and finally, by his giving himself in death for mankind's redemption. Put into words that may help to convey the thought to us: the eternal Word could not die; but as the Word made flesh, Christ died that men might live. This truth is admittedly a mystery, difficult to comprehend; but it need not disturb us in a world in which life itself is an unfathomable mystery. Saint Paul, whose interpretation of the Incarnation and the Cross is woven into the fabric of the gospel tradition, declared that Christ took Death into captivity, put it into chains, so to speak, and took away its sting.[15] The Apostle found in the death of Christ a fact of cosmic significance: by it the corruptible in the order of creation, and in man, has the promise of being changed into incorruption. To return to our former statement: the man Jesus died; but Christ the Word died not. For the Word is more than the man. It is eternal. Let us call to our aid here the words of the great church father Athanasius:

> The body of the Word, then, being a real human body, in spite of its having been uniquely formed from a virgin, was of itself mortal and, like other bodies, liable to death. But the indwelling of the Word loosed it from this natural liability, so that corruption could not touch it. Thus it happened that two opposite marvels took place at once: the death of all was consummated in the Lord's body; yet, because the Word was in it, death and corruption were in the same act utterly abolished.[16]

Such was the meaning of the death of Christ to his followers of the first centuries. We of the modern day, lacking the background for its more profound theological consideration, may —though without taking any pride in our ignorance—content ourselves with the simple statement that Christ died for his love of mankind. That fact, accepted by faith, is the gospel's beginning and its end. By this faith many, through the Christian

---

[15] I Corinthians 15:55.
[16] *De Incarnatione Verbi Dei*: "The Incarnation of the Word of God." Translated by *A Religious* of C.S.M.V.S. 1946. Th., p. 49. Used by permission of the publisher, The Macmillan Co.

centuries, have lived and died, a multitude of them as witnesses and martyrs, counting their lives and their sufferings on earth as a small price to pay for this rich and eternal inheritance. Saint Paul was one of the greatest of them. This demonstration of love, "this coming of God to meet him," as some recent writer has said, "broke him down utterly." It elicited from him a response that has been one of the historic wonders of the world. After a period of violent opposition, followed by his conversion, and a considerable time in retirement to "think it through," and a longer period of successful evangelism among Asiatic, Greek, and Roman Gentiles, he could say, with finality:

> I am crucified with Christ:
> Nevertheless I live;—
> Yet not I, but Christ liveth in me;
> And the life which I now live in the flesh
> I live by the faith of the Son of God,
> Who loved me, and gave himself for me.[17]

The climax of Jesus' agony on the Cross is followed in the Gospel record by the stillness on Calvary and the story of the burial. Joseph of Arimathea, aided, John says, by Nicodemus, took Jesus' body from the Cross and laid it in a tomb newly hewn out of the rock in the garden near the place of the Crucifixion. There is a sad irony in the carefully preserved inference that all that Pilate, at last, did was to surrender to Joseph Jesus' dead body. Joseph brought the linen winding sheet; Nicodemus contributed the precious myrrh; while the women, Luke tells us, went to the village to prepare other spices and ointments for the burial. But the Evangelists, together, note that the day was now far spent; the sun was setting toward beginning of the Sabbath; and the ministration of the burial must be ended before the day of rest began. Matthew—not forgetting, as he writes, the continued Jewish opposition to the newly risen Christian faith—is careful to add that when the door of the tomb had been sealed by a great stone, a detachment of soldiers was set there to guard the body against being stolen. As the darkness slowly settles on Golgotha, we find Mary Magdalene,

[17] Galatians 2:20.

and the women with her, seated on the hillside overlooking the tomb. Luke closes the account, no doubt wondering as he writes: "And on the sabbath day they rested, according to the commandment." Christian tradition has enriched the story with the much portrayed scene of the descent from the Cross; and millions, brooding on the events of that first Good Friday, still ask if there be "any sorrow like unto my sorrow."

Chapter 29

THE LIVING CHRIST

I
THE STORY OF THE RESURRECTION

The modern age has witnessed a strong tendency to reduce Easter to a pagan holiday. The return of the sun, the renewal of life in the opening bud, and the general awakening of all nature are hailed as its recurrent signs. Its most natural association is with the vernal equinox. The season of spring is its controlling motive. And it has sometimes seemed, in the eyes of many, to be most appropriately observed by an exhilarating show of animal spirits and a suitable pageantry of fashion. The underlying cause of this trend has been the turn of modern man's thinking from an historical-theological to a naturalistic-secular point of view. The practical result has been a daily preoccupation with the contemporary scene. Among more thoughtful people it has led to a contemplation of the perennial cyclical return and repetition of all things.

This fact is regrettable. For Easter is a peculiarly Christian festival. Together with Christmas, it is an outstanding symbol of our Christian faith. The birth and the resurrection of Christ indicate to us what was begun and brought to completion by his coming into the world. At the first Christmas, John the Evangelist tells us, the eternal Word in the person of Christ became flesh, thereby assuring us that God Himself had come to dwell with us in the midst of our human mortality. At the first Easter, Christ arose from the dead, not leaving us in our mortality to lament his departure, but taking with him in his risen body the whole of God's creation, including our earthly bodies, into an immortal and eternal life.

The observance of Easter, therefore, does not simply teach

us that the soul is immortal. Other noteworthy and pagan
faiths tell as much. The ancient Egyptians and Greeks were
sustained in spirit by their philosophies of the soul's immortality. Saint Paul, a scholar acquainted with the religions of
the pagan world, knew this very well, and indicated that fact in
his well-known address at Athens and in his letters to the
Corinthian churches.[1] We note, for example, that the Atheni-
ans, listening to Paul, followed him easily as he talked of things
of which they knew, when he said: "For in Him—in God—we
live, and move, and have our being." But when they heard the
Apostle speak of "the resurrection of the dead," some mocked,
while others said: "We will hear thee again of this matter."
The resurrection of Christ did not simply provide Paul with
further valuable evidence to add to the teaching of Plato and
the Roman Stoics concerning the soul's immortality. It was
the very foundation of his faith in the resurrection of the dead,
and in the ultimate regeneration and restoration of the world.
For this reason Paul—to whom the primitive Christian tradition
was from the beginning indebted for his interpretation of the
events of gospel history—was wont to speak of Christ's risen
body as the "first fruits" of the resurrection, by which he meant
not only the immortality of the saints but also the final and
corporate re-creation of the entire natural order. This, as the
Apostle conceived it, was the divinely ordained End of the created world. It was the realized goal of the kingdom of God in
all its perfection and glory.[2]

As a background for our study, therefore, Paul's teaching
presents us with this threefold fact concerning the resurrection
of Christ: first, that it is the assurance of our own immortality,
with and through him; second, that in Christ's risen body we
have the symbol of our spiritual regeneration, and of our adop-
tion into the newborn and living fellowship of believing persons
who constitute the church; and third, that the risen and living
Christ is, to a world now bound and rooted in sin, the "first
fruit" of a new and ultimately to be perfected order of divine

---

[1] Acts 17:15-32; I Corinthians 15.
[2] Romans 6:36, 8:11-23; II Corinthians 5:1-4; I Thessalonians 4:14;
Colossians 2:12.

creation. Against this background let us now turn our attention
to the Gospel writer's story of the Resurrection.

Mark the Evangelist begins his account by saying that the
two Marys and Salome were thinking only of the tragic fact
that Jesus was dead. They had spent the Sabbath in deep and
mournful silence. And now in the morning of the first day in
the week they were come to the tomb, bringing with them the
spices and ointments to bestow their last act of reverence on his
dead body. Everything seemed ended. Jesus' death seemed to
be all that remained of a great and fond dream. Their deeper
thoughts are not recorded. Their chief immediate concern was
a practical one. "Who," they said among themselves, "shall
roll away the stone from the door of the tomb?" We can see
them looking down and talking as they walk into the garden
toward the place of burial. Then, Mark tells us, "looking up,
they see that the stone is rolled away"; and he adds that it was
"exceeding great." We can see through the veil of the language that the Evangelist uses the dramatic, and perhaps symbolical, intent with which the first apostles must often have
narrated the event in the days that followed. The stone is indeed a heavy one, lying on the disciples' hearts. They enter the
tomb and they see "a young man sitting on the right side,
arrayed in a white robe." They are amazed. But the young
man—was he Mark himself?—says to them: "(1) Be not affrighted. (2) Ye seek Jesus of Nazareth which was crucified.
(3) He is risen; he is not here. (4) Behold the place where
they laid him."

The story seems obviously to be from the memoirs of Peter.
It shows the signs of the Apostle's own recollection of the
event. Peter himself—according to Luke's account—was astonished. He is clearly trying to report what actually happened. That Christ had arisen and was alive was at this time
a strange miracle to him. He needed time to reflect on it all.
Was it not just as Jesus had himself predicted: the fanatical
action of the chief priests; the vacillating demonstration of Roman justice; and, over and above them, the strange manner in
which Holy Scripture had been fulfilled? Mark resumes the
story by saying that the women "fled from the tomb." Sud-

denly, what had been their chief concern, which was to anoint the dead body of Jesus, became a forgotten thing to them. They had unexpectedly come upon the great truth of the resurrection of their Lord. Instantly, all was changed. Mark, simply reporting the plain fact, says that "trembling and astonishment had come upon them." And he adds, as if recording a point of detail carefully preserved in the tradition, that "they said nothing to any one; for they were afraid." [3]

But that is not Mark's whole story. His Gospel does not end there. A recent writer,[4] commenting on the record, reminds us that in Christian heraldry "it is not rare to find lions blazoned with two tails. The lion of Saint Mark is such a creature. Mark's Gospel has two endings." The one is called the shorter, the other, the longer ending. It will be remembered that the closing section of the Gospel was lost, the most satisfactory explanation being that a wide circulation of the original manuscript among the early churches had caused the ending to be worn and severed from the Gospel document. The longer ending is recorded in Mark 16:9-20. A version of this longer ending is to be found in the so-called Freer Manuscript, now preserved in Washington and identified as document W. A typical form of the shorter ending is preserved for us in Nestle's New Testament.

Matthew's Gospel, as we have learned, depends strongly on that of Mark. The story of the Resurrection is no exception. The reference to the earthquake, recorded in Chapter 28:2, is distinctly Matthean. So also is the statement that an angel descended from heaven to roll away the stone from the tomb, and the further reference to the watchers who "did shake, and became as dead men." The angel's command, "Go quickly and tell his disciples that he is risen from the dead," is a version of Mark's record; likewise also is the report that, when in the dawn of that first Easter the risen Christ came to meet them, the disciples, kneeling before him, "held him by the feet and worshipped him." Matthew adds that, while the disciples wor-

[3] Mark 16:1-8.
[4] See T. W. Manson, H.D.A. Major, and C. J. Wright, *The Mission and Message of Jesus* (New York: The Macmillan Co., 1941), p. 206.

shipped Jesus, "some doubted." After that, and finally, the First
Evangelist indicates his world outlook for the future of the
newborn faith in the following command of Christ:

> Go ye therefore,
> And teach all nations;...
> And, lo, I am with you always,
> Even unto the end of the world.[5]

Turning to Luke's account, we find an interesting variation
from, together with a verification of, the other Synoptic narratives. Luke records that the women "found the stone rolled
away from the tomb," and that they "entered in, and found not
the body of the Lord Jesus." When the women are "per-
plexed" and "affrighted," they are told: "Why seek ye the living
among the dead? Remember, how he spake unto you when he
was in Galilee, saying the Son of man must be delivered into the
hands of sinful men, and be crucified, and the third day rise
again." [6] And Luke adds further that "they remembered his
words." It is the women who tell the disciples. They *remember*.
Some of the company are reported as saying: "This is idle
talk." But the Evangelist does not forget Peter who, as he
says, abruptly leaves, runs to the tomb, and "stooping down,
he beheld the linen clothes," and he goes to his home "wondering . . . at that which was come to pass." [7] All that has happened is so strange, yet so naturally told. Once more, as in the
birth story, divine history is represented as a natural phenomenon. God's ways are wondrous, but they belong to the record
of human events.

Luke now adds to his account of the Resurrection an incident
taken from his particular Palestinian source. It has to do with
the two disciples on their way to Emmaus.[8] The town is near
to Jerusalem. The two disciples are talking to one another of
the things that have so recently happened in the temple court,
before Pilate's palace, and at Golgotha. The events seem to
them to be utter tragedy. Luke, with his skill in vivid portrai-

[5] Matthew 28:19-20.
[6] Luke 24:7.
[7] Luke 24:12.
[8] Luke 24:13-35.

ture, says that they walked together, and reasoned, and were sad. Then Jesus, unrecognized, joins them. They are deeply involved in a discussion of the event of the resurrection. They have been informed, but they do not understand. Only when Christ—though in disguise to their eyes—himself speaks to them, does the truth begin to dawn. It is interesting, also, to note that their insight comes to them by the light of Old Testament prophecy. "Ought not Christ to have suffered these things, and to enter into his glory?" [9] is what they hear their unrecognized companion say. But it is by the sign of the new covenant, "in the breaking of bread," that they know him as their risen Lord.

> He blessed the bread, but vanished at the word,
> And left them both exclaiming, " 'Twas the Lord!
> Did not our hearts feel all he deigned to say,
> Did they not burn within us by the way?" [10]

II

THE FAITH OF THE EARLY CHURCH

Writing in the Book of the *Acts,* Luke continues the account of what occurred when the resurrection of Christ was accepted as an accomplished fact. Things began to happen, he says, which linked the earthly life of Jesus—his mighty acts and words—with his presence among the apostles after his resurrection: first, in giving proof that he was alive; then, in his commission to them to preach the gospel of the kingdom of God; and finally, in his promise that the Holy Spirit would come upon them, after which they were to be empowered to be his living witnesses in the world until his coming again. The Book of the Acts is the story, principally, of two such outstanding witnesses: (1) of Peter, at Jerusalem and in greater Palestine; and (2) of Paul, at Antioch and throughout the Mediterranean world.

We have already learned that the disciples could not at first believe that their Lord was risen from the dead and was alive.

[9] Luke 24:26.
[10] William Cowper, "The Walk to Emmaus."

The Evangelists record that they were amazed at the report, that when the women told them of what had occurred and they had gone to verify the truth for themselves, they fled from the tomb in trembling and astonishment. Mark, who here almost certainly speaks for Peter, adds that "they said nothing to any one; for they were afraid." [11] Here, we have noted, Mark's Gospel breaks off—the last pages, through frequent circulation, having gotten worn and lost. But the circumstances of the event are clear. Peter, like anyone of us would be, was dumb-founded. He was a forthright, honest man. He thought that with Jesus' death all was over and ended. John the Evangelist, years later, in an appendix to his Gospel, records that Peter could think of nothing else to do; and so, turning to the men who with him had been Jesus' followers, he indicated that they would best recover from their fond dream and return to their occupation of fishing. [12] But for Peter—as for the Christian church of which he was to be the first great leader—what he thought to be the end was but the beginning. He was prepared to bury his hope with Jesus' dead body. He had, until now, not counted on the fact that what had begun as an act of God was not to end in a tomb in Palestine. Before Peter could act, Jesus spoke, and all was changed. The night, with all of Peter's sad remembrance, including his denial, was over. It was morning. Christ met him at the dawn. That was enough. Peter had become a rock; he was now an apostle.

What Peter did thereafter is recorded in outline for us in the Book of the Acts; what he believed is indicated in the two New Testament letters that bear his name. He became, according to Luke's testimony, the new church's first great leader. It was a remarkable beginning for this little community of souls—these initial pilgrims of eternity who, by the way now open to them through Christ, were setting out to seek a city not made with hands, and to establish among the nations that were to rise and fall the spiritual and enduring kingdom of God. Peter and the other eleven disciples—Matthias had been chosen to take the place of Judas the traitor—were gathered together in Jerusalem.

[11] Mark 16:8-9.
[12] John 21:3.

It was on the day of Israel's ancient feast of Pentecost, of the ingathering of the first fruits of the wheat harvest. [13] Suddenly, Luke relates, the Holy Spirit descended upon the little company. Prophecy was fulfilled; the church was born; and Peter arose to preach. What he said on that occasion is especially noteworthy; for Luke the historian's account of it is presented to us as typical of the gospel as it was preached and believed among the first Christians. [14]

The Apostle's sermon began with an appeal to Old Testament prophecy, setting forth the hope of Israel for the coming of Messiah. That coming was to be at a time of which, for ages, young men had had visions and old men had dreamed dreams. It was to be characterized by "wonders in heaven above, and signs in the earth beneath"—by which we see that the story of the earthly life of Christ was, from the beginning of the apostolic age, presented to the people in an eschatological setting.[15]

After this appeal for a recognition of the divine plan of human history, the Apostle's message turned to the public ministry of Jesus. His teaching, as preserved for us, for example, in the Sermon on the Mount, was not ignored; but the stress of the discourse was on the manner in which what Jesus said and did was approved of God: Jesus' words and deeds, to quote Luke's words of Peter, were "signs which God did by him, in the midst of you, as ye yourselves also know." [16] There, clearly before Peter's listeners, was the original survey of the Jesus of history, complete and authenticated—and the briefest ever composed.[17] The sermon then turned to the signal event of Christ's passion, of which Peter the evangelist said two things: first, that Jesus was "crucified and slain" by "wicked hands"; second, that he was delivered into the hands of evil men "by the determinate counsel and foreknowledge of God."

But it was with the story of the Resurrection that the discourse at Pentecost reached its climax. God raised up Jesus from the dead, "having loosed the pains of death, because it

[13] Leviticus 23:17-20; Exodus 23:19; Deuteronomy 26:2-10.
[14] Acts 2:14-47.
[15] Acts 2:19.
[16] Acts 2:22.
[17] Acts 2:22.

Courtesy of The Art Institute of Chicago.

7. THE RESURRECTION (from THE GREAT PASSION). Albrecht Dürer.

Courtesy of The Art Institute of Chicago.

8. The Last Judgment (from "Seelen-Wurzgarten" published in Ulm). Anonymous.

was not possible that he should be holden of it." Referring, as was proper, to the poet-king David, Peter quotes him as saying that God Himself would not let His "Holy One to see corruption." Once again, to refute any unbeliever who might be listening to him, Peter said: "This Jesus hath God raised up, whereof we all are witnesses." Finally, to assure his hearers that this event was not the end of divine historic revelation, the Apostle declares that Jesus was not only risen from the dead but was now exalted by the right hand of God, by Whom he has been made "both Lord and Christ."

The discourse ended with the Apostle's declaration that the dispensation of the Holy Spirit had begun—that this was now the age of Grace; and that all who repented of their sins and were baptized should "receive the gift of the Holy Ghost." Luke adds that those who believed did, principally, three things: "They continued steadfastly (1) in the apostles' doctrine and fellowship, and (2) in breaking of bread, and (3) in prayers." [18] Besides these things, they divided their earthly possessions, lived with singular gladness of heart and in the good favor of all the people. Such, according to Luke, was the state of faith in the apostolic church.

But the witness to the living Christ, begun with the preaching of Peter, quickly rose to a culminating tide of testimony in the extraordinary life and ministry of Paul. His activity extended beyond that of Peter in two main respects: first, in its theological exposition of the Christian faith; second, in its appeal to the Gentile world. Wherever Paul preached, whether on his arduous missionary journeys or as a prisoner before Festus and Agrippa, the theme of his discourse was on the death and resurrection of Christ. He had himself, he said, been loosed from the chains of sin and death and he wished all men who heard him to live the new life he now lived by faith in Christ the Lord. But, as we have already noted, his message did not end there. The world, he realized, lay in a dreadful and helpless bondage to sin. The whole creation, he wrote to the Roman church, was in travail, to be "delivered from the bondage of

18 Acts 2:42.

corruption into the glorious liberty of the children of God." [19]
And those, particularly, who through their faith in Christ had
already come to an experience of spiritual liberty, "groaned
within themselves" for the redemption also of their natural bodies. This was indeed a cosmic view to take of the kingdom of
God. But Paul, looking on the world in its entirety and with
penetrating eyes, did not hesitate in declaring it. For this
deliverance of the whole creation from bondage to death was
to him the transcendent goal of divine history. It was God's
plan interpreted in terms of a philosophical conception of the
universe.

It is important to note the manner in which Paul presented
his gospel message. The Apostle consistently began his discourse with a review of Israel's history—its Messianic hope,
and the fulfilment of this hope in the coming of Christ—and
ended with an exalted exposition of his view of the world's
redemption. His preaching was profoundly true to the traditional conception of the gospel as history. It was, at the same
time, definitely Christological. Finally, in uniting together the
historical and the Christological aspects of the gospel, he arrived
at an outlook that was unmistakably eschatological.[20] Christ,
and life in him, was to the Apostle the beginning and the end
of all things. His conception of the goal or End of history,
and its association with the return and reign of Christ, is fully
summed up in these words:

> As in Adam all die,
> Even so in Christ shall all be made alive. . . .
> Christ the firstfruits:
> Afterward they that are Christ's at his coming.
> Then cometh the End,
> When he shall have delivered up the kingdom
> To God, even the Father. . . .
> For he must reign,
> Till he hath put all enemies under his feet.
> The last enemy that shall be destroyed is death. . . .

[19] Romans 8:19-23.
[20] Romans 8:11-12, 14:10-12; I Corinthians 4:5, 7:31, 15:1-58; II Corinthians 5:10; I Thessalonians 4:15 ff.; Philippians 4:5.

When all things shall be subdued unto him,
Then shall the Son also himself be subject unto him, . . .
That God may be all in all.[21]

In calling up the witnesses to the faith of the early church,
we ought not to omit a brief mention of the New Testament
letter to the Hebrews. This is an extraordinary Christian document. As we should expect from its title, its background is that
of the Old Testament. In some respects it closely resembles
the letters of Saint Paul, most notably in its cosmic view of the
person of Christ and in its stress on the sacrificial nature of his
death. But there is in it a trend of thought that gives to "faith"
the more intimately traditional character of trust in God as the
divine "Protector and Rewarder." It emphasizes the fact that
Christ's earthly life was lived in such trust, that it was characterized by great patience and pure sinlessness, and that, as the
result of his absolute faithfulness, he has become the divine
Intercessor for mankind at the throne of God. Faith and faithfulness are joined together by the author of the letter to give
us a clear picture of the early church as it began to face persecution under the edict of Rome. As Christ suffered, so the faith
of Christians is tested by suffering; and the heroes of faith,
listed in Hebrews 11, are the types of those who labor and suffer
for an invisible kingdom—who regard themselves as pilgrims of
eternity, sojourners on earth, seeking a city not made with
hands "whose builder and maker is God." The author of the
letter summons his fellow Christians to remember these heroes
who, even though dead, surround their living comrades like a
great cloud of witnesses; and he reaches the climax of his message when he exhorts them to run their earthly race with patience.

Looking unto Jesus
The author and finisher of our faith;
Who for the joy that was set before him,
Endured the cross, despising the shame,
And is set down at the right hand
Of the throne of God.[22]

21 I Corinthians 15:22-29.
22 Hebrews 12:2.

It is now necessary to add but one summarizing word about the faith of the early church as taught in the Fourth Gospel. The Johannine writer, in his story of the Resurrection, indicates how the "Easter Faith" had its direct origin in the "Easter Fact." Christ, from the beginning, had been the Light of the world. He had been the eternal Word incarnate, and that Word had been the light and life of men. As at his birth, so by his death, this light had been momentarily eclipsed.

But now, "while it was yet dark" in the world, Christ arose and revealed himself alive: first, to Mary Magdalene; then, to the disciples behind closed doors; after that, to Thomas, who, having doubted, saw and believed; and finally—in the Gospel's epilogue—to Peter on the shore of the Lake of Galilee. John, in his account of the Resurrection, stresses two facts—the two principal pillars on which the church of the succeeding ages was to be built and to rest. The first is a faith that is not dependent on the sense of sight and so made subservient to it. Instead, it is a faith based on a knowledge of the objective reality of the things no eye can see, and therefore is the prerequisite condition of man's knowledge of things seen. To the religious man, generally, this objective reality is spiritual; to the author of the Fourth Gospel, it is the eternal Word embodied in the risen and living Christ. What this faith, put to the test, signifies is expressed in the words of our risen Lord to Thomas: "Because thou hast seen me, thou has believed. Blessed are they that have not seen, and have believed." [23]

The second fact which John stresses is Love. The assumption that John 21 is an epilogue to the Gospel does not change the picture but accentuates it. Here is the great Evangelist's last word to the church which, in the closing scene, Peter has come to represent. The church, through its apostles, is to be first the Fisher of men, and second the Shepherd of souls. This is Christ's double command to it: (1) "Cast your net"; (2) "Feed my sheep." The ever recurrent question to the disciple is: "Lovest thou me?" And, to every inquiring soul, intent on discovering the will of God, there comes, now as ever, the repeated call: "Follow me."

[23] John 20:29.

Saint Augustine, living at a time when Christianity was beginning its historic conquest of western Europe, has left us these celebrated words as a summing up of the gospel story and its meaning to all subsequent ages:

But, our true Life came down hither, and bore our death, and slew him, out of the abundance of His own life. And He thundered, calling aloud to us to return hence to Him into that secret place, whence He came forth to us: first in the Virgin's womb, wherein He espoused the human creation, our mortal flesh, that it might not be forever mortal; and thence like a bridegroom coming out of his chamber, rejoicing as a giant to run his course. For he lingered not, but ran, calling aloud by words, deeds, death, life, descent, ascension: crying aloud to us to return unto Him. And He departed from our eyes, that we might return into our heart, and there find Him. For He departed, and lo, He is here. [24]

[24] From the *Confessions,* Book V. Translated by Dr. E. B. Pusey (New York: F. A. Stokes & Co., 1838).

THE CHRISTIAN WORLD
IN THE APOSTOLIC AGE
35-100 A.D.

300 MILES

TRM

QUESTIONS AND TOPICS FOR DISCUSSION

Chapter 1. History as Divine Drama

Can all history be interpreted in terms of nature?
Examine the word "drama," as used in this chapter, and apply it to the idea of a divine providence in human history.

Chapter 2. The Gospel as History

Can world history be interpreted in terms of what is contained in the Gospels? Or are the Gospels simply the product of a movement in history? Do you think that history, viewed in perspective, has a meaning? If so, how is that meaning to be discovered? Can it be discovered simply by looking for it? Or is history's meaning made plain to those who have somehow found the key to its unfolding plan?

Chapter 3. The Earthly Life of Christ

Is it possible to view the life of Christ in terms of a concept so great as world history in its entirety?

Chapter 4. The Historic Christian Church

Think of the Christian church first as a purely historical movement. Then consider it as a divine institution. Do these two ideas represent the same thing or is there a difference between them? If so, where does that difference lie?

Chapter 5. The Roman World

Consider the historical and geographical circumstances of the rise of Christianity. Does the location of Palestine have anything to do with the manner in which Christianity came to be the religion of the empire?

Looking at the events occurring within the Roman empire, can we say that the time was at hand for the coming of Christ?

Chapter 6.   The Primitive Christian Community

What picture do we get from the Book of the Acts of how the early Christian community was founded and of how the early Christians lived?

Note how the early Christians looked backward upon Israel's history, while at the same time they looked forward to the establishment of the Church in the empire.

Chapter 7.   The Earliest Gospel

What advantage is there in being able to trace the Christian faith to its earliest beginnings?

What is meant by the statement that the gospel story was preached before it was written?

Chapter 8.   From Tradition to Literature

Should we expect the four Gospels to be identical in literary style and structure in order to regard them as authentic?

Does the divine inspiration of Holy Scripture imply verbal agreement among its writers?

If the Gospel Evangelists depended upon documentary sources in composing their narratives, does this fact increase or lessen their authenticity as Holy Scripture?

Chapter 9.   The Gospel of Mark

Observe the resounding note of urgency in Mark's Gospel. How does this note develop into the Evangelist's note of the Kingdom of God?

Chapter 10.   The Gospel of Matthew

If Matthew's narrative depends greatly on that of Mark in its main story, what makes the Gospel of Matthew so rich and meaningful to Christians today?

Note how Matthew's narrative combines two main elements of the early gospel tradition: the ethical and the eschatological. What

is meant by the term "eschatological," and how does it dominate the ethical in almost every chapter?

Chapter 11. The Gospel of Luke

Why is Luke especially called the Gospel historian? Are the other Gospels less historical than his? Or is Luke more touchingly emphasizing the humanity of Jesus in his account of the events?

Chapter 12. The Gospel of John

What are we to infer from the way in which John begins his Gospel? Why is this Gospel treasured by so many Christians to-day? Note, for example, as you read the Gospel, the great symbols of bread and water as these are used by the Fourth Evangelist.

Chapter 13. Looking at the Life of Jesus

Is it enough for us to have a biography of Jesus? Or must we read the four Gospels from another point of view? If so, what must this point of view be? Concentrate your attention on the actual reasons for which the Gospels were written.

Chapter 14. The Voice of Ancient Prophecy

This chapter has to do with the fundamental relationship between the Old and the New Testaments. Note how what we call gospel history is rooted in the prophetic writings of the Old Testament.

Are we supposed to believe that the first Christians were acquainted with the Old Testament and its prophetic message?

Does such a prophetic view of history differ from the idea of looking on history as the practical operation of the natural law of cause and effect?

Chapter 15. The Messianic Vision

What, precisely, is meant by the term "Messianic"? Can we trace the signs of a Messianic hope throughout the entire Old Testament? What about such early references as those found in Genesis, in the story, for example, of the temptation and fall of man?

Note how in the course of time the Messianic and the apocalyptic hopes become united, as we pursue our reading of both the Old and the New Testament.

Chapter 16.   The Record of Beginnings

Compare the infant stories of Matthew and Luke. Note the special importance of each.

Why does Mark omit an account of the birth and infancy of Jesus?

Does John's record of the Incarnation, in the beginning of his Gospel, presuppose his knowledge and acceptance of the current tradition of the birth of Jesus?

Chapter 17.   Days of Preparation

How is the earthly ministry of Jesus here associated with the preaching of John the Baptist? Did Jesus himself require baptism at the hand of John?

How does the fourth Gospel interpret John the Baptist's relationship to Jesus?

Does the story of the temptation mean something more than the fact that Jesus was human? If so, how are we to interpret it?

Chapter 18.   Preaching and Healing in Capernaum

Note that it was the Kingdom of God around which both the preaching and the healing of Jesus were centered. Did Jesus heal people simply because he pitied them? Or, by healing men's bodies and minds, did he wish to show what things would be like when the Kingdom was fully come? How may such healing be thought of as the restoration of a sinful and fallen world?

Chapter 19.   Jesus Among Scribes and Sinners

We are not to forget here that Christ came not to destroy the law but to fulfil it. Are we to infer that Jesus preferred the company of the sinners to that of the scribes? Or is the point to be made here that sinners were attracted to Jesus? If so, why?

Chapter 20.   Evangelism in Galilee

Why, besides desiring their company, did Jesus call men to be his disciples?

Did the disciples comprehend the meaning of what he was saying to them and doing in their presence? If not, how were they to be made ready to become apostles after his death?

What is meant by the note of urgency so strikingly present in the preaching of Jesus at this time? What also of the note of gladness, of which the Evangelists write?

Chapter 21.   Discourses on the Kingdom of God

Observe that this chapter and those that follow center in the concept of the Kingdom of God. Note that this concept is presented as gradually unfolding before the eyes of Jesus' disciples.

Did the idea of the Kingdom of God also gradually unfold itself before Jesus? Or was he conscious of its meaning from the beginning? How, in consequence, are the discourse and parables on the Kingdom to be interpreted?

Chapter 22.   The Sayings and Parables of Jesus

Note the distinction between the sayings and the parables of Jesus.

Does the fact that these stories and sayings were easy to remember furnish us with any evidence of the authenticity of the records? If so, why and how?

What is the difference between saying that Jesus spoke in living words to his hearers and that he was himself the Living Word? Explain the distinction between the terms "grace" and "judgment" as they were applied to the parables.

Chapter 23.   The Galilean Crisis

How was the crisis brought on by the attitude of King Herod? Is there any difference between recognizing such an outward crisis in the history of Palestine and saying that the Kingdom of God had its own crisis—that it was itself characterized by crisis? In what way does the Miracle of the Loaves reflect this crisis and point to Jesus' death on the Cross?

Chapter 24.　The Galilean Crisis (Continued)

What was Peter's great confession?

What did Jesus' Messiahship imply?

How does the idea of suffering enter into the Messianic concept?

In what way could such a concept of suffering be associated with the glory of Jesus' Messiahship?

Why are Moses and Elias brought into the picture of the Transfiguration?

Chapter 25.　In the Borderland of Perea anl Judea

The Evangelists tell us that by this time a strong wave of unpopularity was overtaking Jesus. Yet they also say that he was now more popular than ever. How are these contrasting facts to be interpreted? Do they suggest that the drama of redemption was nearing its climax? Does this situation suggest a great separation among the people into what Jesus in one of his parables called "the wheat and the tares"? If so, does this thought suggest to you the idea of a great last judgment? How is the overshadowing Cross the symbol of world judgment as well as world redemption?

Chapter 26.　Hostility in Jerusalem

Jerusalem was the citadel of Judaism. Now it was to be also the center of Jesus' most intense period of activity. Does that fact indicate how close together Judaism and the Christian faith were or how far apart they had come to be?

How could the Christian Gospel be an outgrowth of Israel's faith and yet be, as the Evangelists imply, a divine judgment on that faith?

What do you think of the view that Jesus in his discourses of Judgment was undertaking to cleanse the old Israel and to prepare it to become the nucleus of the new Israel which was later to be known as the Christian church?

Note here the story of the cleansing of the temple.

Chapter 27.　Jesus Alone with His Disciples

Note here the complete change of atmosphere in comparison with that of the preceding chapter.

Here, we may say, is the new Israel. The church is born. It consists of the fellowship of those who partake of the last supper with Jesus. What is meant by the bread and the wine as Jesus interprets their use at the close of the Passover meal?

Looking at the farewell discourses in John's Gospel, what can we say of the faith and the fellowship by which the first Christians lived?

Chapter 28. The Account of Jesus' Passion

Note how the whole story which the Evangelists have to tell comes to a climax with the story of Jesus' suffering and death. Observe the length and the close similarity of the four records. Are we justified in inferring from this fact that the story of Jesus' passion served as the foundation of the early preaching of the apostles? If so, can we draw any inference as to the most important thing for Christians today to believe about Jesus Christ?

Chapter 29. The Living Christ

The Resurrection is the great climactic event of the Gospel. But note how naturally the story is told. What inference are we to draw from this fact? Has not the whole Gospel account been presented to us in this same natural but miraculous manner? Does this truth present the story of Jesus to us in a new light? If so, what kind of history is the Gospel?

We have called it divine history. Has that term now come to have a new meaning to you, a meaning comparable to that which was in the minds of the early Christians?

In consideration of what we have discovered, against what background and with what attitude should the Gospels be read by us today?

BIBLIOGRAPHY

ADAMS, DAVID E. *Man of God.* New York: Harper & Bros., 1941; Toronto: The Musson Book Co. Ltd., 1941.

AULÉN, G. *Christus Victor.* New York: The Macmillan Co., 1931.

BAAB, OTTO JUSTICE. *Jesus Christ Our Lord.* Nashville: Abingdon-Cokesbury Press, 1937.

BACON, B. W. *The Gospel of the Hellenists.* New York: Henry Holt & Co., Inc., 1933.

————. *The Gospel of Mark.* New Haven, Conn.: Yale University Press, 1925.

————. *Studies in Matthew.* New York: Henry Holt & Co., Inc., 1930.

BARNETT, ALBERT E. *The New Testament, Its Making and Meaning.* Nashville: Abingdon-Cokesbury Press, 1946.

BATTENHOUSE, HENRY M. *New Testament History and Literature.* New York: The Ronald Press Co., 1937.

————. *The Bible Unlocked.* New York: Appleton-Century-Crofts, Inc., 1928.

BRANSCOMB, B. H. *Jesus and the Law of Moses.* New York: Harper & Bros., 1930; Toronto: The Musson Book Co. Ltd., 1930.

————. *The Gospel of Mark.* London: Hodder & Stoughton, Ltd., 1937.

————. *The Teachings of Jesus.* Nashville: Abingdon-Cokesbury Press, 1931.

BUNDY, W. E. *The Religion of Jesus.* Indianapolis: Bobbs-Merrill Co., 1928.

BURKITT, F. C. *The Gospel History and Its Transmission.* New York: Chas. Scribner's Sons, 1925.

BURNEY, C. F. *The Poetry of Our Lord.* New York: Oxford University Press, 1925.

CADBURY, H. J. *Jesus, What Manner of Man.* New York: The Macmillan Co., 1947.

CADOUX, C. J. *The Historic Mission of Jesus.* New York: Harper & Bros., 1943.

CASE, S. J. *Jesus, a New Biography.* Chicago: University of Chicago Press, 1927.

CHAPMAN, JOHN. *Four Gospels.* London: Sheed & Ward, Ltd., 1944.

CHARLES, R. H. *Religious Development Between the Old and New Testaments.* New York: Henry Holt & Co., Inc., 1914.

CHARNWOOD, LORD. *According to St. John.* Boston: Little, Brown & Co., 1925; London: Hodder & Stoughton, Ltd., 1925.

COLWELL, ERNEST C. *An Approach to the Teaching of Jesus.* Nashville: Abingdon-Cokesbury Press, 1947.

CRAIG, CLARENCE TUCKER. *The Beginning of Christianity.* Nashville: Abingdon-Cokesbury Press, 1943.

331

————. *Jesus in Our Teaching.* Nashville: Abingdon-Cokesbury Press, 1931.

————. *The Study of the New Testament.* Nashville: Abingdon-Cokesbury Press, 1939.

CREED, J. M. *The Gospel According to St. Luke.* New York: The Macmillan Co., 1930.

DEISSMANN, G. A. *The New Testament in the Light of Modern Research.* London: Hodder & Stoughton, Ltd., 1929.

DIBELIUS, MARTIN. *From Tradition to Gospel.* New York: Charles Scribner's Sons, 1935.

————. *Gospel Criticism and Christology.* London: Nicholson & Watson, Ltd., 1935.

————. *Jesus.* Philadelphia: Westminster Press, 1949.

————. *The Message of Jesus Christ.* New York: Charles Scribner's Sons, 1939.

DOBSCHUTZ, E. VON. *The Eschatology of the Gospels.* Doubleday & Co., 1910.

DODD, C. H. *The Apostolic Preaching and Its Developments.* Chicago: Willett, Clark & Co., 1937.

————. *History and the Gospel.* New York: Charles Scribner's Sons, 1938; Toronto: The Musson Book Co. Ltd., 1938.

————. *The Parables of the Kingdom.* New York: Charles Scribner's Sons, 1936; London: James Nisbet & Co. Ltd., 1935; Toronto: The Musson Book Co., Ltd., 1935.

DUNCAN, GEORGE S. *Jesus, Son of Man.* New York: The Macmillan Co., 1949.

EASTON, B. S. *Christ in the Gospels.* New York: Charles Scribner's Sons, 1930.

————. *The Gospel According to St. Luke.* New York: Charles Scribner's Sons, 1926.

————. *The Gospel Before the Gospels.* New York: Charles Scribner's Sons, 1928.

EDERSHEIM, ALFRED. *The Life and Times of Jesus the Messiah.* New York: Longmans, Green & Co., 1883.

FERRÉ, NELS. *Evil and the Christian Faith.* New York: Harper & Bros., 1947.

FILSON, FLOYD V. *Origins of the Gospels.* Nashville: The Abingdon-Cokesbury Press, 1938.

GLOVER, T. R. *The Jesus of History.* New York: Association Press, 1917.

GOGUEL, M. *Life of Jesus.* New York: The Macmillan Co., 1933.

GOODSPEED, E. J. *The Life of Jesus.* New York: Harper & Bros., 1950.

HEADLAM, A. C. *Life and Teaching of Jesus the Christ.* London: John Murray, 1936.

HOLLAND, H. S. *The Fourth Gospel.* New York: E. P. Dutton & Co., 1923.

HORTON, W. *Our Eternal Contemporary.* New York: Harper & Bros., 1942.

HOSKYNS, SIR EDWARD, and DAVY, NOEL. *The Riddle of the New Testament.* London: Faber & Faber, Ltd., 1931; New York: Harcourt, Brace & Co., 1932.

HOWARD, W. F. *The Fourth Gospel in Recent Criticism and Interpretation.* London: The Epworth Press, 1931.

Hügel, Frederick von. *Essays and Addresses on the Philosophy of Religion.* New York: E. P. Dutton & Co., 1921.

Kepler, Thomas. *Contemporary Thinking about Jesus.* Nashville: The Abingdon-Cokesbury Press, 1944.

Klausner, J. *Jesus of Nazareth, His Life, Times, and Teaching.* New York: The Macmillan Co., 1929.

Knox, John. *Christ the Lord.* Chicago: Willett, Clark & Co., 1945.

———. *The Man, Christ Jesus.* Chicago: Willett, Clark & Co., 1941.

Lagrange, M. J. *The Gospel of Jesus Christ.* London: Burns, Oates & Washburne, Ltd., 1938.

Lake, Kirsopp. *Six Collations of New Testament Manuscripts.* Cambridge, Mass.: Harvard University Press, 1932; New York: Oxford University Press, 1933.

Lebreton, J. *The Life and Teaching of Jesus Christ, Our Lord.* London: Burns, Oates & Washburne, Ltd., 1935.

Lewis, C. S. *Miracles.* New York: The Macmillan Co., 1947.

MacGregor, G. H. C. *The Gospel of John.* New York: Harper & Bros., 1929.

MacKinnon, J. *The Gospel in the Early Church.* New York: Longmans, Green & Co., 1933.

———. *The Historic Jesus.* New York: Longmans, Green & Co., 1931.

Major, H. D. A., Manson, T. W., and Wright, C. J. *The Mission and Message of Jesus.* New York: E. P. Dutton & Co., 1938.

Manson, Thomas Walter. *The Teaching of Jesus.* New York: The Macmillan Co., 1932.

Manson, William. *The Gospel of Luke.* New York: Harper & Bros., 1930; London: Hodder & Stoughton, Ltd., 1930.

———. *Jesus the Messiah.* London: Hodder & Stoughton, Ltd., 1943. Philadelphia, The Westminster Press, 1946.

McGiffert, A. C. A. *History of Christian Thought.* New York: Charles Scribner's Sons, 2 vols., 1932.

McNeile, A. H. *Introduction to the Study of the New Testament.* New York: Oxford University Press.

Minear, Paul S. *Eyes of Faith.* London: Lutterworth Press, 1948; Toronto: Ryerson Press, 1948.

Moffatt, James. *The Historical New Testament.* Edinburgh: T. T. & T. Clark, 1901. *New Testament.* New York: Doubleday & Co., Inc., 1922; London: Hodder & Stoughton, Ltd., 1922.

Montefiore, C. J. G. *Rabbinic Literature and Gospel Teachings.* New York: The Macmillan Co., 1930.

———. *The Synoptic Gospels.* New York: The Macmillan Co., 1927.

Moore, G. F. *Judaism in the First Centuries of the Christian Era.* Cambridge, Mass.: Harvard University Press, 1930.

Oesterley, W. O. E. (ed.) *Judaism and Christianity.* New York: The Macmillan Co., 1937.

Otto, R. *The Kingdom of God and the Son of Man.* Grand Rapids, Mich.: Zondervan Publishing House, 1938.

Palmer, A. W. *The Light of Faith.* New York: The Macmillan Co., 1945.

Parsons, E. W. *The Religion of the New Testament.* New York: Harper & Bros., 1939; Toronto: The Musson Book Co., Ltd., 1939.

PITTENGER, W. N. *Christ and Christian Faith.* New York: Round Table Press, 1941.

RATTEY, B. K. *Growth and Structure of the Gospels.* New York: Oxford University Press, 1935.

RAWLINSON, A. E. J. *Christ in the Gospels.* New York: Oxford Book Co., 1944.

REDLICH, E. BASIL. *Form Criticism: Its Value and Limitations.* New York: Charles Scribner's Sons, 1939.

————. *Student's Introduction to the Synoptic Gospels.* New York: Longmans, Green & Co., 1936.

RICHARDSON, ALAN. *The Gospels in the Making.* London: Student Christian Movement Press, 1938.

ROBINSON, T. H. *St. Mark's Life of Jesus.* London: Student Christian Movement Press, 1937.

SANDAY, W. *Outlines of the Life of Christ.* New York: Chas. Scribner's Sons, 1931.

SCHWEITZER, ALBERT. *The Mystery of the Kingdom of God.* New York: Dodd, Mead & Co., Inc., 1914.

————. *The Quest of the Historical Jesus.* New York: The Macmillan Co., 1910.

SCOTT, E. F. *The Ethical Teachings of Jesus.* New York: The Macmillan Co., 1948.

————. *The Validity of the Gospel Record.* New York: Charles Scribner's Sons, 1938.

————. *The Varieties of New Testament Religion.* New York: Charles Scribner's Sons, 1943.

SHARMAN, H. B. *Son of Man and the Kingdom of God.* New York: Harper & Bros., 1943; Toronto: The Musson Book Co. Ltd., 1943.

SMITH, DAVID. *The Days of His Flesh.* New York: Harper & Bros., 1933; London: Hodder & Stoughton, Ltd., 1933.

SMITH, G. A. *The Historical Geography of the Holy Land.* London: Hodder & Stoughton, Ltd., 1931; New York: Harper & Bros., 1932.

STANTON, V. H. *The Gospels as Historical Documents.* New York: The Macmillan Co., 1920.

STREETER, B. H. *The Four Gospels.* New York: The Macmillan Co., 1924.

TASKER, R. V. G. *Nature and Purpose of the Gospels.* New York: Harper & Bros., 1944; Toronto: The Macmillan Co., Ltd., 1944; Toronto: The Musson Book Co. Ltd., 1944.

TAYLOR, VINCENT. *Behind the Third Gospel.* New York: Oxford University Press, 1926.

————. *The Formation of the Gospel Tradition.* New York: The Macmillan Co., 1933.

————. *The Gospels: A Short Introduction.* London: The Epworth Press, 1948.

WADE, G. W. *New Testament History.* New York: E. P. Dutton & Co., 1922.

WARSCHAUER, JOSEPH. *The Historical Life of Christ.* New York: The Macmillan Co., 1926.

WEISS, BERNHARD. *A Commentary on the New Testament.* New York: Funk & Wagnalls Co., 1906.

WEISS, J. *History of Primitive Christianity.* New York: The Macmillan Co., 1937; Elmira, New York: Primavera Press, Inc., 1937.

WERNLE, P. *Sources of Our Knowledge of the Life of Jesus.* Boston: The Beacon Press, 1907.

WILDER, AMOS. *Eschatology and Ethics in the Teaching of Jesus.* New York: Harper & Bros., 1939; Toronto: The Musson Book Co., Ltd., 1939.

WILLOUGHBY, HAROLD. *The Study of the Bible Today and Tomorrow.* Chicago: University of Chicago Press, 1947; London: Cambridge University Press, 1948.

WREDE, WILLIAM. *Origin of the New Testament.* New York: Harper & Bros., 1909.

INDEX